ON
SEXUALITY
AND
POWER

—

Between Men ~ Between Women

On
Sexuality
and
Power

ALAN SINFIELD

Columbia University Press   New York

326038

COLUMBIA UNIVERSITY PRESS

Publishers Since 1893

New York   Chichester, West Sussex

Copyright © 2004 Columbia University Press

Library of Congress Cataloging-in-Publication Data

Sinfield, Alan.
On sexuality and power / Alan Sinfield.
p. cm — (Between men—between women)
Includes bibliographical references and index.
ISBN 0–231–13408–8 (cloth : alk. paper)
ISBN 0–231–13409–6 (pbk. : alk. paper)
1. Homosexuality, Male—Psychological aspects.
2. Power (Social sciences) 3. Sex (Psychology)
4. Gays in literature. 5. Homosexuality and literature.
I Title. II. Series.

HQ76.S545   2004
306.76'6—dc22   2004052773

Columbia University Press books are printed on permanent
and durable acid-free paper.

Printed in the United States of America

Designed by Lisa Hamm

c 10 9 8 7 6 5 4 3 2 1
p 10 9 8 7 6 5 4 3 2 1

BETWEEN MEN ~ BETWEEN WOMEN

Lesbian, Gay, and Bisexual Studies

Terry Castle and Larry Gross, Editors

Advisory Board of Editors

Claudia Card

John D'Emilio

Esther Newton

Anne Peplau

Eugene Rice

Kendall Thomas

Jeffrey Weeks

Between Men ~ Between Women is a forum for current lesbian and gay scholarship in the humanities and social sciences. The series includes both books that rest within specific traditional disciplines and are substantially about gay men, bisexuals, or lesbians and books that are interdisciplinary in ways that reveal new insights into gay, bisexual, or lesbian experience, transform traditional disciplinary methods in consequence of the perspectives that experience provides, or begin to establish lesbian and gay studies as a freestanding inquiry. Established to contribute to an increased understanding of lesbians, bisexuals, and gay men, the series also aims to provide through that understanding a wider comprehension of culture in general.

CONTENTS

ACKNOWLEDGMENTS

I am grateful for books, comments, and conversations to Peter Burton, Alex Evans, John Fletcher, Gowan Hewlett, Ann Rosalind Jones, Vicky Lebeau, Linda Logie, David Marriott, Vincent Quinn, Nick Rees-Roberts, David Rogers, Lynne Segal, Mark Sinfield, Peter Stallybrass, Chris West; students on the Sexual Dissidence and Cultural Change program at the University of Sussex. They are not responsible for the ideas.

Parts of this book have appeared in other forms in *Critical Inquiry* and *GLQ* (*Gay and Lesbian Quarterly*); Richard Phillips, Diane Watt, and David Shuttleton, eds., *De-centering Sexualities* (London: Routledge, 2000); and David Alderson and Linda Anderson, eds., *Territories of Desire in Queer Culture* (Manchester: Manchester University Press, 2000).

Gregory Woods's poem, "Under where Catullus toyed," is quoted with permission from the Carcanet Press. John Minton's painting "Painter and Model" is used on the cover with permission from the Royal College of Art and the Russell-Cotes Art Gallery and Museum, Bournemouth, England.

ON
SEXUALITY
AND
POWER

——

1

INTRODUCTION

Reginald Shepherd is, he says, the person no one wants to know about: a black (African American) gay man with an unappeasable attraction to white men. "I am in love with the image and idea of white manhood, which is everything I am not and want to be." Why is this such a fearful condition? Because of the historic oppression of blacks by whites. Shepherd is under no illusion about the role of power in his attraction: "I think many gay men worship the power that oppresses them; I think too that all sexual relations in our society are about power over another or the submission to the power of another."[1]

Shepherd's sexual desire is hinged on to racial difference, the most fraught political, economic, social, and cultural issue in the United States and Britain, and in many other countries. At this juncture, unavoidably, the psychic meets the social, fantasy meets history, desire meets politics. No wonder our societies find the subject hot to handle. We experience a marked unease about all hierarchical liaisons—not only of race but also of age, gender, and class. In metropolitan contexts today, it is often said, gay people favor egalitarian relations. Shepherd himself seeks commonality in everything but racial difference: his dream lover is "some beautiful cultured blond named Troy with whom I'd have everything in common, everything but that" (56).

Yet power differentials are remarkably persistent, in gay fantasies and in the stories about gayness that circulate. I discern three reasons for this. One is that, while we may like to think of fantasy as free-ranging, in fact it often shows astonishing fixity. Shepherd's desire is by no means comfortable, but it appears ineluctable. "So I hate him and desire him, fearing him and myself, too often despising both. So I continue to want him" (56). Second, our desires are not ours alone; they are embedded in the power structures that organize our social being. Shepherd would like to step out of his personal history, but that would be "to step out of the history of the nation." It would be to say: "This is not America." The entire social system is tending to maintain his fantasy. And, anyway, who would he then be? "The catch is that 'myself' is a product of that history both general and very particular. . . . What and who would I be without the burden of the past?" (57; my elision).

A third reason for the persistence of hierarchy in relationships, I will argue, is that *it is sexy*. Racial difference is not just a major influence on or component in Shepherd's sexuality, it is intricately implicated with what turns him on. "I am in love with the image and idea of white manhood, which is everything I am not and want to be, and if I cannot be that at least I can have that, if only for the night, if only for the week or the month" (54–55). For Shepherd, whiteness is sexy, despite or because of its bond with oppression.

It would be absurdly presumptuous to suppose that a (white) commentator might begin to unravel Shepherd's intimate experience. However, he has placed it, boldly, in the public domain, and I can record that it is there. A project of this book is to reexamine the implication of sexuality and power. I propose a framework for this in chapter 4, and continue with chapters that explore binary relations founded in gender, age, class, and race. These formations, as Jonathan Dollimore says, quoting Jacques Derrida, are "violent hierarchies": "one of the two terms forcefully governs the other."[2] They structure our societies; they constitute our psyches also.

The late and still-lamented Allon White, a keen Freudian, and I were talking about the unconscious. I was attempting to substantiate a materialist position which I associated with Jean-Paul Sartre, namely that human behavior may be explained without resort to the idea of a reservoir of unconscious repressed experience which could only be reached through the ministrations of the analyst. In order that traumatic experiences may be repressed into the unconscious, they have first to reach the threshold of the conscious, which is where they are censored as unacceptable. The images which Freud dredged up in his hysterical patients were not unavailable: rather, the patients did not want to admit to them. So there is no reason to posit an unconscious as such.[3] "That's right," cried Allon, puckishly. "Some people have no unconscious. And you're one of them." I felt that at some not very subtle level I had lost the debate. Even a materialist needs a theory of psychic life. Chapters 2 and 3 of this book make a start on sketching what the terms for that might be.

My approach is broadly *cultural materialist*. It seeks to raise questions about cultural production, addressing typically the relations between dominant and subordinate cultures; the scope for dissidence; how far male dominance might be able to accommodate feminism and dissident sexualities; how culture is negotiated through institutions, including those which govern the definition and circulation of art and literature; how subcultural groups constitute themselves in and through culture. Cultural materialism is a kind of Marxism, and does not pretend to political neutrality. It looks for the transformation of an exploitative social order.[4]

Cultural materialists believe that historic forces and the power structures that they sustain determine the direction, not just of our societies, but ultimately of our selfhood. Yet there is little agreement on how to describe the links between the psyche and the social order. Raymond Williams, who announced the main themes of cultural materialism in the 1970s and 1980s, placed his understanding of personal attachments in his novels, rather than his theory. Louis Althusser seeks to explain how the human subject is persuaded to recognize him- or herself as hailed (interpellated) by the norms of society, while experiencing him- or herself as a free individual.[5] This sounds like the beginnings of a theory of subjectivity and psychic life. However, Althusser is ready to cede the individual psyche to Freud and his followers. He accepts that the unconscious and its effects are the specific object of psychoanalysis. "History, 'sociology' or anthropology have no business here." Nevertheless, questions remain, for Althusser, about how historical origins and socioeconomic conditions affect psychoanalytical theory and technique.[6]

The most ambitious theory has sought to combine Freudian and Marxian principles. Herbert Marcuse in *Eros and Civilization* (1955) sought to reverse what was usually taken as a central Freudian principle—that repression of natural instincts is a necessary condition for the development of civilization.[7] Marcuse argued that while some repression is inevitable, modern societies experience *surplus repression*, that is, repression in the service of domination. Further, what is specially repressed is sexuality, and especially insofar as it is restricted to genital organs and reproductive purposes. Marcuse wants us to retrieve the *polymorphous perversity* that we experienced as infants: this, he holds, will threaten the overthrow of the order of procreation and the institutions that guarantee it. This was a theory for the exuberant and optimistic 1960s. Writing a little later, in 1976, Michel Foucault is more aware of the "polymorphous techniques of power." A Marcusean "great Refusal" of the system supposes power to be unitary and solely oppressive. Rather, the opposite has come about: "there is a plurality of resistances."[8]

Anyway, rather than repressing sex, Foucault points out, we have talked of almost nothing else, since Victorian times. This "veritable discursive explosion" (96) has been the cause and effect of diverse taxonomies of sexual and gender dissidence, especially in the traditions of anthropology and psychoanalysis; I mean to draw upon both. Anthropologists have observed structural correlations in diverse societies: same-sex passions, they find, are organized through age difference (commonly, an older partner initiating a younger partner) and gender difference (one partner takes the role of a man, the other of a woman). I have added race and class to age and gender.

For feminists, and lesbian and gay activists, psychoanalytic texts are fraught with problems. My emphasis on age, class, and race, as well as gender, has to resist a Freudian propensity to suppose that proper analysis of any sexual relation is likely to disclose a version of the ultimate drama through which the castrating father (allegedly) installs gender hierarchy. Consider Joan Riviere's much-cited essay, "Womanliness as a Masquerade." An analysand who grew up in the American South reports a dream in which she is threatened by a black man, and resists him with the secret intention of attracting him. Riviere comments: "The meaning was that she had killed father and mother and obtained everything for herself (alone in the house), [and] became terrified of their retribution."[9] Although she mentions the American South, Riviere's interpretation involves no thought of the horrific violence that was enacted against black men accused of violating white women. One allegedly hostile man is pretty much like another, and it all comes back to your father.

Other commentators have made a similar point. Michael Warner demands: "Why is gender assumed to be our only access to alterity? It is not even the only line of sameness and difference that structures erotic images. Race, age, and class are capable of doing that as well."[10] Lynne Segal traces a difficulty in articulating class to Lacanian psychoanalysis and points out that some feminists "have addressed the significance of differences other than those of gender, noting that class, race, ethnicity and sexual orientation, for example, have no place in psychoanalytic formulations of subjectivity."[11]

My aim is not to attack or defend psychoanalysis; there is little point, at

this date, in doing either.[12] A hundred years after the principles were enun-
ciated, it is still difficult to imagine what a rival theory would look like.
Getting beyond this point is going to require a paradigm shift, a wholesale
reconception from a new stance. In the meantime, the omnipresence of
Freud's ideas makes him the inevitable reference point. My approach here
is pragmatic, perhaps appropriative. While setting aside theories which
seem to me unfounded and unhelpful, I mean to make positive use of some
Freudian concepts, including the distinction between desire-for and
desire-to-be, the demarcation between gender identity and sexual object-
choice, and the role of narcissism in structuring gay desire.

In this book elucidations and qualifications of theorists will be balanced
and tested by more nuanced, complex, and perhaps vulnerable insights,
quarried from works of fiction (novels, stories, and films) and autobiography. (I say little about theater because I have written about it elsewhere,
albeit from other points of view.)[13] Some of my references to fiction are
quite brief, designed to support claims that such-and-such an attitude is
commonly held. They are synoptic and symptomatic, borrowing purposefully from disparate sources in order to indicate that it is not just Hollywood writers, or just writers concerned with AIDS, or just male writers,
who hold this-or-that position. Other discussions are larger, and are
designed to show the complexity and subtlety of engagement that occur in
certain writings, and, by inference, in human lives.

I am not trying to write literary history, which seems to me impoverished in its defining assumption—that literature is sufficiently self-contained to constitute, ultimately, a self-sustaining system. Nor am I interested in establishing literary value. I am captivated by some contemporary
and recent fiction not because it tells us transcendent truths, but because
it offers sophisticated narratives for exploration, reflection, and action.
The literary is often seen as opposed to action, but I remain loyal to the
cultural materialist idea that any writing of ambition might be more important than that. As Bertolt Brecht wrote of theater, "it sets out society's
experiences, past and present alike, in such a manner that the audience
can 'appreciate' the feelings, insights and impulses which are distilled by
the wisest, most active and most passionate among us from the events of
the day or the century."[14]

Reports of gay experience indicate repeatedly that fiction enlarges our
sense of our potential. American novelist Jim Grimsley is typical:

The very first book I read in which gay men appeared was Mary Renault's *Fire from Heaven*, in which Alexander and Hephaistion become lovers in the second half of the book. I was still in high school, probably 1970 or 1971. The fact that I could find some kind of affirmation that there were—or had been—other men like me was enthralling and I read the book over and over again. One of the ironies of that era was that the best books about gay men were all by women. Soon after that I would find John Rechy's *City of Night*, which was extraordinary and powerful and which shook me deeply with its portrait of a gay man's narcissistic sexuality and indifference to commitment.[15]

I have argued elsewhere that the narratives which we revisit compulsively (in literary writing and many other forms) are those which in our cultures are unresolved: I call them *faultline stories*.[16] When a part of our worldview threatens disruption by manifestly failing to cohere with the rest, then we reorganize and retell its story, trying to get it into shape—back into the old shape if we are conservative-minded, or into a new shape if we are more adventurous. Faultline stories address the awkward, unresolved issues; they find their way, willy-nilly, into texts. There is nothing mysterious about this. Authors and readers want writing to be interesting, and these unresolved issues are the most promising for that. This is true in the culture at large, and in subcultural formations also. I deploy some of the techniques of poststructuralist literary criticism, but my aim is to explore how gay experiences have fed into books, films, plays, and cultural commentary, and how we, in turn, have read and pondered them, and reframed ourselves through them. In recognizing the plausibility of a story (Yes, I would act like that in those circumstances; or No, if he takes that line he's asking for trouble), we recognize ourselves, both individually and, implicitly at least, as part of a subcultural formation. We don't have to agree; the point is to have the conversation.

To be sure, I am exploiting different kinds of texts—different genres, different media. A romance is likely to mobilize different impressions of gayness from a thriller. Yet each exerts a claim for plausibility within its own criteria, and readers learn to read accordingly. My main interest is in writing of the last thirty years, but contemporary writing is not necessarily the most influential. I discuss Walt Whitman, Oscar Wilde, Thomas Mann, Radclyffe Hall, E. M. Forster, and Jean Genet because they still bulk large in our collective imaginations. The aim is not to deduce facts from fiction, but to explore ideas and images; the kinds of representations that have been circulating. These texts display what people (gay and otherwise) have been saying about lesbians and gay men; or rather—for writing must be

seen as an intervention in a contested space—what they have wanted readers to believe. In my concluding chapter I ponder whether there may be
some use in the idea of a lesbian and gay canon.

It will be sensible to clarify a few other aspects of my approach. Much of
what I have to say may easily be applied to heterosexuality. I have framed
my thoughts and study in terms of gay subcultures because I know them
better and am personally engaged there; because they offer a substantial
and up-to-date body of work to build upon; and because there are plenty of
books about sex from a straight point of view. It may be that a queer stance
will be of wider relevance. Centers, after all, are defined by margins; dissident sexuality, being not the default position, is by definition always already
problematized.

I cannot envisage an effective study of gay men that will not be aware of
what lies at the most immediate boundaries, those with lesbians and transgender people. I have drawn upon these neighboring discourses when it
has seemed instructive to do so. I refer to both *gay* and *queer*, tending to
use the former in modern and subcultural contexts, the latter in cases with
more of a casual, provocative, and inclusive slant. *Sexual dissidence* is at
once vaguer, more purposeful, and more inclusive.[17] *Same-sex* aspires to
neutrality. *Female* and *male* are always to be understood as the prevailing
normative concepts, as are the notions of *masculinity* and *femininity* that
conventionally accompany them.

I have tried elsewhere to write about the interface between metropolitan and nonmetropolitan constructions of same-sex passion. The idea was
not to find a universal model, still less to legislate for other peoples, but to
gain a critical perspective on metropolitan assumptions, revealing them as
a local and temporal creation—one that tends to disavow, repudiate, or
repress large areas of actual sexual opportunity.[18] In this book my concern
is mainly with gay subcultures that have arisen in the cities of North America and northwestern Europe, and to some extent with local versions of
them as they have been distributed through other parts of the world by
global interaction.

In practice, as it transpires, although this book was largely conceived
and written in Britain, many of my texts are from the United States. As I
have observed elsewhere, most of the metropolitan imagery of gayness is
"American"; blue-jeans and T-shirts, short hair and mustaches, have been
adopted into British gay subculture; so have candlelit vigils, quilting, bud-

dying, and photo-obituaries.[19] Because it is located in a more violent and fractured society, and because the AIDS emergency struck more precisely in more clearly demarcated communities, writing from the United States often seems to present the dilemmas of gayness with a special intensity. When I refer to "our cultures" I mean those of the United States and north-western Europe.

2

TAXONOMIES

POSSIBLE AND PLAUSIBLE

In a recent essay designed to kick-start gay history, David Halperin proposes a new categorization of same-sex relations. He distinguishes the *modern* concept of homosexuality, and four *prehomosexual traditions*. These latter are found in specific European contexts—from ancient Greece through early-modern Italy and France, and the molly houses of the eighteenth century, on into the emergence of the concept of "sexual inversion" in the writings of late-nineteenth-century sexologists. They are: (1) effeminacy, (2) pederasty or "active" sodomy, (3) friendship or male love, (4) passivity or inversion.[1] The key factor linking these prehomosexual traditions, Halperin says, is the privileging of gender over sexual identity (defined by object-choice).

In "modern" homosexuality, which develops in the mid-twentieth century, it is the other way around. Both partners in a same-sex scenario are regarded as gay and neither need be positioned as feminine. Today, Halperin says, "Homosexual relations cease to be compulsorily structured by a polarization of identities and roles (active/passive, insertive/receptive, masculine/feminine, or man/boy). Exclusive, lifelong, companionate, romantic, and mutual homosexual love becomes possible for both partners."[2] However, traces of earlier patterns linger, and hence the confusions in some current ideas of gayness. Conversely, we may read modern egalitarian expectations back into earlier periods. Astutely, Halperin observes an inconsistency in Jamie O'Neill's acclaimed novel, *At Swim, Two Boys*: while the Irish situation is presented with careful historical responsibility, the relationships between the gay boys are presented in the modern manner.[3]

Halperin's model is relatively local—it charts particular social and historican contexts within Western European and classical tradition. He concedes that his "categories are heuristic, tentative, and ad hoc," that his patterns "do not reduce to a single coherent scheme."[4] Bruce Smith's analysis of early-modern England and George Rousseau's account of Enlightenment Europe are in similar vein: they chart same-sex liaisons more or less in the terms in which they were regarded contemporaneously.[5] In fact, their models may be regarded as local elaborations of the more general model advanced by anthropologists such as David Greenberg, Stephen Murray, and Gilbert Herdt. From a wide survey, they discover two main patterns of male same-sex relations: gender difference (one party is "masculine," the other "feminine") and age difference. Like Halperin, they find that a new type—egalitarian partnerships founded in similarity—has been developing lately in metropolitan settings.[6] More elaborate homosexual taxonomies, Jeffrey Weeks notes, have been generated by psychologists, such as Clifford Allen's twelve types (including the compulsive, the neurotic, and the alcoholic) and Richard Harvey's forty-six types (including the religious, the bodybuilder, and the ship's queen).[7]

Anthropological approaches have afforded a valuable way of reminding post-Stonewall gays that their way of doing things is not universal. I mean to take another route, trying to assemble a more abstract model—one that will seek to map the range of *possible* sex and gender positions, aspiring to coherence and even completeness. The *plausible* positions, at any time and place, will be a particular selection and development from the possible positions. For instance, Halperin believes that while it was plausible in earlier centuries to have a close male friend, and to cross-dress, to combine the two in one person was almost inconceivable. However, it is always possible, and nowadays a drag queen may have close friends of all kinds.

It should not be supposed that the plausible modes delimit the totality of current behaviors. At present, for instance, there is no extant moral or legal ratification for the serial killer. Even psychologically, it is quite hard to envisage what gratification he or she might be obtaining. Nonetheless such people exist. Plausibility locates what can be said and done within normal parameters but, necessarily, it supposes the coexistence of varying degrees of implausibility, threatening always to infiltrate or shatter the normative. A more abstract taxonomy may remind us that the immediate evidence will not anticipate all possibilities.

I do not intend this as an antihistorical, nor an ahistorical work. My aim is to explore frameworks within which historical differences may be better comprehended (especially, in the present study, the relations between the present and the recent past). The detecting of taxonomies is not a trivial matter. Eve Sedgwick suggests that it may contribute to "the making and unmaking and remaking and redissolution of hundreds of old and new categorical imaginings concerning all the kinds it may take to make up a world."[8]

THREE PROBLEMS WITH FREUD

The other established taxonomies are in the Freudian tradition. Kenneth Lewes derives four "explanations" of male homosexuality from Freud's work; C. A. Tripp eight; Kaja Silverman three (one of them in two variants).[9] As Silverman remarks, "the various theories Freud proposes to account for the etiology of homosexuality are far from consistent, and it is often difficult to determine whether one is supposed to extend, supplement, or supersede those that came before" (362). My intention is not to rehearse these theories, nor to attack or defend Freud, but to reconsider problems and opportunities for a materialist elucidation of dissident sexualities.

Freud makes a number of gay-friendly utterances: most famously, that "all human beings are capable of making a homosexual object-choice and have in fact made one in their unconscious."[10] However, some of his ideas about homosexuality occur in the course of surprisingly flimsy essays (such as the one on Leonardo da Vinci).[11] Lesbians and gay men have found three tendencies in Freudian theory particularly hard to deal with. One is the implication that gay men are in some fundamental way feminine, and lesbians correspondingly masculine. For many sexual dissidents, it should be said at once, this implication is not at all unsatisfactory. They are happy to think of themselves as embodying a significant element of the "other" sex. However, many are not. Gay men in particular have often appealed to David and Jonathan, the Theban Band, and Walt Whitman in order to establish that, so far from being effeminate, same-sex love may be quintessentially manly. Maurice, in E. M. Forster's novel, believed he had "brought out the man in Alec, and now it was Alec's turn to bring out the hero in him."[12] Notwithstanding, Silverman, expounding the Freudian corpus, warns that the gay man may have to accept that "an identification with 'woman' constitutes the very basis of his identity, and/or the position from which he desires."[13]

As one might expect, many lesbians object to the idea that they might be "really" male. Sheila Jeffreys opposes bitterly the ascription of masculine roles to women.[14] Teresa de Lauretis makes an elaborate case, broadly from within psychoanalysis, for freeing lesbians from the imputation that they are castrated and yearning for phallic maleness. The infant, she says, experiences a castrating loss (such as Freud posits), but it is the loss of the female—of the mother—not of the phallus. De Lauretis instances *The Well of Loneliness* (1928), where Stephen's mother finds her daughter's body repulsive. This maternal withholding, which Stephen cannot address directly, is displaced onto a fetish: manliness. Her masculine bearing, therefore, signifies not phallic pretension but "Stephen's desire for the (lost) female body."[15] The difference from traditional Freudian versions is that Stephen's cultivation of male identity is linked only incidentally to the phallus. It is the adjustment that the sex/gender system makes available: "The popularity of *visible* masculine signifiers as lesbian fetish in Western cultures is directly proportionate to the latter's enduringly hegemonic representation of lesbianism as phallic pretension of male identification" (308).

Probably Elizabeth Grosz is right to say that this attempt to render psychoanalysis lesbian-friendly still carries too much Freudian baggage.[16] Nonetheless, de Lauretis' separation of gender from heterosexuality sets off reverberations that may be heard through the present study. My aim at this point is not to evaluate such theories but to note the firmness with which some lesbians repudiate Freudian arguments that would position them as second-class men. Molly in Rita Mae Brown's *Rubyfruit Jungle*, encountering a butch/femme bar, exclaims: "That's the craziest dumbass thing I ever heard tell of. What's the point of being a lesbian if a woman is going to look and act like an *imitation man*? Hell, if I want a man, I'll get *the real thing*, not one of these chippies."[17] This is perhaps the kind of incident Judith Butler has in mind when she insists that homosexuality is not a *copy* of heterosexuality. "As a young person," she confesses, "I suffered for a long time, and I suspect many people have, from being told, explicitly or implicitly, that what I 'am' is a copy, an imitation, a derivative example, a shadow of the real."[18]

A second problematic tendency in Freudian theory concerns "arrested development." As Freud elaborates his idea of an Oedipus complex and adapts to it his experiences of homosexuality, the congenital claims of Havelock Ellis and the inversionists are largely replaced by a developmental model. In his famous letter to a mother about her son's homosexuality, Freud assured her that it was "nothing to be ashamed of, no vice, no degradation." Nonetheless, he felt bound to say, it was "produced by a certain arrest of sexual development."[19] "How does it come to be taken as self-evident that homo-erotics is really an arrested form of interest in oneself?" Michael Warner demands.[20]

What is so revealing is the point at which the arrest is supposed to occur: it is at that moment in the Oedipal process at which the individual is caught in the "wrong" gender identity. In a note added to the *Three Essays* in 1910, Freud declares:

> In all the cases we have examined we have established the fact that the future [male] inverts, in the earliest years of their childhood, pass through a phase of very intense but short-lived fixation to a woman (usually their mother), and that, after leaving this behind, they identify themselves with a woman and take *themselves* as their sexual object. That is to say, proceeding from a basis of narcissism, they look for a young man who resembles themselves and whom *they* may love as their mother loved *them*. (56)

In other words, the homosexual behaves as his mother did (or as he wanted her to). Carole-Anne Tyler glosses: "if a man desires another man, he must do so as a woman."[21]

For women the Oedipal sequence is more complicated, but the outcome is similar. In his essay on "Female Sexuality" (1931), Freud sketches three lines of development for the girl as she "acknowledges the fact of her castration. . . . Only if her development follows the third, very circuitous, path does she reach the final normal female attitude." Otherwise she may arrive at "a general revulsion from sexuality," or she may "cling with defiant self-assertiveness to her threatened masculinity," perhaps resulting in "a manifest homosexual choice of object." In a footnote Freud grants cheerfully that "men analysts with feminist views, as well as our women analysts, will disagree."[22]

A third problematic tendency, for many lesbians and gay men, is located around the term *narcissism*. The mythical Narcissus is a beautiful youth who refuses to be wooed, embracing only himself; gazing at his own reflection, he starves to death. Not the kind of guy you want as a role model.

In his essay "On Narcissism: An Introduction" (1914), Freud distinguishes *anaclitic* (other directed) and *narcissistic* love. According to the anaclitic type a man may love the woman who feeds him, and the man who protects him. According to the narcissistic type a man may love versions of himself—what he is, what he was, what he would like to be, someone who was once part of himself. Freud straightaway mentions, but does not develop, "the significance of narcissistic object-choice for homosexuality in men."[23]

On Freud's own account, narcissistic love is far less limited than the name suggests. Like anaclitic love, it requires two people, and only in one variant are they supposed to be *the same*; otherwise there is a significant difference. In practice, a relationship with an individual who represents the person you have been, or might become, is likely to involve ceaseless negotiation. You are faced continually with both the distinctiveness of the other person (the extent to which s/he does not embody your ideal self) and the contradictions and failures in your own yearning (your ideal self is not as likable, coherent, or attainable as you might wish to suppose). In fact "anaclitic" doesn't mean independent, but *attached*; specifically, "leaning-on," Freud's editor explains, "by analogy with the grammatical term 'enclitic,' used of particles which cannot be the first word in a sentence, but must be appended to, or must lean up against, a more important one." Narcissism, then, may operate in an anaclitic way. Freud does not offer them as opposed types: "We have, however, not concluded that human beings are divided into two sharply differentiated groups." Nor, according to Freud, is narcissistic love distinctively gay. It characterizes many women, who, "especially if they grow up with good looks, develop a certain self-contentment which compensates them for the social restrictions that are imposed on them in their choice of object. . . . Such women have the greatest fascination for men."[24] Freud instances also the narcissism of parents and children.

Notwithstanding, followers of Freud have tended to conclude that homosexual love is narcissistic and therefore at best immature, at worst pathological. It seems likely to involve age and status difference (a man loves what he was, what he would like to be), and hence to violate the modern egalitarian ethos. The common inference, as Kenneth Lewes puts it, is that homosexuality is "not truly object-related, that it involves impoverished object relations and consequently operates through a primitive and defective superego, and that its mental organization is basically preoedipal."[25] It is not surprising that lesbians and gay men have been uneasy at being labeled "narcissistic." The only relation of difference that is validated is gender, and then only when a male and a female are involved.

Even so, in my view Freud's four variants of narcissistic love do offer an intuitively relevant model for some kinds of lesbian and gay passion. Elements of hero worship and idealization, in or of a younger partner, abound in the histories we have created for ourselves, from Socrates and Sappho to Shakespeare, and on to Wilde and Forster. This is not just a male thing. Sarah Ponsonby was thirteen and Eleanor Butler nearly thirty when they made the commitment that was to become the Ladies of Llangollen. Stephen is thirty-one and Mary twenty-one when they fall in love in *The Well of Loneliness*. Audre Lorde in *Zami* tells how she passed for thirty-five when she was actually twenty so as to take the protective role in her relationship with Muriel.[26]

DESIRE-FOR AND DESIRE-TO-BE

In pursuit of a more effective and more materialist taxonomy, I mean to resort to another Freudian construct—one which is, I hope, less ideologically loaded than those I have discussed so far. In the essay *Group Psychology and the Analysis of the Ego* (1921), Freud draws a distinction between *desire-for* and *desire-to-be*. Typically, he says, the boy develops an anaclitic attachment to (desire-for) the mother. At the same time, also, he experiences an identification toward (desire-to-be) his father. These are "two psychologically distinct ties: a straightforward sexual object-cathexis toward his mother and an identification with his father which takes him as his model." Propelled by "the irresistible advance toward a unification of mental life, they come together at last; and the normal Oedipus complex originates from their confluence."[27]

For Freud it is crucial, if your Oedipus complex is to work out properly, to get desire-to-be and desire-for the right way round:

> A little boy will exhibit a special interest in his father; he would like to grow like him and be like him, and take his place everywhere. We may say simply that he takes his father as his ideal. This behaviour has nothing to do with a passive or feminine attitude towards his father (and towards males in general); it is on the contrary typically masculine. It fits in very well with the Oedipus complex, for which it helps to prepare the way.[28]

However, it may not work out so conveniently. The father may be taken as the object of a feminine attitude, or the boy may develop an identification with his mother. The process, Freud admits, is precarious and hard to understand:

> It is easy to state in a formula the distinction between an identification with the father and the choice of the father as an object. In the first case one's father is what one would like to *be*, and in the second he is what one would like to *have*. The distinction, that is, depends upon whether the tie attaches to the subject or to the object of the ego. The former kind of tie is therefore already possible before any sexual object-choice has been made. It is much more difficult to give a clear metapsychological representation of the distinction. (135)

What does seem clear is: (1) desire-to-be must be kept apart from desire-for, (2) this quarantine is unreliable, and (3) the consequence is sexual and gender dissidence. This insistence upon a precarious separation is Eve Sedgwick's theme in *Epistomology of the Closet* where, she says, the idea was "to demonstrate that modern, homophobic constructions of male heterosexuality have a conceptual dependence on a distinction between men's *identification* (with men) and their *desire* (for women), a distinction whose factitiousness is latent where not patent."[29] Judith Butler also addresses the topic: "The heterosexual logic that requires that identification and desire be mutually exclusive is one of the most reductive of heterosexism's psychological instruments: if one identifies *as* a given gender, one must desire a different gender."[30]

So how does passion cross the barrier between desire-to-be and desire-for? The answer: very easily! Wayne Koestenbaum observes: "I spent much of my childhood trying to distinguish identification from desire, asking myself, 'Am I in love with Julie Andrews, or do I think I *am* Julie Andrews?' I knew that to love Julie Andrews placed me, however vaguely, in heterosexuality's domain; but to identify with Julie Andrews, to want to be the star of *Star!*, placed me under suspicion."[31] John Fletcher declares: "There can be no clear cut distinction between identification and desire, being and having, in the early stages" of infant development; it is only a presumed Oedipal polarity that requires it.[32] Noncompliance with this heteronormative demand is presented by Fletcher as a positive opportunity for gay relations:

> What is refused [in male homosexuality] is not masculinity or the phallic in itself, but the polarity at the heart of the Oedipal injunction: "You cannot *be* what you desire, you cannot *desire* what you wish to be." The "narcissism" that characterizes certain gay male erotic scenarios, turning on images and terms of traditional masculinity and phallic positioning, often can be seen to have a reparative function, restoring an *alliance* between being and having, identification and desire. (114; Fletcher's emphasis)

Like de Lauretis in her argument for gender identity as fetish, Fletcher cleverly reorients the Oedipal calamity so that it becomes a gay advantage.

Now, it is not necessary to tangle with psychoanalytic intricacies and purported explanations of gender and sexuality in order to find illumination in the distinction between desire-to-be and desire-for. The pattern has a formal aptness; it will admit, at least in the abstract, all the models I have discussed so far. It reorganizes, in relatively neutral terms, the gendered and narcissistic models of homosexuality which have troubled lesbians and gay men in psychoanalysis. It may be mapped onto, though not contained by, the schema posed so precisely by Sedgwick in *Epistemology of the Closet*, of inversion (women's souls in men's bodies and vice versa) and gender separatism (same-sex bonding).[33] It offers to connect up Halperin's four prehomosexual traditions. For instance, the effeminate man may be seen as cultivating desire-to-be of the feminine gender, while experiencing desire-for either women or men. Or, again, an "active" sodomite cultivates a desire-to-be male while experiencing desire-for a boy or man.

For the conventional model of heterosexuality you need a man who has desire-to-be male and desire-for a female, and a woman who has desire-to-be female and desire-for a male:

| A man has: | desire-to-be M | desire-for F |
| A woman has: | desire-to-be F | desire-for M |

The structure appears complementary at every point—as it should do, for the terms are designed to ratify heteronormativity. You desire-to-be yourself (i.e., your own gender), which seems only right. You have desire-for-another, who is indeed other (another gender). Changing any of the positions disrupts the model. Such disruptions may be experienced, variously, as shameful weakness, moral dilemma, nervous strain, exhilarating kinkiness; some of them will produce gender identifications and object-choices which our cultures call homosexual.

It may be that the dichotomies I am invoking will strike you as a blunt instrument; so they do me. Their usefulness, it will emerge, resides largely in what we can learn from their inadequacies. My goal is not to fit the range of our relations into them, but to use them to disclose salient features of that range. For a start, the terms "M" and "F" must be problematized. They are to be understood as the prevailing normative concepts of male and female, together with the norms of masculinity and femininity that commonly accompany them. It is not my assumption that they are the positions that we have to occupy, but they are the positions we have to negotiate. In the initial, simple version of the model, it is supposed that gender identity will correspond to anatomical sex; however, this may not be so. In practice, little is uncontested in these matters. Some people referred to Margaret Thatcher as "that bloody woman," others said she wasn't really a woman at all; interestingly, I don't remember anyone calling her a lesbian. Again: is it manly or cowardly for a man to assault his wife? Our cultures are not agreed on that.

MODEL (g)

Two main dissident models initially appear. For the sake of simplicity, and because I feel more confident there, I am writing them as they apply to men. However, I believe they may admit lesbian experience as well; I indicate this from time to time, drawing upon instances and scholarship from lesbian traditions. In an attempt to evade preconceived historical and geographical notions, I call the two initial dissident models (c) and (g).

The former, model (c), is often associated with the ancient Greeks and endorsed by many gay men today. It shows males, without relinquishing their masculine gender identities, desiring other males:

(c) A man has: desire-to-be M   desire-for M

This model flies in the face of a (Freudian) inclination to impose a cross-sex pattern upon same-sex relations by distributing a same-sex couple as one pseudo-male and one pseudo-female. However, it may be authenticated (for Freudians) by Freud's recognition of desire-for the same gender in his account of narcissism. If the two men are more or less equal, they fit the modern egalitarian ethos. I return in a while to some of the complications in model (c).

The second dissident model, model (g), looks like this:

(g) A man has: desire-to-be F   desire-for M

This is the classic inversion model of the "passive" male homosexual: he wants to be female, and his desire, like that conventionally expected in a woman, is for a man. He may be said to have a woman's soul in a man's body, or a negative Oedipus complex. In the popular imagination, still, effeminacy is the badge of gayness. For instance, in Ned Cresswell's romance of small town to stardom via sexual intrigue, *A Hollywood Conscience*, neither Brik nor Ryder has shown any sign of effeminacy. However, once Brik's gayness is recognized, camp becomes the inevitable marker of this knowledge. If Ryder is getting married he will want a matron of honor, Brik suggests. " 'Guess you'll have to wax your legs,' " Ryder responds. The topic is not pursued by the boys; it is too risky, they pull back to their customary protocol.[34] I trace some of the history of dissident gendering in chapter 5. Model (g) is about sexual dissidence organized around gender; we may call it the *gender* model.

Many gay men and lesbians, I have suggested, are uncomfortable with this model; it often appears in context with some element of disavowal or, at least, unease. In James Robert Baker's novel *Tim and Pete*, Pete is a garage mechanic, performs heavy metal, and passes for straight. Tim is a film archivist. He likes Pete because he is not simply gendered—not "just a mechanic or a rock musician or a cute, butch guy. . . . It could be a long time before I met someone else with Pete's sensibility and humor."[35] Meanwhile Tim risks being too effeminate, Pete accuses: " 'The day we went to Monte Carlo you looked like a fruit.' " " 'Only in your mind. I was wearing a totally masculine, faded green tennis shirt and a sloppy straight guy's khaki shorts,' " Tim retorts. " 'With your collar turned up like a queen,' " Pete insists; two German guys made antigay remarks (73). However, neither of them is as feminine as Victor, who is British, lives with his mother, and likes Barry Manilow and Liza Minnelli.

Further, model (g) proves significantly inexact, in ways that indicate just how tangled and resistant to categorization gender is in our sex/gender system. Consider: the obvious *partner* for the man in model (g), who desires that he himself should be feminine and that his partner should be masculine, is:

A man who has: desire-to-be M   desire-for F

Of course, this image is familiar: it represents the "normal" heterosexual man! Actually, that is not so strange. In the mid-twentieth century, men such as Quentin Crisp believed that effeminate homosexuals sought "to win the love of a 'real' man." So the ultimate ideal partner was indeed a straight-identified man who desired the feminine. Unfortunately, desiring the feminine in the masculine form called the straightness of this man into question: "A man who 'goes with' other men is not what they would call a real man."[36] So the maneuver is bound to fail. In Latin cultures, however, this seems less of a problem: a masculine-identified man may manifest desire-for both women and effeminate men.[37]

If, in one aspect, model (g) discloses a congruency with heterosexual desire, in another it fails to distinguish between the "effeminate" male homosexual and the transsexual anatomical male who feels that he really is female. Each manifests desire-to-be F, and may well experience desire-for M. This confusion is paradoxical, because one advantage of separating desire-to-be from desire-for is that it becomes easier to see the specificity of transgender.[38] The ultimate distinction is that whereas the male homosexual priority is to get a man (desire-for), the transgender priority is to establish a dissident identity (desire-to-be). In Leslie Feinberg's *Stone Butch Blues*, Jess has a dream which "wasn't about being gay. It was about being a man or a woman."[39] Judith Halberstam reports the case of Danny, a pre-operative female-to-male transsexual: Danny finds sexual satisfaction with men, but only so long as it is understood to be "gay" sex—so long as s/he is "recognized" as a man.[40] Don Kulick has observed a comparable attitude among male-to-female *travestis* in Brazil. They choose their macho boyfriends not for sexual fulfillment but because having such a man in the house reassures the *travesti* that s/he is female.[41] In fact, transsexuals are not necessarily homosexual, and their model has to be written:

(g) A man has: desire-to-be F   desire-for M/F

The transsexual also problematizes the initial term in the diagram, "a man" (or "a woman"), for s/he may regard hirself as a male, a female, a mixture of the two, or neither. Notice that when we speak of the transsexual as a man who has desire-to-be a woman, that this is a loaded way of putting it—a way that prioritizes anatomical gender. We might instead term this person a woman who has been born into the wrong body, prioritizing psychological gender.

As Jay Prosser observes, some transsexuals are refusing absolute gender categories. Kate Bornstein remarks: "I identify as neither male nor female, and now that my lover is going through his gender change, it turns out I'm neither straight nor gay."[42] This is not new. Theresa, Jess's lover in *Stone Butch Blues*, calls herself a lesbian and urges Jess to join the women's movement—" 'You're a woman!' " she exclaims. But Jess denies this: " 'No I'm not,' I yelled back at her. 'I'm a he-she. That's different.' "[43] The transsexual is complicated also as a partner: is desire-for about hir masculinity, hir femininity, or both? Such relationships may be straight or gay, depending how you look at it.

Application of the categories "M" and "F" has been thrown into further disarray by recent academic and political attention to "intersexuality"—approximately, what has been called hermaphroditism—bearing anatomical indications of both genders. The Intersex Society of North America is objecting to the practice of surgeons who, coming upon infants whose sex appears mixed or indeterminate, intervene to construct what they regard as more satisfactory gender characteristics. The society urges that medically unnecessary surgery be deferred until the child can make an informed decision from within a supportive environment.[44] Intersex people may feel themselves to be "F," "M," neither, or both. Clifford Geertz presents atti-

tudes toward intersexuality in different cultures as an instance of the constructedness of common sense.[45] The fact that transgender resists my dia-
grams is not surprising; it is an index of the difficulty our societies have in
conceptualizing it.

One consequence of constructing a model that prompts a serious recognition of transgender is that the situation of the more typical lesbian or gay
man comes more clearly into focus by comparison. Many such people
experience a degree of dissident gender identification. However, they do
not behave or regard themselves as thereby *not-male* (for men), or *not-
female* (for women). Rather, they see themselves as embodying an element
of the alternate gender. So camp men generally have more in common with
other men than they do with women (women know this). Correspondingly,
contributors to Sally Munt's collection *Butch/Femme* insist that while
butches allude to masculinity, and even masquerade as men, their purpose
is to pursue their particular ways of being women.[46] Judith Butler writes:

> Within lesbian contexts, the "identification" with masculinity that appears as
> butch identity is not a simple assimilation of lesbianism back into the terms
> of heterosexuality. As one lesbian femme explained, she likes her boys to be
> girls, meaning that "being a girl" contextualizes and resignifies "masculinity"
> in a butch identity. As a result, that masculinity, if that it can be called, is
> always brought into relief against a culturally intelligible "female body."[47]

Halberstam cites Butler's argument, but reasserts that there are other positions: "While some girls are content with boys who retain genetically female
bodies, others desire the transgendered or cosmetically altered body."[48]

I am minded to conclude, from these complexities, that the difference
between lesbian or gay and transgender variants of model (g) is one of
degree. They all point toward a dissident gender identity, but they range, in
a person of predominantly male anatomy, from sensitivity, through the
screaming queen, to the person who seeks gender reassignment surgery. In
the diagram

(g) A man has: desire-to-be F,

therefore, the terms comprise variable intensities in a continuum. If this
argument feels wrong—threatening to situate you close to something that
you feel is not-you—bear in mind that it is the proximate that demands
most assiduous policing. Stephen Maddison, in *Fags, Hags, and Queer Sisters*, suggests that we regard (some kinds of) homosexuality and transgen-

der as "alternative responses to similar conditions," adding: "The two movements share a heritage."[49] That is right: the diaries of Anne Lister and *The Well of Loneliness* figure in both lesbian and transgender discourses (I develop this argument in chapter 5).

What has made it difficult to unravel the diversity of the gender model is Freudian absolutism, which is committed to a distribution of psychic life between two poles: father/mother, male/female. For instance, in "A Case of Homosexuality in a Woman" (1920), Freud's analysand had "entirely repudiated her wish for a child, her love of men, and the feminine role in general." The outcome was "extreme": "She changed into a man and took her mother in place of her father as the object of her love."[50] But the extremism is Freud's: not wanting a child, a male partner, or a feminine role does not turn a woman into a man! Again: finding at the end of puberty that the time has come for "exchanging his mother for some other sexual object," a young man "identifies himself with her; he transforms himself into her, and now looks about for objects which can replace his ego for him, and on which he can bestow such love and care as he has experienced from his mother."[51] Such language ("he transforms himself into her") encourages the inference that the homosexual who develops a dissident gender identity *really has*, at some level, changed gender.

In fact most gender-dissident individuals in the gender model, transsexuals apart, should be apprehended as aspiring, quite informally, to some kind of *mixing* of gender identities, whereby a person may appropriate "other" gender attributes, without seeking to abandon his or her initially ascribed gender. I had thought to call this "androgyny," meaning not a semimystical transcendence of gender and the body, but simply a strategic appropriation. However, Halberstam critiques Martha Vicinus' usage on this: "The androgyne represents some version of gender mixing, but this rarely adds up to total ambiguity; when a woman is mistaken consistently for a man, I think it is safe to say that what marks her gender presentation is not androgyny but masculinity."[52] So androgyny and female masculinity are distinct.

The wider point here is that a range of degrees and types of commitment may occur within the gender model, and only the most extreme should be understood as amounting to gender transformation. Desire-to-be is a relative matter, then, not an absolute difference. Perhaps the idea, as Maddison suggests, is not to be a woman but to disaffiliate from dominant heterosexual modes of manhood.[53] For many or most gay men, desire-to-be in the gender model should be represented not by "F" but by "RF," *relatively feminine*:

A man has: desire-to-be RF   desire-for M

While "RF" does embrace the carefully fashioned appropriation of the drag queen or king and the punk gender-bender, for the most part it entails the ordinary, day-to-day effects of an uneven gender identification. Indeed, it may have little to do with object-choice, and be compatible with a heterosexual desire-for. Desire-to-be "RF" is available for diverse disaffections of males from heavily masculine commitments: leisure-class men affecting a dandified style; schoolboys wanting to be aesthetes rather than athletes; artists, priests, and dons choosing to signal unworldliness; the present-day "New Man." Halberstam points out that rural women may be considered masculine by urban standards, but merely practical in their own community.[54]

In most cases I have written the dissident models as they locate individuals, but identities are interactive and the partner (long or short-term, actual or fantasized) is important because s/he is the person who, above all, is expected to confirm one's own identity. In conventional heterosexual couples this may work contrastively: the man may feel more masculine in contrast with the woman, and vice versa. Plainly a lot of normative masculinity depends on that process; indeed, while it is conventionally supposed that a man has to be masculine in order to impress a woman, it may be the other way around—the woman is called upon to ratify his masculinity. This is a point made by feminists. Today in metropolitan contexts the obvious partner for a man who has desire-to-be "RF" is *a man who has desire-for "RF."* In fact *both partners* may experience desire-to-be "RF" *and* desire-for "RF." This does not mean that such couples will be symmetrical. The "RF" element may be distributed unevenly, producing complementarity at some points, conflict at others. Further, "M," "F," and "RF" are likely to be relative between the partners. In a butch/femme couple, for instance, the partners may be gender-marked mainly as measured against each other, not in absolute terms of masculinity and femininity.

The relative nature of many gender-dissident identities points toward the diversity of innumerable actual lesbian and gay relationships. I think its occurrence is sufficiently pronounced to justify terming it the *relative-gender* model, or model (rg). Insofar as it posits a weaker element of gender dissidence than has often been supposed, it begins to converge on model (c)—to which I now return.

MODEL (c)

A man has: desire-to-be M   desire-for M

In the most obvious version of (c), each man is attracted to someone who is very like himself. They may admire and inspire one another's masculinity, perhaps emulously, as between Shakespeare's Coriolanus and Aufidius, or in the gym. (When Aufidius calls Coriolanus "boy," at the climax of the play, he ejects him from manly equivalence.) Somewhere around this point, many accounts of (c) and (g) seek to justify one and condemn the other. Adherents of (c) are accused of doubling phallic maleness, colluding with heteronormativity, and despising women; adherents of (g) are accused of being effeminate, colluding with heteronormativity, and (secretly) despising women. A taxonomist is not obliged to evaluate—though in fact the terms I have been using are replete, inevitably, with premature evaluations; there is no neutral language.

As with model (g), for some men the positions in (c) might better be apprehended as "RF" or "RM" (relatively feminine or masculine). However, this does not affect the viability of the model. The main structural inadequacy in (c) is that diverse relations are incorporated together. If this model may be labeled narcissistic, that does not mean that a monochromatic sameness prevails. For very many gay men, it is crucial that the desired object in model (c) should be *male and different*—different, above all, in class, and/or age, and/or race. Let's take examples.

At the start of the film about David Hockney and his friends and lovers, *A Bigger Splash* (Jack Hazan, 1974), we see a good-looking young man, hands behind his head, face composed. The camera swings between him and Hockney; they look pleased with themselves. Hockney speaks partly toward Joe, partly to camera:

> How could I describe Joe? He's, erm, erm, he's tall; he's about my size [*Hockney smirks and Joe giggles*], erm, he's handsome. He's got a complexion similar to mine. He's [*they laugh*] witty, erm, he's, erm, sexy. And—what else? He's artistic: I've decided you're artistic, Joe.

"When did you decide that?" Joe asks—"When I said I liked your work?" Joe suggests.

Hockney emphasizes the physical similarity of the two men; their complicit laughter allows the viewer to suppose that they are talking partly about genital equipment. However, everything else in the exchange speaks status difference. We don't need to have Hockney described because we know who he is and, anyway, the entire film is about him. He has the authority to decide who is to be called artistic; they have been to Paris with some of his pictures. Joe, we may gather, is stirred by Hockney's fame. At the end of the film we are in the same scene; Joe is talking about Hockney's paintings: "They were so beautiful. And I said, 'My God, I know the painter that did that.' And I knew the person thought I was lying." Joe's admiration is flattering for Hockney who, though I deem nice-looking, is not a pinup boy; age is not mentioned, but Joe is clearly younger. The difference in status, I think for both men, is part of the attraction.

Class difference was very common in mid-twentieth-century queer relationships, where it was often associated with (middle-class) effeminacy and (working-class) masculinity; I have written about this in various places.[55] Some women cultivated it as well. Stephen in *The Well of Loneliness* begins by falling in love with Collins, the maid. Ominously, in respect of her later sacrifice of Mary, Stephen prays to be allowed to take Collins's housemaid's knee, Christlike, upon herself; when praying doesn't work she tries kneeling for long periods. Disillusionment sets in when she comes upon Collins necking with the footman; she handles it by transferring her affections to her new pony, which she names "Collins." As Prosser points out, Stephen is of a higher class than her lovers, Angela and Mary.[56] Consider also Virginia Woolf's romance with aristocracy, as well as with Vita Sackville-West, for instance as displayed in *Orlando*. I am taking "class" approximately, as comprising hierarchies of wealth, status, and cultural sophistication, and their markers in attire, decor, and general lifestyle; it is in my view quite wrong to suppose that we have grown out of all that.

Class hierarchy is disavowed and then acknowledged in *Tim and Pete*. Both men are into movies, but whereas Tim is an archival researcher and, as I have remarked, at risk of appearing effeminate because of his college-educated manner, Pete is an automobile mechanic, fronts an aggressively political band, and is passing as straight in his rough (lower-class) apartment building. Pete has misled Tim about his " 'middle-class background' ": "the neighborhood was more lower-middle class or blue collar." Pete implied that he studied at Yale, when actually he'd only lived in New Haven with a history professor (class and age hierarchy there). Tim realizes that Pete had "exaggerated so that we'd seem more equal."[57] But does Tim really want Pete to be more equal? "Once I'd sucked Pete's cock while he was only wearing his Yale T-shirt. Afterward he'd said, 'So do you like me better as a brilliant student or a dumb mechanic?' " Tim had replied: " 'I like *you*' "—the correct response for the modern, egalitarian gay man. But now he wonders whether it was true (37). When they saw the film of *Maurice* they went home and acted joke variations on the roles (" 'Oh, Scudder. You're stretching me. My word' "). Their parody effected a "homoerotic catharsis . . . a genuine guilty pleasure" (39; my elision). The endurance of class mobility as a theme is evident in *The Talented Mr. Ripley* (Anthony Minghella, 1999) and *AKA* (Duncan Roy, 2002), films in which desire-for and desire-to-be cross over to intriguing effect.

If model (c) sexualities may be regarded as narcissistic, and hence as involving what one was, would like to have been, or would like to be, then age difference is a likely component (it is a factor in *A Bigger Splash* and *Tim and Pete*). In Felice Picano's novel *Like People in History*, a young ACT UP activist is surprised to find Wally and the older narrator together: " 'I could never figure out why a great-looking guy like Wally would get involved in a transgen thing.' " "Read trans-generational," the narrator says to himself. "Read I'm old enough to be his father but neither look it nor act like it. Read eternal Peter Pan."[58] The age model flourishes notwithstanding. It figures in many of the most influential texts of our time—*The Immoralist* (André Gide), *Death in Venice* (Thomas Mann), *Maurice* (E. M. Forster), *Funeral Rites* (Jean Genet), *Hemlock and After* (Angus Wilson), *Variation on a Theme* (Terence Rattigan), *Sweet Bird of Youth* (Tennessee Williams), *Entertaining Mr. Sloane* (Joe Orton), *A Single Man* (Christopher Isherwood), *The Swimming-Pool Library* (Alan Hollinghurst), *Ready to Catch Him Should He Fall* (Neil Bartlett), *Frisk* (Dennis Cooper), *The Night Listener* (Armistead Maupin). Its ordinariness is manifest in innumerable contact ads. In *The Beautiful Room Is Empty* by Edmund White, the narrator has a substantial relationship with Lou, but it doesn't work out: Edmund is "too big and educated to be the boy, and too much younger to be the man."[59]

De Lauretis' founding of lesbianism in the loss of the mother seems likely to produce relationships characterized by age difference. She reports how the Milan Women's Bookshop Collective found disparities (social, educational, economic) among their reading group: some women "were seen as authoritarian 'mothers' prevaricating over the preferences and interpretations of the others, who thus felt cast in the role of daughters."[60] The collective decided not to outlaw this element of hierarchy, but to validate relations of *entrustment,*

> in which one woman gives her trust or entrusts herself symbolically to another woman, who thus becomes her guide, mentor, or point of reference. . . . Both women engage in the relationship—and here is the novelty, and the most controversial aspect of this feminist theory of practice—not in spite, but rather because of and in full recognition of the disparity that may exist between them in class or social position, age, level of education, professional status, income, etc. (21–22; my elision)

And this, de Lauretis observes, is "contrary to the egalitarian feminist belief that women's mutual trust is incompatible with unequal power" (24). Working with disparities enables a proper recognition of the diversity of women.

An interesting corollary of the age version of model (c) is that it offers a way for lesbians and gay men to reproduce their kind: some girls and boys may pass through, serially, to the woman's or man's position, and so on from generation to generation. This is anticipated by Freud in his comments on the Greeks: "As soon as the boy became a man he ceased to be a sexual object for men and himself, perhaps, became a lover of boys."[61] Jean Genet is a notable individual who was involved in such a sequence. People hostile to homosexuality become especially distressed at the prospect that we might have our own, same-sex way of breeding.

In my discussion of the gender model (g), it was possible to recognize a range of desires by horizontal substitution—complicating rather than changing the received terms of the model ("M" and "F"), and then adding "RF" and (rg). In model (c) vertical substitution is required. For instance:

(c) A man has:	desire-to-be M	desire-for M
	who is old	who is old
	young	young
	old	young
	young	old

The asymmetry between the two models occurs because (g) is about gender, whereas in (c) gender tends to obscure other factors. I propose calling model (c) the *complementarity* model, taking this to include both the sense of lack in narcissism and the potential affinity in difference; it may be particularized as *race complementary*, *class complementary*, and *age complementary*.

As with the gender model, the mapping of such elaborations discloses further complications. With the complementarity model there is no convenient starting assumption as to who does what. A boy in the age version, for instance, might be rough and "active" or docile (tractable, agreeable) and "passive"; indeed, he might be rough and "passive" or docile and "active." Nor are these matters stable: a relationship may start in one vein and modulate into another. Delving further into the intimate potential of both fantasy and practice would produce more elaborate systems.

BISEXUALITY

A blatant disturber of neatly gendered models is bisexuality. Traditionally, lesbians and gay men have been suspicious of bisexuality, regarding it as a way of evading the stigma of gayness. This may have been partly true. It is plain, however, that very many people entertain, simultaneously or successively, divergent desires, both for and to-be. In *Gay and After* I argue that in the 1970s and 1980s, to declare yourself gay or lesbian was such a strenuous project that to blur the effect by adding that sometimes you were a bit straight after all seemed just too complicated, and scarcely plausible. The notion that there are two distinct populations suited straights because it helped them to avoid contamination, and gays because it facilitated political and economic organization. However, since the mid-1990s, some young people are less daunted by such pressures. Meanwhile some noted lesbian and gay activists, who can hardly be accused of running scared, have been venturing beyond customary identities.[62]

Taxonomical thinking discloses an interesting symmetry: compare the position of the bisexual with that of the transsexual. Both are in-between—irregular combinations of "M" and "F." However, one is structured in desire-for, the other in desire-to-be.

The scope for entertaining, more or less together, formally incompatible desires is represented positively in Aiden Shaw's self-consciously contemporary novel, *Wasted*. At the beginning David and Joe are together, though David was with Flora before. David also loves his nephew, Ryan (age sixteen). Ryan is with Leila, but experiments in going to bed with David. Flora takes up with Don, who is straight but nonetheless drawn to Joe. David dies, and Joe connects with Flora as an artistic collaborator. Flora falls for Josie. Joe finds an immediate sexual rapport with Dylan, a student friend of Ryan. " 'Yeah. Meet the family,' said Flora."[63] These are families of choice. Scarcely an eyelid is batted at these diverse developments. David is worried that his feelings for his young nephew are sexual (50); however, for Ryan it's cool: " 'You sound like an old queer from the Fifties.' He held out his arms to hug David. 'Why should it bother me?' " (52). Flora doesn't hesitate with Josie: "It felt so right in Josie's arms. Complete. Already it felt like the next phase in life" (200); " 'What! Flora a dyke?' " Ryan exclaims. " 'Fuck! That one's full of surprises' " (218). Joe and Dylan feel obliged to defend the age difference between them (fifteen years), but it's no big deal. Among the younger generation more or less anything goes. Indeed, Ryan finds that in fantasy he can fill in the blank of David's former lover with diverse interchangeable images, including himself, like morphing in a pop video. In Ryan's drugged dream the characters of the book merge into each other: "Leila was David. David was Leila, now both just one person. Sexual. Passionate. Loving. Breasts turned into arse cheeks, their dicks into syringes. Dylan also became a part of them. He merged with David and Leila. Ryan loved them, physically and mentally" (257).

However, free-ranging is not the only game in town. As a counterpart to the equable families of choice, *Wasted* displays a preoccupation with involuntary sexual experience. David tells Ryan how he has been obsessed with him—"'hundreds of times I have jerked off about you . . . nine years of jerking off, and the different images I've had of you in my head during that time'" (142; my elision). There is one rape in the novel, probably two. Also, as well as the usual array of clubbing drugs, the characters experiment with a sleeping tablet through which one person subjects himself to an oblivion in which anything can be done to him. "'But he could have done anything.' 'Exactly. Sexy, huh?'" (9). It is a mechanism of trust, but also of exploitation. More ominously, the closing episode of the book indicates that not everyone in the city is cool. The amiable, freewheeling milieu has no resources to match obsessional sexual violence.

The outcome is merely frustrating in a rueful instance offered by Sarah Schulman in her novel *Empathy*. Anna, a woman, and a man have been drinking and decide to play a game: "each one would say their fantasy and the other two would fulfill it." The man goes first, and wants the two women to suck his dick, so they do. The woman wants Anna to be fucked by the man, so she is. However, when Anna wants the man to leave the room so she can make love to the woman, the woman says no.[64]

My goal in this chapter has been to generate models of gender and sexual experience quite abstractly, so as to afford a possible frame within which the more local, empirical categories of Halperin, Smith, Rousseau, and anthropological scholars may be comprehended. I have derived desire-for and desire-to-be from Freudian writings, while trying to avoid the Freudian tendency to essentialize and absolutize gender. The dominant categories that emerge in my analysis are gender difference and gender complementarity. *Gender difference* comprises heterosexuality, together with a range of intricate same-sex relations of identity and desire, in which a person with at least some biological male characteristics is apprehended, either by himself or his male partner, as feminine (and the other way about for women); gender difference turns out, often, to be *relative. Gender complementarity* delineates relations where two men or two women have both desire-for the same gender and desire-to-be the same gender; while it may be addressed as a kind of narcissism, it emerges as preoccupied with hierarchies of class, age, and race, within ostensible sameness.

Arguably, I have myself colluded with heteronormativity by retaining versions of "F" and "M" as starting points in my models. Perhaps we should be taking more seriously a desire-to-be wealthy, taller, a doctor, or Barbra Streisand. Or this:

A man has: desire-to-be not-M   desire-for God

Identity might not be about gender, sexuality might not be genital. Many erotic practices are relatively diffuse—involving pleasures of touch and smell. Some sadomasochists, fetishists, and pedophiles may be able to find satisfaction with either male or female partners. Concepts such as beauty, intelligence, sense of humor, and even virtue may be stimulating; they are not altogether in thrall to ideology. The point of my taxonomy, I have said, is not to limit identity or desire but, rather, to offer a base from which the specificity and multiplicity of the potential combinations and interactions may coherently emerge.

Even with these provisos, I suspect that for many readers my brisk modeling feels too regulated, too standardized. It goes against the general postmodern-poststructuralist truism, that *any* identity is, and should be, provisional, unstable, fuzzy around the edges, occupied only through processes of anxious iteration. Taxonomy refuses the ideology which asserts that we are all individuals, and that our sex lives belong to a private, personal, individual realm into which it is better not to inquire. At least (it may be averred) Freud produces an air of mystery. I have to say that I have never found individualism a very appealing or reassuring idea. As David Evans observes, capitalism invites us to see ourselves as "unique individuals with needs, identities and lifestyles which we express through our purchase of appropriate commodities."[65] In fact, advertisers and other cultural producers know how to corral us into niche markets where we can be conveniently targeted; individual choice is disturbingly congruent with the idea that the right designer label will enable us to complete our happiness. At the same time, it is only by combining that ordinary people gain any potential for political action—for understanding, even. Insistence upon individuality amounts to a naive reluctance to acknowledge that oneself is actually quite like a lot of other people.

The presumption behind my models is that our behavior falls into patterns, and that they are not unconnected with those disclosed by surveys and focus groups. Sexuality is social. However, I do believe that those patterns are immensely complex. In *Stone Butch Blues* Theresa protests when Jess decides to begin taking male hormones in order to pass as a man. " 'I'm a woman, Jess. I love you because you're a woman, too,' " Theresa avers. " 'I just don't want to be some man's wife, even if that man's a woman.' "[66] This is not just a matter of object-choice. Theresa experiences her identity as interdependent with that of her partner: " 'I'm a femme, Jess. I want to be with a butch.' " Otherwise her lesbian character is at stake: " 'If I'm not with a butch everyone just assumes I'm straight. It's like I'm passing too, against my will. I've worked hard to be discriminated against as a lesbian' " (151).

3

FANTASY

DISSIDENT IDENTITIES

After decades of collaboration and occasional sexual experimentation together, Esther Newton and Shirley Walton realized that the reason they had never really got off was that, despite appearances, they both were tops. What is needed, they argue, is "a more precise vocabulary to take us out of Victorian romanticism in sexual matters and toward a new understanding of women's sexual diversity and possibility."[1] The categories Newton and Walton discover are:

> sexual preference (from which gender you usually select your partners)
> erotic identity (how you image yourself)
> erotic role (who you want to be in bed)
> and erotic acts (what you like to do in bed)

What you prefer to do in bed cannot be inferred from whether you appear to be cultivating a masculine or a feminine image, or whether you are the older or the younger partner. My investigation of taxonomies entailed an admittedly schematic tendency; this chapter will involve a corrective assessment of the disorderly operations of fantasy, which challenge, solidify, and divert established identities and orthodox desires.

Your fantasies may run quite counter to your self-presentation; they may be indelible, or fairly flexible; they may be conventional or, at least to others, radically inventive. There is, writes Vicky Lebeau, "no limit to the reach of fantasy, its role in our attempts to contain the trauma, as well as the banality, of our lives."[2] Fantasies are not, as I use the term, typically unconscious, though they may be. Leo Bersani declares their practical importance: "What positions, what activities, what identifications excite us? What imagined object best helps the masturbatory process along? What do we prefer the other to be doing—to us, for us, alone, with someone else?"[3]

By fantasy I mean the scenarios that we cultivate in our imaginings, typically of empowerment and humiliation (I seek to justify this emphasis on power in the next chapter). Fantasies are not necessarily sexual in form or origins; as I have indicated, a scenario of class or racial identification or domination is not necessarily to be *reduced to* the sexual. Their most intense expression *may be* sexual, however; that is where they enter the most vivid sites of pleasure and control. Fantasies are not necessarily solitary, secret, manipulated, or frustrated; the term includes attempted and successful realization in action, perhaps in collaboration with another. Getting someone to share your scenario is not only fun, it may help to make it plausible to you. Perhaps, as Aristophanes suggests in Plato's *Symposium*, the desire to find one's lost other half is fundamental not just to love and desire, but to humanity. Fortunately, a consensual partner may be found for most practices. Conversely, Jean-Paul Sartre's vision of hell, in his play *Huis Clos* (*No Exit*; 1944), is three people trapped together and prevented by their incompatible psychic needs from confirming each other.

Regrettably, that is not all. You can be at ease with yourself and with your partners, but if the social and political system is stigmatizing and criminalizing you, then you still have a problem. Consider the men in the British "Operation Spanner" case, who were found guilty of consensual S/M practices about which they felt personally very happy.[4]

Sophisticated analysis of these topics often begins at the intersection of psychoanalysis and film studies, with "the gaze." A comparison may be broached between the way the subject locates him- or herself in the reading of a film (or other) narrative, and in a fantasy scenario. Laura Mulvey inaugurated much of this work by arguing that in Hollywood cinema male viewers are invited to identify with a male protagonist in looking at and desiring women as objects, while women are to identify with the female figures passively looked at.[5] Such an analysis answers well to an intuitive sense of Hollywood as a monstrous dream machine for the industrialization of culture, dedicated to the preservation of conventional male and female roles. However, it seems to make women passive, not to say stupid, in their reading of film. Also, it makes the system appear more monolithic than is plausible.

Subsequent work—including by Mulvey herself—has consisted of theorizing a way past the implications of the gaze, involving three main
points.[6] First, Hollywood does seem to offer more diverse possibilities. An
instance that has delighted many gay men is the chorus, "June Is Bustin'
Out All Over," in Richard Rodgers and Oscar Hammerstein's *Carousel*
(Henry King, 1956). In the film's choreography, the girls dance with the fish-
ermen and the sailors, but then the boys dance with each other, in pairs,
and for each other as complementary groups; the girls watch the boys, the
boys watch each other. Diverse spectatorial positions are available here for
women and gay men. Unfortunately, *Carousel* strives ultimately to contain
such gender exuberance: the plot is resolutely heterosexual, and even comradely relations between men are shown as dishonest, violent, criminal,
and fatal. Such a contradiction is not unusual in the Hollywood musical.
But audiences do not have to respect closures; they may dwell imaginatively on the episodes that excite them. June may bust out.

Second, as Jean Laplanche and Jean-Bertrand Pontalis observe in a key
formulation, fantasy "is not the object of desire, but its setting." This means
that the subject may locate him- or herself at more than one point in a scenario. A seduction fantasy, for instance, "is a scenario with multiple entries,
in which nothing shows whether the subject will be immediately located as
daughter; it can as well be fixed as *father*, or even in the term *seduces*."[7]
Desire-for alternates, overlaps, and tangles with desire-to-be. Freud is
often credited with noticing this potential mobility of identification and
desire in his essay " 'A Child Is Being Beaten.' "[8] There is a nice instance
of it in James Robert Baker's novel, *Boy Wonder*, where a leading theme is
obsessional fantasy investments. "As the film [*Rebel Without a Cause*]
reached its climax, and Sal Mineo died on the observatory steps, Shark
wept. 'I felt as I *were* Sal Mineo,' he said, 'but also Dean. In the end more
Dean, the survivor, than Mineo, the martyr. But a *part* of me died on those
observatory steps.' "[9]

Chris Straayer considers how a Mulveyan viewing regime may be
adapted to accommodate a lesbian spectator and her partner. In films such
as *Entre Nous* (Diane Kurys, 1983) and *Voyage en Douce* (Michel Deville,
1979), the male in a triangular relationship with two women may be
regarded as an "intermediary" for the feeling between the two women.
Through hints such as the exchange of significant glances, a space for
"female bonding" may be discovered.[10] Again: Dorothy Allison notes that
the clippings pinned above her desk include a young woman in a black lace
dress and feathered hat, and a samurai woman sweeping her long sword.
"Some days I want to become one or the other of them. Some days I want

to write the story of how they become lovers. Other days I can't stand to look at them at all."[11]

Third, any assumption that people want to identify with the nearest equivalent to their ostensible selves is unsatisfactory. On the contrary, fantasy is likely to be the place where we try out alternative identities and desires. Constance Penley has observed how women contributors to *Star Trek* fanzines invest their libidinal energies in heroic, romantic, and sometimes sexy stories about Captain Kirk and Dr. Spock, rather than in women characters. Penley takes this as evidence "that one can, no matter what one's gender, identify with either the man or the woman, or the entire scene itself, or the fictional place of the one who looks on to the scene."[12] The motives of these women seem to be mixed. They are witty and self-parodic; fooling about, experimenting, conducting their own enterprising voyage into the unknown; they are also in earnest. They are claiming male freedoms in their imaginations, while refusing to announce themselves as feminists and rejecting the female body; they are happy to see men as erotically involved but reluctant to contemplate gayness. The main point, however, is perhaps that very many people are far more inventive and adaptable than has often been supposed.

Cross-gender identification is an obvious instance of unruly fantasy. In some aspects at least, it seems to be more disturbing to heteronormativity than dissident object-choice. The notorious version is the traditional gay male devotion to female stars such as Judy Garland and Maria Callas. The death of Garland is usually reckoned to be one of the direct stimuli for the 1969 Stonewall Riots. According to Richard Dyer, Garland "could be seen as in some sense androgynous, as a gender in-between." Further, "she sings of desire for men and of relationships with men going wrong. Male singers could not (still largely do not) sing of these things."[13] Stephen Maddison posits two explanations. The gay man adopts the position of the woman— perhaps, we might confess, elbowing her aside—so as to commandeer her desire for the man. Also, a broadly "feminine" emotional stance is desired and the entire scenario is embraced.[14] Lately many gay men have admired women such as Barbra Streisand and Madonna, who appear to have more control over their destinies.

At this point it seems appropriate to recall my argument in the previous chapter, that individuals who cultivate an element of gender dissidence, stopping short of a transsexual adjustment, do not want to be a different gender; they should be apprehended as aspiring, quite informally, to an amalgamation of gender attributes. Gay men who gain pleasure and strength from a vivid engagement with Streisand don't believe that they *are* her. They are pirating aspects of the image for their own purposes. For gender is a negotiation, not a possession; there are innumerable reasons for trying to feel definite about it, but any such attainment is provisional. Fantasy should be understood, not as an absolute demand, nor as a unified core, but as a sequential, piecemeal, strategic adaptation. David Wojnarowicz remarks: "Fantasized images are actually made up of millions of disjointed observations collected and collated into the forms and textures of thought."[15]

If a mood of feminine emotional indulgence and sexual attraction has appeal for some men, the freedoms associated with masculinity have an obvious appeal for women. Lynne Segal describes how her path to a heterosexual and feminist identification passed through gay fiction: "The lustfully desirous fantasies of my own youth were—as they remain—most easily aroused and fed by the words and images of male homosexual authors." Segal was drawn particularly to the black, and hence doubly forbidden, author James Baldwin. His gay characters afforded a more attractive route to desire for the male than many of the available images of women.[16] Cora Kaplan describes a comparable youthful investment in Baldwin's writing. She appreciated

> the lowered threshold he provided for fantasies that were not about the fixing of gender or sexual orientation but about their mobility and fluidity. Women could take up shifting and multiple fantasy positions within his fictional narratives: that possibility, itself wonderfully if terrifyingly liberating, allowed an identification not just with specific characters but with the scenarios of desire themselves.[17]

Images of gay men offered a way to gain a more flexible foothold among the extant sex and gender scenarios, evading a premature consolidation of fantasmatic desires and identifications within the limits of Cold War gender ideology.

Some lesbians report a youthful, transitional reliance on male gay scenarios. They signaled, in the context of a relative sparsity of lesbian images, at least that not everyone is straight. For Cheryl Clarke, an African American, Baldwin figured the prospect of queer, black authorship. *Another Country*, despite having nothing positive to say about lesbianism, "made me imagine freedom from traditional monogamous heterosexuality and set me to thinking about the possibility of a 'variant' life."[18] As a prominent dissident intellectual—one who preferred not to live in the land of the free—Baldwin represented broader prospects of alternative thought. Bia Lowe describes a double displacement, whereby she invested in actors who were admired for their virility while implicitly embodying an element of gayness. Lowe got from her mother the idea that actors such as Laurence Olivier and Rock Hudson

> were men with enormous sex appeal and, now I realize, not without that certain je ne sais quoi [sic]. Was I unknowingly drawn to gay men because of the model of my mother? Or because, as a budding Miss H, I was protected by them from the failure of heterosexual contact? Because gay men reminded me more of brothers than of fathers? Until I came out, I might as well have been a gay man, for male was the only gender I would spot in the "pathology" of same-sex love. I read *Giovanni's Room*, saw *The Boys in the Band*. I eyed my mother's string of interior decorators. I listened for clues to my own stirrings in the swells and swirl of Tchaikovsky's music.[19]

As well as race, class identifications may tangle with sexuality and gender. Sue-Ellen Case says she became queer through an adolescent identification with Arthur Rimbaud.[20] Valerie Walkerdine remarks how, watching *Rocky II*, she found that her identification was taking an unexpected path. She had not expected to enjoy its "macho sexism," but she found herself identifying with the class feeling that informs it. "The film brought me up against such memories of pain and struggle and class that it made me cry. . . . I too wanted Rocky to win. Indeed, I *was* Rocky—struggling, fighting, crying to get out."[21] Class feeling overwhelmed gender principles—or, rather, enabled a more complex experience of them.

There may be downsides to these irregular identifications. As always with appropriations, one gets more than one had bargained for. For Kaplan, to read Baldwin in the context of the limited ideology of femininity that prevailed in the late 1950s meant engaging "not only in an empathetic, even desiring, identification with the figures of masculinity in his texts, but also (if only subliminally) in a repudiation of the feminine, if not exactly of women."[22] Segal pursued her interest in gay men to the extent of becoming pregnant by and marrying one; it didn't work out.[23]

SUBSTITUTIONS, CONFLATIONS, REVERSALS, LOOPS

Anthropologists have held that some societies organize same-sex passion around age, others around gender. In chapter 2, correspondingly, a complementarity model and a relative-gender model emerged. But these models are not always discrete. In Pai Hsien-yung's Taiwanese novel *Crystal Boys*, the prostitutes are all boys and the punters are older men; the informing imagery, in this militaristic society, is of fathers and sons. This seems to be a same-sex community structured primarily around age. Nonetheless, the boys are called "fairies," even the ones who might seem masculine: one who is "husky as an ox" is called "Little Fairy," and one with "a wonderful physique"— "broad shoulders, and a muscular chest"—is called "the Butch Queen."[24]

What seems to be happening here is a *conflation* or *substitution* of roles: since both boys and women figure subordination, they may be blurred together, or the one may stand for the other. It is beyond the scope of this book to track the range and intricacy of fantasy. In this section I mean to unravel some exemplary instances of fantasmatic maneuvering and explicit role-play, discovering a nexus of complications that seem especially prominent as ways of elaborating gay psychic experience. I distinguish substitutions, conflations, reversals, and loops.

Sometimes roles are substituted for (allegedly) tactical reasons. In single-sex institutions one male may fuck another without losing status, so long as he takes the "active" part and the other is regarded as a stand-in woman. In 1922, Alec Waugh invoked the substitutability of boys and women as an explanation for homosexuality in boarding schools:

> In this environment there is nothing unnatural about the attraction exercised by a small boy over an elder one. A small boy is the nearest approach possible to the feminine ideal. Indeed a small boy at a Public School has many of the characteristics that a man would hope and expect to find in a woman. He is small, weak, and stands in need of protection.[25]

That is a heteronormative way of putting it, of course; we might say that the attraction of women resides in their "boyish" characteristics. Boy-love as a substitute for girl-love is widely displayed in prison dramas, including *Little Ol' Boy* by Albert Bein, *"Now Barabbas . . ."* [sic] by William Douglas Home, *Deathwatch* by Jean Genet, and *Fortune and Men's Eyes* by John Herbert.[26]

Freud's comment on same-sex passion among the Greeks finds that love of boys is really about love of women. "What excited a man's love was not the *masculine* character of a boy, but his physical resemblance to a woman as well as his feminine mental qualities—his shyness, his modesty and his need for instruction and assistance."[27] So gender hierarchy is maintained after all—so long as you go along with the Victorian notion of what "a woman" is like. Foucault believes the opposite of the Greeks:

it was the juvenile body with its peculiar charm that was regularly suggested as the "right object" of pleasure. And it would be a mistake to think that its traits were valued because of what they shared with feminine beauty. They were appreciated in themselves or in their juxtaposition with the signs and guarantees of a developing virility.[28]

Commenting on an earlier version of some of the ideas in the current study, David Halperin insists that not all systems conflate all subordinations, or in the same way.[29] This is indeed my point; the conflations I observe are particular strategic adjustments, not instances of an essential process.

It is noticeable that substitution and conflation of roles are more commonly posited of subordinate figures. The masculine, together with the adult, the established, and the white, appears simply as itself, and claims the authority to reposition its others. Pai Hsien-yung's crystal boys, having run away from home, are lower class as well as young and feminine. Arthur, in Alan Hollinghurst's *Swimming-Pool Library*, is black, and also younger and considerably poorer. Such conflations illustrate the malleability of fantasy, but also the ruthlessness of its appropriations, and its disregard for the stability of the subordinated person. If relative femininity and youth are regarded as metonymic, or perhaps even the same, then the conflation of roles may enable a more elaborate fantasmatic discourse; alternatively, it may lead to a confused identity.

Edmund White reports: everyone on the New York scene was doing it: "We were all obsessed with fantasies back then, which we kept exploring until they became absurd. One boy even said to me: 'I do father-son, sailor-slut, older brother–younger brother, black rapist–white secretary, trucker-hitchhiker, and a virgin couple on their wedding night.'"[30] You can slot into one or the other; it's all the same kind of thing; hierarchy is the point, as much as the particular terms in which it is framed. Perhaps it is a mistake to suppose an original menu of discrete dominations and subordinations, wherein everything was simply itself. In fact, an attraction of same-sex relations may reside in their potential to invoke, simultaneously, several social hierarchies in complicated combinations.

The fantasy identifications discussed so far seem to involve fairly simple substitutions; a person is able to cultivate feelings, typically of empowerment or submission, that would be hard to access through his or her regular identity. Of course, fantasy is not always so conveniently labeled or so comfortably experienced. Often in psychic life there is a tendency for roles to be *reversed*—such that one fantasizes oneself as the other. As Jacqueline Rose puts it, with case histories of Jewish Holocaust survivors in view, "being a victim does not stop you from identifying with the aggressor; being an aggressor does not stop you from identifying with the victim."[31] Role reversal was common in the cross-class liaison of the mid-twentieth century, where the bit of rough trade might be called upon to fuck his social superior.

I remarked at the start of this book how Reginald Shepherd's desire for men is entangled with his experience of racial hierarchy. Shepherd both desires white men and has himself always wanted to be white. He asks, "How much of wanting another man is the desire to be that man?" The connection works quite literally: by being seen with a white lover, Shepherd becomes "an honorary white man." He believes that sex is about dominance and submission: "For a gay man both roles are simultaneously available."[32] Gary Fisher, with similar issues in mind, ponders *Billy Budd*: Melville might have been "a bit more generous; he might have asked us to feel instead of to just watch, feel what it is to be victim and victimizer; white victim and then black victim; white victimizer and black victimizer; asked us to feel, to study and enjoy all the permutations, all the variations on a theme in this text."[33]

Such reversals may be facilitated in gay relations. In the previous chapter I followed John Fletcher's argument about the breaking of the fragile barrier between identification and desire, to show that such confounding of the distinction between desire-to-be and desire-for is endemic in same-sex passion. Earl Jackson Jr. frames this factor in a revision of Mulveyan, cinematic terms: whereas the viewing pleasures of the heterosexual male may most easily entail identification with the man and objectification of the woman, the gay viewer "regularly identifies with the figure he sexually objectifies. In other words, he experiences a coalescence of drives that are radically dichotomized in his heterosexual male counterpart." This is specially true in pornography.[34] In my view Jackson may underestimate the perversity (to use the normative term) in much heterosexual passion; in horror films men may identify with the female victim.[35] But we should take Jackson's point, that gay people may more readily cross the heavily policed line between identity and desire, making it relatively convenient to cultivate complex scenarios. In Robert Chesney's play *Jerker, or the Helping Hand*, J. R. declares his engagement with both the prince and the princess: "I was always more interested in *him* than in the fairy tale princesses— Snow White, Cinderella, whatever. *I* identified with the Sleeping *Beauty*: *I* wanted that kiss."[36] J. R. is committed to both characters: he wants to be both the prince who kisses and the princess who gets kissed—and awakened into sexual response, such that the prince gets kissed in return.

Finally, we may observe instances in which passion takes a *loop* through one kind of identification or desire, in order to gain a role in relation to another. This was a resource for the young Edmund White, as he struggled with adolescent passion. In *A Boy's Own Story* he falls for the gym teacher, Mr. Pouchet, and imagines himself to be Pouchet's girlfriend. White was prepared to be "Julie or Helen or whoever else, just so long as I was in his mind somehow."[37] His desire loops through the desire of the teacher and the person of the girlfriend.

Jonathan Dollimore describes a threesome in which a bisexual male (I call him "the protagonist") watches a man fucking with a woman:

> His identifications here are multiple: he identifies with the man (he wants to be in his position, having sex with the woman) but he also wants to be her. And I mean *be* her: he doesn't just want to be in her position and have the man fuck him as himself (though he wants that too); no, he wants to be fucked by the man with himself in the position of, which is to say, as, the woman.[38]

The protagonist has desire-to-be the man, but this is for a purpose: "he wants to be in [the man's] position, having sex with the woman." He wants to fuck the woman, and imagines doing it through the agency of the man. His masculine activity is routed through another. Elsewhere, we have found desire-for and desire-to-be to be autonomous, in the sense that nothing about the one can reliably be inferred from the other (drag artistes may be straight). In this case, one facilitates the other:

desire-to-be the man ⟶ desire-for the woman

Both these desires seem to secure the masculinity of the man. This, however, is not the protagonist's goal, Dollimore insists: "he also wants to be her. And I mean *be* her."

desire-for the man ⟶ desire-to-be the woman

Bisexuality is usually glossed, quite simply, as a static split: desire-for both genders. This is not an adequate account of the positionings of Dollimore's protagonist: he is performing an elaborate psychic loop through the possible permutations. He knows the pleasure of being fucked by a man, he adds, but in this scenario "he also wants to be the woman; he wants to be fucked by the man in a way he imagines—fantasizes—only a woman can be." This way of putting it implies another variant:

$$\text{desire-to-be the woman} \longrightarrow \text{desire-for the man}$$

"Maybe he desires the man through her."

Is this the goal, then? For the bisexual protagonist, Dollimore admits, "the sexual attractiveness of the male is heightened by the fact that the latter is apparently desired by the woman; he excites the more because he is desired by her" (529). Should we declare the protagonist in bad faith, then? His desire-for and desire-to-be take him in a loop through the woman, but his true goal is to share the identity and desire of the man (Dollimore is aware that the woman might be the most objectified figure in the scenario as he presents it; indeed, she might be in effect extinguished). However, I believe that would be a false inference. The care with which the sequence is elaborated indicates that the pleasure is in the entire process, not in any singular end product. Indeed, having reached the point of desiring the man, the protagonist may well go back to the beginning and, from the position of the man, desire the woman.

Guy Willard's novel *Mirrors of Narcissus* offers a complex sequence of the desires and identities that one young man might experience. We first see Guy looking at his reflection after working out, and enjoying the thought that women in the dorm opposite can see him through the window. His desire-to-be appears suitably masculine, and adequately depends on heterosexual validation. However, desire-to-be crosses into desire-for when he masturbates over a picture of a bodybuilder. He likes the thought of other men fancying his girlfriend, Christine. "It was as if she were my doll and I was dressing her up to please the guys. And my pleasure in it was ignited by a process of reflection: the other boys' excitement excited me." So far so good, though the other boys seem rather prominent in the fantasy. Then identification turns to desire: "I imagined that all the male attention she drew to her stuck to the surface of her skin, so that when I caressed her, I was caressing those male glances. . . . This was the only way I could get close to a boy."[39] Guy contrives the positions of Christine and himself in lovemaking so that she appears like a boy: "I lay on my back and she sat atop me straddling my thighs, the better to stroke my erection. From the way she was sitting it looked as if my upthrusting penis were hers, completing the illusion that she was a boy" (26). The consequent orgasm may be credited to all three of them. Christine sees that Guy is turned on; she is open-minded, but he conceals the extent of his gay interest.

Thus far, Guy's desires may be represented like this:

$$\text{desire-to-be M} \longrightarrow \text{desire-for F} \longrightarrow \text{desire-for M}$$

Guy manages to lever the woman out of the loop when he is invited to model as Narcissus by a gay artist, Peter. Guy is excited by the thought that Peter desires him. When the painting is finished, Guy finds himself aroused by the image of himself (mirroring again the Narcissus in the painting, of course).

Guy falls for his straight roommate, Scott, who, in the manner we have seen elsewhere, is slightly feminine—though not, of course, effeminate: "The eyes were what held my attention. They were large and soulful, and hinted of artistic sensibilities. As if to confirm this, his skin was very fair, a shade too delicate for a boy, though it didn't make him effeminate in any way" (63). Guy seeks to approach Scott by suggesting to Christine that they help him to lose his virginity. She refuses to do this; instead, she and Scott sleep together and discover their love for one another. For Guy, though only in imagination, this completes a loop: "Through the channel of Christine's body, Scott and I were now one, linked by the most basic bonds vouchsafed to unrelated strangers. My skin, in nakedness, had touched Christine's, and her skin, in nakedness had touched his" (169).

$$\text{desire-for F} \longrightarrow \text{desire-for M}$$

The implication in the novel is that Guy was really gay all along, and using loop strategies, exploitatively, to sort himself out. Thus any playful or adventurous potential in his fantasies is set aside. Christine's refusal to collaborate is wise, according to the narrative; Scott, despite his responsiveness to Guy's advances on one occasion, is "Perfectly normal" (187). The simplest models are adequate after all. *Mirrors of Narcissus* finally offers a traditional view of dissident fantasy.

THE SUBJECT IN POSTSTRUCTURALISM

As film theory has repudiated the deterministic notion of spectatorship found initially in Mulvey, it has sometimes imagined a free play of identities. Penley declares: "An important emphasis has been placed on the subject's ability to assume, successively, all the available positions in the fantasmatic scenario."[40] The mobility and intricacies of fantasy tend to undermine expectations of stability, thereby facilitating an elaborate range of libidinal investments. This account is too voluntaristic for Teresa de Lauretis. She objects to

> the optimistically silly notion of an unbounded mobility of identities for the spectator-subject; that is to say, any spectator would be able to assume and shift between a variety of identificatory positions, would be able to pick and choose any or all of the subject-positions inscribed in the film regardless of gender or sexual difference, to say nothing of other kinds of difference.[41]

Even in these postmodern times, identity has to have some kind of structure, however provisional. I have shown readers investing in diverse aspects of scenarios, but that does not mean there are no constraints; indeed, movement within a scenario may help to keep it in place. This issue is the theme of this section.

The potential for mobility in psychic identifications has been a persistent motif in queer and poststructuralist thought (queer theory is best understood as a kind of poststructuralism). Judith Butler concludes *Gender Trouble* with the prospect that we might evade the oppressions of difference by elaborating a multiplicity of fantasies and practices: "Cultural configurations of sex and gender might then proliferate or, rather, their present proliferation might then become articulable within the discourses that establish intelligible cultural life, confounding the very binarism of sex, and exposing its fundamental unnaturalness."[42] If we recognized innumerable sexualities, norms and stigma would collapse. Henning Bech reaches a compatible conclusion in his book *When Men Meet*. He argues that the admiration of gay men for masculinity has now become a harmless style choice:

> the more the surfaces are detached and become autonomous, the more the roles are severed from nature, the more accessible they become for staging and pleasure, the more they can be treated *as* surfaces, *as* roles, *as* images. . . . We can finally reach the point at which the dangerous in masculinity is maintained all the while it's suspended, the violence, the domination, the power display; it can stop when it isn't fun any more.[43]

The more we experiment with masculinity, in other words, the less significance it has. Bech foresees the demise of the masculine/feminine hierarchy.

I am struck more by the repetition and fixity of fantasy, in the experience of very many people. I conceded in chapter 2 that my juggling of "M" and

"F" might impress the reader as too standardized. It goes against the general postmodern/poststructuralist truism that *any* identity is, and should be, provisional, unstable. I do believe that psychic life is manufactured out of the typical building blocks of gender, age, class, race, and sexual orientation. These are the structures in which we live, and ongoing psychic life is an attempt to cope with the attendant triumphs and humiliations. I envisage our selfhoods as constructed through a kind of *bricolage*—the term proposed by Claude Lévi-Strauss to describe the development of cultures in anthropology. In John Clarke's account this means a piecemeal, appropriative process: "the re-ordering and re-contextualisation of objects to communicate fresh meanings, within a total system of significances, which already includes prior and sedimented meanings attached to the objects used."[44] As I have said, it is because the permutations are so numerous and so intricate that the outcome is experienced by many as implying the uniqueness of the individual, and, often, his or her ultimate freedom from the constraints of history and ideology.

What is difficult to articulate, in the models I have been using, is the fourth dimension: time. In the formation of an individual subject, there will be moments of crystallization, in which a specific set of identifications and object-choices will become established, while others are repudiated. Fantasies attempt to manage those traumatic moments, often in tangled form; the individual subject, at any point of time, is the product of a sequence of pioneering and entrenched selves. Through these successive engagements, the subject is constituted.

The postmodern notion that one might manage better without some kind of working identity is intensely romantic. R. D. Laing, the 1960s theorist of damaged identity, remarks: "It is difficult to imagine many who would choose unlimited freedom within a nexus of personal relations, if anything they did had no significance for anyone else. Would anyone choose freedom if nothing he did mattered to anyone?"[45] Would a boundless indeterminacy be sexy? Dollimore invokes the German film *Taxi zum Klo* (*Taxi to the Toilet*: Frank Ripploh, 1981), where Frank passes a note through to the next cubicle asking, "What are you into?" The reply is, "Everything. Anything." Frank walks out in disgust.[46] No opposition, no substance, no turn-on. It is one of Foucault's key insights: power always entails—is experienced only through—resistance.

Identity, according to Laing, is neither essential, nor something you adopt and proclaim, like a political slogan. More fundamentally, it is "that whereby one feels one is *the same*, in this place, this time as at that time and at that place, past or future; it is that whereby one is identified. I have the impression that most people tend to come to feel that they are the same continuous beings through womb, to tomb. And that this 'identity,' the more it is phantasy, is the more intensely defended" (86; Laing's emphasis). Because gay people may be out of touch with their birth families and closeted at work, they may appear to be unconstrained. A potential for anomie in gay culture is the theme of Andrew Holleran's *Dancer from the Dance*. "We are free to do anything, live anywhere, it doesn't matter. We're completely free and that's the horror," Malone opines. " 'Perhaps you would like a Valium," Sutherland responds.[47]

The extent to which one might be bound to an identity, and the consequences of abandoning it, are explored in Kevin Smith's film *Chasing Amy* (1997). Placing his friendship and artistic collaboration with Banky in jeopardy, Holden falls in love with Alyssa, although he knows she is a lesbian. His feelings become unbearably intense, so he tells her of them. Alyssa's response is to climb out of the car and start hitchhiking. Has she no comment? Yes: "Fuck you!" It is unfair of Holden to unburden his soul to her, because by ignoring her declared lesbianism he is refusing to take her seriously: "Do you remember for one fucking second who I am?" "People change," Holden replies. "Oh, it's that simple. You fall in love with me and want a romantic relationship. Nothing changes for you. . . . I can't just get into a relationship with you without throwing my whole fucking world into upheaval" (my elision). There's bound to be a period of adjustment, Holden replies. "There's no period of adjustment, Holden, I am fucking gay. That's who I am, and you assume that I can just turn all that around because you've got a fucking crush!" She follows him back to the car, however; they embrace heavily; next thing it's morning and they're sleeping on the couch together.

Alyssa does seem able to abandon her declared identity after all. The outcome is notably uneven, however, as Holden falls into complacent assumptions. He is devastated to learn that Alyssa's adaptable identity includes a history of experimentation with boys at school. Also, he presumes that he can reengineer his relations with Banky, who is evidently jealous, by inviting him to explore his (alleged) latent homosexuality. In some circumstances some people may be able to change some parts of their identities in some directions, but they will still be carrying all kinds of debris, and indeed esteem, from their former selves, and the outcome may be uncomfortable.

Generally, erotic imagery proves amazingly stubborn, as people who have tried to change through psychotherapy and religious devotion know. In a memorable formulation, Lynne Segal presents intrepid fantasmatic adventuring as characteristic of psychic life: "We insert ourselves, whatever our sex, at one and the same moment as both active and passive, powerful and powerless, giving and receiving: desire flows through binaries in all directions at once, all of the time."[48] Yet I can also envisage a case for the opposite extreme: the fixation. The obsessional fetishist may be living more intensely than people who gain an easy, moderate pleasure, either from unconsidered custom, or from almost anything.

Jeanette Winterson's protagonist in *The PowerBook* supposes that the idiom of the computer adds a new impetus to the idea of freedom to be who you will, if only for one night. This prospect is emblematic of our ability to rewrite the stories in which we figure: "there is always a new beginning, a different end. I can change the story. I am the story."[49] We assume that the screen we have open at the moment represents our lives, but there is another, less familiar window behind that, and yet another beyond that. "We think of ourselves as close and finite, when we are multiple and infinite" (103). However, *The PowerBook* does not actually exemplify such freedom. Ali (as the narrator is most often called) engages in a sultry affair with a married woman, who is reluctant to leave her husband. This passion governs Ali's electronic explorations: "That's why I trawl my screen like a beachcomber—looking for you, looking for me, trying to see through the disguise. I guess I've been looking for us both all my life" (64). This is hardly freedom, and hardly the sign of a new electronic age. It is a quest as purposeful and traditional as those pursued by the heroic knights of epic and romance—whose stories are intercut with Ali's affair. The challenge to forsake everything, follow your heart, and live for the magical twosome is hardly a new narrative motif.

The invocation of freedom sits oddly with the air of obsession in *The PowerBook*. Indeed, links with other novels by Winterson suggest that she herself (like very many authors) is working out some compulsive stories of her own. The angry invocation of narrow childhood circumstances is reminiscent of *Oranges Are Not the Only Fruit*, and her lover's flaming red hair and autocratic husband recall Louise in *Written on the Body*. Indeed, the latter novel and *The PowerBook* suggest a dynamic, whereby the narrator is a masculinized figure (in *Written on the Body* it is unclear whether s/he is a woman or a man) who feels impelled to compete with the husband. The narrator in *The PowerBook* identifies herself with male heroes, permitting little sense of herself as a woman; she doesn't allow that any particular pressures might attend a lesbian affair. In *The Passion*, Henri venerates Napoleon, while Villanelle makes love to another woman in the guise of a man, and has to endure the sight through a window of the domestic affection of her lover and her husband. The patterns in Winterson's writing mark the extent to which we do not control our own stories.

It may be observed also that *The PowerBook* affords an instance of the thesis I develop in the next chapter, concerning the effacement and ineluctability of power in our relationships. Ali insists that there is no legitimate overlap between power and love. However, the main narrative shows her seeking to control her lover by imposing her idea of how they should proceed. She complains specifically when she feels herself unable to exclude her lover's husband. "The only power I have is the negative power of withdrawal. . . . A relationship where one person has no power or negative power, isn't a relationship, it's the bond between master and slave" (187; my elision). Of course, this would explain Ali's male identification: men have power. While fantasy may prove transformative, it may also trap the subject in fruitless and perhaps dangerous compulsions.

THE FRONTIERS OF FANTASY

The psychic investments discussed thus far in the present chapter are in fact less about freedom than the discovery of a flexible, but apparently suitable, identity. In other contexts, the scope of the fantasy scenario is a problem: it harbors rapists, stalkers, habitual familial abusers, serial killers. Not all roles can be legitimated, even within the superpermissive regime of Queer. There is a persisting problem with individuals who want to force their practices upon others. This should not surprise us. While the hierarchies of gender, age, class, and race often appear benign, and may afford opportunities for rewarding sexual adventures, it is evident that the social and political system, which sponsors such fantasies, can operate in intimidating and brutal ways when a serious threat is perceived. As these hierarchies are internalized by individuals and groups, often as competing psychic and social demands, they are bound to produce strenuous techniques of psychic management and vehement attempts to gain control of self and others. Violent mental disturbance, in other words, is what you would expect in societies like ours.

Mark Ravenhill's play *Shopping and Fucking* represents the *ménage à trois* of Robbie, Lulu, and Mark as unexceptional but foundering because of Mark's substance abuse. He decides, as part of his cure, to avoid dependency of any kind, but young Gary's story of abuse by his stepfather draws Mark in after all. Gary, however, doesn't want to be loved and protected, he wants to be owned and hurt. So why not gratify him? "When someone's paying, someone wants something and they're paying, then you do it. Nothing right. Nothing wrong. It's a deal," Gary says.[50] Is this right? For Robbie in particular, more or less anything goes. Like him, many of us are learning to acknowledge and accommodate a range of "perverse" practices that previously would have been thought embarrassing, if not disgusting. But does that mean we can have any experience that we can afford to pay for? When they operate a telephone chat line, Lulu is eventually sickened when a scenario comes too close to life. The question, then, is this: How far is fantasy liberating, how far constraining?

The protagonist in *Frisk* by Dennis Cooper is drawn "uncontrollably" to a particular "physical type."[51] Ever since the age of thirteen, when he saw photos of an apparently murdered model, the desires of the narrator, Dennis, have been fixed on such a boy and such a scene ("It looked as if someone had set off a bomb in his rectum"; 27). The photos, he says, "went on to completely direct or destroy my life" (30). Five years later Dennis meets Henry, who claims to have been the model: the photos were fakes. But that doesn't dispel the fantasy.

The novel takes place at this interface between actuality and fantasy. Samson is Dennis's ideal type, so he maintains his fantasy scenario in his imagination during conventional lovemaking: "In reality I was caressing him. In my head I'd be grabbing objects off the night table, crashing his skull, then mutilating his body, especially his ass, while he tried to dissuade me from murdering him in a brain-damaged voice" (34). One night Dennis loses it with Samson and punches him repeatedly. Samson isn't upset: " 'I was *so* out of it. And you were *so* weird' " (35; Cooper's emphases). However, Dennis is afraid, and for a few years avoids

serious, ongoing relationships as a precaution. It wasn't that I didn't fantasize murdering hustlers. It's just that I tend to be too scared or shy the first few times I sleep with someone to do what I actually want. The worst that could, and did, happen was I'd get a little too rough. But the hustler would stop me, or I'd stop myself, before things became more than conventionally kinky, as far as he knew. (36)

What is inhibiting Dennis from acting out his fantasies? He seems to have no trouble getting boys to go with him, especially when they are on drugs; he has money (his parents send it to him). He writes a story, in which Joe's wish to be hurt has placed him in the power of Gary, who fantasizes about murdering people. " 'But something usually stops me. I think it's beauty. But whatever it is, it's not there with you. I really want to kill you,' " Gary says (63). He is not impressed by the conventional S/M notion that the bottom is in charge. " 'Well, um, you shouldn't do it, because I don't want you to, and I'm half of this,' " Joe protests. " 'If I don't do it,' Gary said, 'that'll be why. But it's the only reason, which is strange, because there should be others, right?' " (64).

We live in a world, *Frisk* is showing, in which it is not easy to supply better reasons. This is not a new dilemma (" 'I mean, I know there's no God' "— Dennis; 69). Compare Dorian Gray's exclamation when Lord Henry is executing his initial seduction: " 'Stop!' faltered Dorian Gray, 'Stop! you bewilder me. I don't know what to say. There is some answer to you, but I cannot find it.' "[52] Dennis's old friend Julian says he understands the appeal of murder, but is shocked by the idea of doing it. " 'I'm not being moralistic. I'm talking fairness, which is not a particularly bad rule to live by, as rules go' " (112). This seems right, but it scarcely measures up to the intensity of Dennis's compulsion.

Ultimately he is inhibited, more simply, by the very extremity of the gap between ordinary life and his fantasy. Henry wants details of the photos in which he appeared, but they seem preposterous in real-life conversation: "Spoken aloud, the descriptions seemed much more pretentious, ridiculous, amoral . . . something, than they'd ever been in the secret, uncritical world of my fantasies" (30; Cooper's pause). This gap between what you can imagine and what you can actually, plausibly, say or do is neatly illustrated when Dennis fantasizes about sacrificing a boy called Finn on the top of an Aztec pyramid. "Part of me wanted to kill and dismember him, which I probably could have done without getting arrested," Dennis reports; "but most of me gave him a towel, then humored him until he left" (38).

Dennis writes letters to his old friend Julian, describing how he has been killing boys in Amsterdam. The murders become more violent and disgusting (at least to me). Julian and his younger brother Kevin, who's always had a thing for Dennis, come to rescue him. Kevin lights on the idea of restaging the photos, and hence Dennis's original trauma. "I'd wind up cured or exorcised or something" (121). It appears to work; Julian goes home to his partner, while Kevin and Dennis stay together. But is Dennis cured? It all depends, as Claudia Card says of S/M generally, on whether the cathartic or the addiction model is correct. The former means that occasional controlled indulgence may enable painful psychic material to be disposed of safely; the latter that enactment may produce a need for more intensity or more frequency.[53] The closure of *Frisk* depends on the cathartic model (Dennis's need to act out his desires diminishes), but elsewhere in the novel Dennis's obsessions feed on themselves and the addiction model appears to reign; certainly it seems to claim intense imaginative energy. Nor is mere indulgence in fantasy without eventual consequence. Dennis explains why he was unfazed by the first (pretended) murder: "I guess I'd fantasized killing a boy for so long that all the truth did was fill in details. The feeling was already planned and decided for ten years at least" (92). *Frisk* does not flinch from the thought that fantasmatic desires may prove overwhelmingly addictive, no matter how repulsive they are.

In fact, although he has not actually murdered anyone, Dennis's motives in writing the letters were not therapeutic: "I realized at some point that I couldn't and wouldn't kill anyone, no matter how persuasive the fantasy is." He was trying to attract an accomplice—someone to "come here, and give me the courage or amorality or whatever to actually kill somebody in league with them" (123). Notice also the ambivalence in Dennis's key statement, that the snuff photos "went on to completely direct or destroy my life" (30). "Destroy" speaks Dennis's revulsion, but "direct" is more complacent.

Dennis's unrepentant streak nourishes and is nourished by a disturbing cross-current in the novel: the idea that the boys he approaches are neither uninterested nor unwilling. Henry is still eager to please, eager to be appreciated; Joe at the last moment appears to consent to his own murder; Pierre's partner predicts that a boy who has escaped from a "kiddie porn ring" will be terrified, but he blows a kiss to media reporters (86). One might argue, anyway, that consent is often no more than *internalized ideology*. For instance, when in the marriage service the partners say "I will," this is perhaps because they are taking it for granted that matrimony is their natural destiny. It would be open to the sexual dissident to interrupt with an impediment, namely that marriage colludes with the wish of the state to control reproduction by fixing gendered and sexual roles. The bride and groom believe they are choosing freely, but they have been systematically conditioned. Where we consent, therefore, we may be most deluded. Not much can be done about this, but it undermines any straightforward reliance upon consent as an ethical and political principle.

Nonetheless, many readers may reflect that the ascription of readiness to the boys is all too convenient for Dennis. A novel is a kind of fantasy scenario, in which the characters may be arranged to suit an imaginative contrivance. The novel says, "this is how people are," but readers may declare the outcome implausible or immoral—merely (we may say) a fantasy. *Frisk* actually draws attention to the contrivance of fiction. The narrative slips repeatedly between invention and (pretended) reportage, first and third person. Dennis presents himself continually as if he were in a film. "I should include some reaction shots here," he says, meaning some indication of how he reacted to his own manic assault on Samson. "But I doubt I had many. I felt numb, blank, so my face probably followed suit" (34). He watches slasher movies avidly; his most substantial conversation is with Pierre, a porn star and hustler whom he has hired. He admits that writing down his fantasies " 'was and still is exciting in a pornographic way' " (123). Such an explicit preference for fantasy over reality does not encourage the reader to trust Dennis's perceptions of other people. It is, however, a logical outcome to the indulgence in fantasy that some theorists are encouraging; *Frisk* is about how you police fantasy when experimentation is offered as a good in itself.

In his next novel, *Try*, Cooper presents similarly violent scenarios, but largely from the viewpoint of the teenager. Ziggy is used sexually by his adoptive fathers, Brice and Roger:

> Ziggy's happy. It's drug-induced, no doubt. Still, for whatever reason, he suddenly knows, like, for sure, that a huge part of . . . sexual abuse, at least for him, is how he loves being a target for such intense feelings, especially from someone who knows him and isn't just stupidly thinking he's cute or whatever. That's why he hasn't killed Brice, or hired a hit man like other abused-type teens do.[54]

We may grant that Ziggy's contentment is an interesting and important phenomenon, but it doesn't justify the exploitation. Indeed, the passage quoted acknowledges the extreme distress which "abused-type teens" may experience. Apart from the power (age and wealth) difference, the use of drugs negates any prospect of informed consent. Ziggy is talked into a threesome he doesn't really want; he is suddenly depressed and bursts into tears, but Roger is oblivious: " 'If you loved me . . .'—Ziggy slugs—'. . . you wouldn't *rim* me while I'm *crying*.' This time he hits Roger's head so violently it's knocked loose. 'That's the *truth*, you . . . *scum!*' " (149; Cooper's pauses and emphases).

The quest for accomplices in Cooper's books discloses a frightening world of desperate, undernourished youngsters, lacking any evident parental or school guidance, oblivious to the risk of AIDS, taking without hesitation any drug they are offered, absurdly possessed by heavy metal bands, and making themselves available to far more powerful men in return for the most meager emotional consolations. Henry, for instance, has commodified himself to the point where he asks everyone he has sex with, " 'If you could change one thing about the way I was acting a minute ago, what would that be?' " " 'You talk too much,' the guy said" (*Frisk*, 8–9).

Frisk constitutes a limit case for any progressive, poststructuralist, or queer wish, that all fantasies might be exhilarating and all sexualities viable. If my contention (which I pursue in the next chapter) about the social and political constitution of desire is right, then it means, on the one hand, that we have to accept as inevitable and only realistic the lineaments of power relations in our sexualities. On the other hand, it means also that gross psychic deformations will appear, even as capitalism and patriarchy produce horrific exploitations. While in the first perspective it is vain to expect that the overwhelming run of our desire can be redirected, in the second perspective there will be perilous consequences to some fantasy scenarios, and it will be necessary to intervene. These consequences will not always be at the gruesome level displayed in Cooper's writings; there are other, meaner, and narrower kinds of fixation, which produce barely tolerable bullying, bigotry, and disconfirmation. *Frisk* and *Try* are valuable books because they take some readers at least into the world of abuse without abandoning them there, but also without harboring impractical prospects for reconciliation of aberrant desire.

A later novel, *Guide*, displays Dennis in a more realistic setting. Alongside murderous fantasies, the narrator exhibits a rather subdued, lovelorn stance. Contrary to the earlier novels, he doesn't get the boys he desires. Luke moves in to his apartment, to the alarm of Andy who has seen the novels: " 'Have you read them? They're all about serial murderers. And all the victims are boys. And all the boys look like you.' "[55] Luke doesn't feel threatened: " 'I think Dennis is more sort of someone who lives in his head,' " he opines (170). Let's hope so.

4

POWER

Men come to the brothel in Jean Genet's *The Balcony* to act out scenarios of power. There is the Bishop and the Penitent, the General and his horse, the Maîtresse and the Beggar, and the Judge, the Executioner, and the Thief.

> There are two kings of France with coronation ceremonies and different rituals, an admiral at the stern of his sinking destroyer, a dey of Algiers surrendering, a fireman putting out a fire, a goat attached to a stake, a housewife returning from market, a pickpocket, a robbed man who's bound and beaten up, a Saint Sebastian, a farmer in his barn . . . a missionary dying on the cross, and Christ in person.[1]

There is no chief of police, as the actual incumbent ruefully observes. However, after he has put down the rebellion, the traditional authority figures wilt and men queue up to enter his scenario. The meaning of this fable is that, traditionally, the imagery of the chief of police is insufficiently charismatic; he is not recognized as part of the establishment, he is too functional. He has not figured in the fantasies of citizens. Now the fascist state has arrived, and the policeman bulks large in the psyches of citizens. His symbol is a man-sized phallus, his counterpart a slave, and his setting a mausoleum. Genet is showing that our sexual fantasies depend on the power arrangements in our societies. This chapter aims to appraise, in outline, the relations between sexual practice and fantasy, social organization, and hierarchies of gender, class, age, and race.

TWO BOYS TOGETHER CLINGING

As a boy, Paul Monette sees his incipient queerness as a failure of manhood. He conceives an attachment to Elizabeth Taylor, he says in his autobiography *Becoming a Man*: "I'm not quite sure what I'd identified with, but it seemed to amount to a kind of *emotional* drag—trying on those steamy, gaudy feelings." He and two friends discover all this for themselves; "If someone had told me I was exhibiting a sensibility, I probably would've frozen in horror, terrified my wrists were going limp." A teacher sees them camping around, and notes: " 'Paul spends too much time acting silly with his day student play-mates. It's not healthy. He's got a lot of growing up to do if he wants to be a man.' "[2]

Paul is not happy with his relatively feminine stance. He "hated the soft androgyny of [his] body, which somehow managed to be both scrawny and plump at once" (70). When he gets fucked he hates himself "for acceding to the *woman's* role, when what I had been so desperate for was to prove I was a man" (144; Monette's emphasis). Class difference is also at issue. Paul's hitherto virtuous life is turned into a more exciting path at the age of nine by his attachment to a lower-class boy, Kite. The "turn-on" was "the twist of his dirty mouth, the punk veneer, the boot-camp father, like an urchin in *Oliver Twist*." The Lawrence who wrote of Lady Chatterley would have understood, and Forster too: "this first fire in my loins was all about class. *Paul is perfect* was slumming." Monette adds: "Maybe Kite was a way of getting out from under the weight of gentility. I've always had a thing for men from unpaved places, not too polished, definitely not English" (22–24; Monette's emphasis). Until his late twenties, Monette's attempts to do something with his unwanted gay sexuality involve class difference. "The laughing man I was looking for was older than I and working-class, certainly no preppie" (194). So there is age difference too, complicated by teaching in private schools, where he is seduced by the boys' flattering attentions and his own loneliness: "I had become the thing the heteros secretly believe about everyone gay—a predator, a recruiter, an indoctrinator of boys into acts of darkness. Sullying my mission as teacher and guide" (197).

Being the seduced boy may be satisfying. Paul enjoys going around with Harold, who is older and wealthier:

> He put on the carnival of events for my sake, treating me like a prince, and even as I raced about laughing on his arm I was thinking how it would be if

this were a permanent thing. To be kept by Harold—no more teaching meat-brain kids, no obligations except to be a poet. Wherever we went, running into Harold's friends, I'd see the flush of pride in his face as he showed me off. No, that's not right. I did all the showing off. (268)

Yet age difference takes Paul only so far: "I needed the seventeen years' difference between us in order to put my trust in his sagacity and worldliness. But I also wanted a man my own age, to discover the world along with me" (269). Paul is uncomfortable with these hierarchies of gender, class, and age. The resolution is his meeting with Roger: they remain together for seventeen years, until Roger's death.

In the continuation of Monette's autobiography, *Borrowed Time*, the emphasis shifts to similarity, even sameness. Roger is a successful lawyer, of compatible professional stature and affluence. They are the same size, and hold shirts, underwear, and socks in common. Neither is relatively feminine; though marriage is invoked, roles are not differentiated. " 'But we're the same person,' " Roger exclaims shortly before death, "in a sort of bewildered delight. 'When did that happen?' " The answer, according to a friend, is that Paul had anticipated the idea: " 'But that's what *you* always used to say in Boston. Roger and you were just two names for the same person.' "[3]

In fact there are significant differences (this will be a recurring pattern). Roger is four years older—thirty-two and twenty-eight when they meet. Paul is frenzied while Roger is calm; Paul is more dependent, Roger more stable and self-contained. "I am the weather, Roger is the climate" (65). Further: "Over the years, relations between us had evolved to a place where he was the grown-up and I the child" (194). Now Roger is sick and Paul cares for him "like a mother" (341). Notwithstanding, Paul insists that these differences are transcended. "Between us we covered the night and the morning watch"; "Being as we were the same person, happily it all balanced out"; "How was it even physically possible to separate us now, with the two of us so interchangeably one?" (29, 41, 315). Some people, Paul acknowledges, regard him as "just a love junkie. What I experience as being known to the core, appetite and aspiration fused, some queers think of as confinement. Doomed to resemble a bourgeois marriage, straight-identified to boot." But Paul learned to love himself, "because someone else finally loved me."[4]

The more serious problem for the love junkie is living up to it all. In *Borrowed Time* this is magnified by Roger's sickness with AIDS.

I ran around the bed and clutched Roger's hand. "We'll fight it, darling, we'll beat it, I promise. I won't let you die." The sentiments merged as they tumbled out. This is the liturgy of bonding. Mostly we clung together, as if time still had the decency to stop when we were entwined. After all, the whole world was right here in this room. (77)

The quality of love must ensure survival. We might notice the echo of John Donne's poem "The Good-Morrow": love "makes one little room, an everywhere." "Whatever dies, was not mix'd equally," the poem continues: Roger's life appears to depend on their equivalence and togetherness.[5] Walt Whitman is there as well:

> We two boys together clinging,
> One the other never leaving.[6]

Poetry and gay tradition may help sustain them.

None of Monette's experiences is uncommon among gay men, though his awareness may be. They amount to a series of anxious negotiations of disjunctions and convergences, positioned around binary differences of gender, class, and age. Positively and negatively, as Monette presents them, these hierarchies constitute the available options; despite aspirations to transcend them in the name of equality, they structure the terms on which intense human interactions become available. Monette prefers to deny, or move beyond, hierarchy, and toward an idealized, egalitarian relationship; yet differentials are still apparent. My case is that hierarchies of gender, age, and class, and race also, are hard to expel from our personal lives because they constitute the principal hierarchies that structure our societies. Differences of masculine and feminine, old and young, upper and lower class, and white and black are not incidental or neutral alternatives. They flow through the power relations that we encounter daily in the world, and through our psyches also; we experience them, ultimately, as empowerment and abjection. Monette's negotiation of hierarchy and equality manifests a persistent strain in gay imaginings.

This proposition facilitates a materialist interpretation of gender and sexuality. Because these elements are so complex, their institutional apparatuses so contradictory, and the permutations so many and so intricate, we experience ourselves as unique individuals; probably that is what we are. Nonetheless, the hierarchies in fantasy and practice derive not from the individual psyche, but from the social relations that define our being. They are continuous with the stories that construct our psychic reality: social being determines consciousness. Egalitarian aspirations also are socially encoded; they are as exciting and difficult to sustain in personal relations as they are in the social order (I return to this in a while). But often, I will show, there is more hierarchy in the frame than is immediately admitted. Such an account of fantasy and power is cultural materialist on three counts: (1) it recognizes the priority of economic, social, and political structures in the constitution of consciousness; (2) it emphasizes the role of ideology; (3) it maintains an awareness of domination and exploitation.

As Foucault argues, power is to be envisaged as pervading the entire social order, in positive as well as negative aspects. It "penetrates and controls everyday pleasure—all this entailing effects that may be those of refusal, blockage, and invalidation, but also incitement and intensification: in short, the 'polymorphous techniques of power.' "[7] To say this is not to overlook the specific and massive apparatuses of government, law, business, and education in our societies. Power is, at once, both intimate and institutional. In *Discipline and Punish*, Foucault seems to repudiate the idea that power relations are "localized in the relations between the state and its citizens or on the frontier between classes." He denies that power may "merely reproduce, at the level of individuals, bodies, gestures and behaviour, the general form of the law or government." This seems to position class, gender, race, and age as superficial modes, whereas power relations are more fundamental, reaching "right down into the depths of society." Yet Foucault does grant "continuity" between the multiple modes of power—not in any predictable analogy or homology, but through "a specificity of mechanism and modality."[8]

If, then, social structures may be said to inform what we experience as our individual sex/gender formations, this is not to imagine some simple transmission of the world into the psyche. Teresa de Lauretis portrays the relations of representation, action, and fantasy as "intimate . . . in the realm of the senses and in that of the law, in sexual practices as well as in the juridical-legislative domain." However, no easy transference should be supposed. We need to observe "the different relations of production."[9] As I remarked in the previous chapter, the erotic deployment of fantasies of power is inevitably tangled into substitutions, conflations, reversals, and loops.

Fantasies of dominance and subjection should be regarded as unsurprising transmutations of prevailing social relations of domination and subordination. Hierarchy is neither an aberration nor a misfortune in desire, but integral with it. Indeed, it may well be that power difference is the ground of the erotic; that it is sexy. That is the insight of Genet's *Balcony*.

THE EGALITARIAN IDEOLOGY

The dominant metropolitan ideology suggests that the most suitable partner, gay or straight, will be of similar age, class, and race to oneself. Gender is the difference that is prized—though only when it figures heterosexually. This ideology of similarity and equality informs the companionate marriage, as it has evolved from the 1920s' endorsement of reciprocity in sexual pleasure, through the 1950s' pram-pushing hubby, to the 1980s' "New Man." Already in 1971, Geoffrey Gorer, reporting on a survey of attitudes toward sex and marriage, was remarking that twenty years previously the dominant model of marriage had been "complementary," resting on a clear division of responsibilities. However, among younger people this was being displaced by a "symmetrical" model, which stresses "comradeship, doing things together, and articulateness." The survey was conducted in England but, Gorer noted, key terms in the new model—"togetherness" and "communication"—were coming from the United States.[10]

Anthropologists and social historians have tracked this development among lesbians and gay men, looking for the emergence of egalitarian relations as a sign of progress. Romantic friendship, in the eighteenth and nineteenth centuries, seems to promise modernity and maturity, even though the equality may be more notional than actual, and the eroticism uncertain.[11] Walt Whitman is celebrated for the dear love of comrades, though his own relationships seem to have been characterized by differences of class and age. The key to David Halperin's sense of modern homosexuality is the opportunity to transcend hierarchy. "Homosexual relations cease to be compulsorily structured by a polarization of identities and roles (active/passive, insertive/receptive, masculine/feminine, or man/boy). Exclusive, lifelong, companionate, romantic, and mutual homosexual love becomes possible for both partners."[12]

A change in expectations along these lines has been confirmed lately among lesbians and gay men by Jeffrey Weeks, Brian Heaphy, and Catherine Donovan. They believe that there was once "a prevalent stereotype about the inegalitarian nature of many homosexual sexual and emotional involvements, defined or fractured by generational, class, racial or domestic inequalities." But now, they find in interviews, "The dominant ethos among lesbians, gay men, and bisexuals is of egalitarian relationships."[13] Even so, "The reality, inevitably, is more complex: non-heterosexuals strive to achieve equality in terms of intimacy, sexual relations and the division of labour in the household against all the inequalities that continue to structure our societies" (109). Actually, around 60 percent of the respondents did not describe their relationships as "equal" (114). Whether they were finding any positive advantage in power differentials is hard to know, since Weeks, Heaphy, and Donovan evidently share the egalitarian ideology, and their interview questions take it for granted that valuable factors, such as "communication, closeness, and intimacy," are scarcely to be found outside equal relationships (110).

To be sure, few people suppose that it is possible to have a totally egalitarian relationship. Notwithstanding, the dominant ideology says that power differentials are unfortunate and should be either avoided or overcome. Indeed, so strong is the ideology of equality that some S/Mers are insisting that their routines are not just "safe, sane, and consensual," but actually egalitarian. Lynda Hart and Joshua Dale note that in some quarters S/M "has become less a polarized expression of a master's power over a slave than a mutual exchange of power." Already in the 1970s, some practitioners began to refer to S/M as "sensuality and mutuality"; by the early 1980s the "mutualists," as Geoff Mains calls them, had become a prime element in the leather community.[14]

Similarity and mutuality correlate with monogamy, respectability, and assimilation in *The Lost Language of Cranes* by David Leavitt. The project of this novel is to sort out the good gays from the unfortunate approximations. The older generation finds it hard to benefit from recent developments in gay selfhood. Owen, who is married to Rose, is unable to talk to anyone about his yearning for gay sex; even at a pornographic cinema, which he visits regularly, he is too ashamed and frightened to speak to anyone or to follow up potential contacts. Two less prominent characters, Derek and Geoffrey, are old-style queens reminiscent of Oscar Wilde; they cultivate British accents, speak of men as "girls," prepare a dinner in which all the food is blue, and include in their circle cultured Europeans who go to Tangiers where it is easy to buy young boys.

All this is regarded with a mixture of distaste and disbelief by the younger generation, represented centrally by Philip, the gay son of Owen and Rose. He had difficulty as an adolescent coming to terms with himself but, the narration suggests, he's doing it more or less right now. He postpones coming out to his parents until he believes he has achieved a gayness he can be proud of: "I wanted to wait until I could show you that a homosexual life could be a good thing."[15] This involves, above all, having a presentable partner: "he had counted on Eliot's presence in their living room to justify all he had said to them, to justify his life" (198). The alternative is cruising and porn movies, but Philip finds little satisfaction there; he meets partners socially, among friends at dinner parties. He has a favorite gay bar, but there is no back room. It is "a friendly place, very social, a place where people go who really are comfortable with being gay, and know it's a lot more than a matter of who you sleep with" (155).

Eliot, Philip's prized partner, proves unreliable. Probably he has been damaged by an overcasual upbringing, and spoiled by superior wealth and connections. However, the resolution, for Philip, is already to hand. Brad, an old school friend, is white, and of the same age, class, and educational attainment; they enjoy spending time together. In due course they find that sex is a natural part of that. When they first kiss, "long and lovingly," it is "spontaneous, without thought" (311). So no sticky, sexually explicit, bathhouse, pickup scene is required; they appear to be a natural couple. They are innocent of gendered roles: there is nothing "frilly or feminine" about Brad (249), and nothing in Philip's appearance "betrayed his homosexuality" (33). Yet when he was at school—although "he hardly fit the stereotype of the sensitive, silent, 'different' boy who knows how to sew, is friends with the teacher and subject to colds"—the other boys "routinely called him 'faggot' or 'fairy' " (74). Plainly Philip was giving some kind of queer signal, but Leavitt cannot say what it was without admitting a demeaning hint of effeminacy. It is easy for the queer reader today to dismiss Philip and Brad as in thrall to a bourgeois, heteronormative lifestyle concept, but twenty years ago it was not easy for young people to accomplish such a thing, in the absence of role models, and even discussion.

The disqualification of hierarchy is confirmed in the stories of the other characters. Owen, prompted by Philip's coming out, does his best to catch up. He makes a suitable choice when he takes up with another married man of similar age and class. Philip's friend Jerene is African American; her adoptive parents—black, middle-class Republicans—reject her when she tells them she is a lesbian. She remains nonetheless nice, good, and wise. However, her new partner is perceived by Philip and Brad as rather a pain, in the manner of characters in Tennessee Williams' *The Glass Menagerie*: "If Laura's looks were Laura Wingfield—fragile and transparent as a tiny glass animal—her temperament was pure Amanda: loud and brash and indiscreet; full of hype and bombast; good-natured, loving, easy to hurt" (251). So Laura is the dominating mother posing as the needful daughter; Jerene is subdued and silenced. These women are still involved in power games; they have not yet arrived at an adequately reciprocal partnership.

Such restagings of difference and similarity as manipulation and maturity are found in many other texts. In the film *An Early Frost* (John Erman, 1985), Michael and Peter form a compatible couple, with just a touch of gender hierarchy: Michael is a lawyer, whereas Peter is artistic, sells collectibles, cooks, wears looser, noncorporate clothes. There are differences, then, but they appear not to signify. It is as if hierarchy is needed to make the relationship plausible, but nothing can be done with it for fear of compromising the image of the good gay. *Hollow Reed* (Angela Pope, 1995) is similar. The issue in this film is Martyn's suspicion that his son is being assaulted by his ex-wife's partner. Meanwhile Martyn and his partner Tom constitute a "good" couple, sharing problems and being sympathetic and sexy for each other; they are a lot nicer than the heterosexuals in the film. There are differences: Martyn is a doctor, he wears a sport's jacket and a tie; Tom keeps a music shop, dresses in jeans, T-shirt, and denim jacket, appears younger and slighter; Martyn drives a car, Tom rides a bike. However, these do not affect the story.

The notoriously sanitized view of gay life in the film *Philadelphia* (Jonathan Demme, 1993) includes a careful negotiation of sameness and difference.[16] Andy and Miguel look about the same age and professional status, and have been together for more than nine years. Miguel appears comfortable with Andy's family; at ease and smart in the courtroom; at home he administers sophisticated medical treatment and is articulate; at a gay fancy dress ball (the opportunity for fantasy to burst forth), they dress the same—as naval officers. The difference is that Miguel looks and sounds Spanish (and is played by the actor Antonio Banderas). However, at no point is this difference registered by anyone.

Jack, a novel by A. M. Homes, rewrites *Catcher in the Rye*.[17] Holden Caulfield was harassed by nauseating perverts; Jack freaks out when he finds that the reason his father left home is that he's gay and lives with Bob. However, there is no need to worry because Bob is entirely presentable: he is a lawyer, Jack's dad is an accountant; they were acquainted socially before they got together, and they are sufficiently respectable to host a party to support a woman who is running for Congress. Meanwhile the apparently normal family of Jack's friend Max turns out to be far from ideal. My account makes it sound worthy, but this is a droll book. For a British instance see Anthony McDonald's romance, *Adam*.[18] Adam (sixteen) falls intensely in love with a young Frenchman (twenty-two). Sylvain is a bit simple—from inbred peasant stock, a child of the woodlands; he can't be introduced to middle-class family and friends. His devotion to Adam proves morbid and dangerous. After all, Adam finds that he has a more mature kind of sexual love with his long-standing school-friend—same age, same class and education, same nationality.

Michael Cunningham's novel *Flesh and Blood* is one that does not take the superiority of sameness for granted. Will, at thirty-five, is "tired of pretty boys" from out of town. His new relationship is with the older Harry:

> he'd be the beauty and Harry the one who paid cool, humorous tribute. Will loved and hated the idea. It surprised him. Here in this expensive but haphazardly furnished apartment, he was the one with the body and no cash. It wasn't where he'd expected to go. . . . It occurred to Will that he could be to Harry what he'd always wanted pretty men to be to him.[19]

The sex is different: "Ordinarily [Will] felt concealed by sex; he disappeared into the beauty of the other man. With Harry he was more visible. Sometimes he liked the sensation. Sometimes he thought he'd get up and leave" (307). They come together initially on a friendly rather than a lustful basis, but they do meet in a gay bar and sex is central.

At the same time, Will and Harry are compatible in every other respect. No racial difference is remarked. Will teaches fifth grade (but went to Harvard); Harry is a doctor (but plays the saxophone). They are both clever; they talk all the time about everything. They both love *Anna Karenina* and *Middlemarch*, and have rebelled against oppressive fathers. They go to movies, eat in restaurants, drive to Provincetown. "Will and he made no declarations; it just unfolded" (307). Alongside Will's turning on to difference, then, Cunningham asserts a natural couple (in the manner of *The Lost Language of Cranes* and *Borrowed Time*). Indeed, they become so compatible as to be interchangeable: Will "lived as himself and he lived as the younger man who was loved by Harry and he lived, obscurely, as Harry, too" (310). However, as in the complementarity (narcissistic) model of gay relations, these convergences are predicated on discrepancy; they secure sameness and difference at the same time.

IMAGE OF AN UNLIMITED EMBRACE

The project of constituting gay respectability around the equal, if pressured, couple is, of course, contested. *The Lost Language of Cranes*, *An Early Frost*, and *Philadelphia* are promoting one position in a cardinal, ongoing dispute. The contrary position values multiple and anonymous partners. Currently the dispute is often framed as one about "gay marriage." I will argue that the two positions actually share a preference for sameness, and a persisting unease about hierarchy.

Positive accounts of multiple and anonymous relations are not so easy to find as one might suppose. Notoriously, such gay classics as *Dancer from the Dance* by Andrew Holleran and *Faggots* by Larry Kramer represent gay subculture as promiscuous and hence necessarily frustrating and anguished. To be sure, pornography often promotes the idea of multiple and anonymous partners. However, it does so from a less prestigious sector of the gay cultural apparatus. Pornography is widely spoken of, by radicals as well as conservatives, as if it were an essential concept (often it is suggested that its images are distinctively objectified). Rather, we should ask what is the history and structure of such a categorization, and what interests it is tending to serve. It is not that this or that practice is bad and therefore pornographic, but that labeling a practice pornographic reflects a decision to regard it as bad. Pornography is not the opposite of worthwhile sexuality, but a way of asserting which sexualities are worthwhile and which are not. Because it is where we put illicit sexuality, pornography cannot confer legitimacy on its images. This outlaw status is reproduced in its irregular modes of circulation. Leavitt, on the other hand, can present the ideas that inform *The Lost Language of Cranes* widely through authoritative media: Alfred A. Knopf, Penguin Books, and the BBC (who filmed the book for television).

In *The Farewell Symphony*, Edmund White makes the important point that the pursuit of multiple and anonymous partners was not a new factor in the 1970s. Cruising was a gay tradition—there was no break with the past. It was the same in England: bear in mind the extensive routines of men such as Tom Driberg, Michael Davidson, and Joe Orton. Nonetheless, White posits a distinctive post-Stonewall ethos: "We saw gay men as a vanguard that society would inevitably follow. I thought that the couple would disappear and be replaced by new, polyvalent molecules of affection or Whitmanesque adhesiveness." "Guys just sort of fell in with each other, buddies rubbing shoulders. We wanted sexual friends, loving comrades, multiple husbands in a whole polyandry of desire."[20]

Samuel R. Delany in *The Motion of Light in Water* recalls the bar, tearoom (public toilet), and truck scenes of the 1950s, but a post-Stonewall orgy at the baths was qualitatively different:

> what *this* experience said was that there was a population—not of individual homosexuals, some of whom now and then encountered, or that those encounters could be human and fulfilling in their way—not of hundreds, not of thousands, but rather of millions of gay men, and that history had, actively and already, created for us whole galleries of institutions, good and bad, to accommodate our sex.[21]

Casual sex might be a vehicle for noble, egalitarian aspirations. David Wojnarowicz finds peace, companionship, and empowerment in a one-off
encounter: "In loving him, I saw men encouraging each other to lay down
their arms. . . . In loving him, I saw great houses being erected that would
soon slide into the waiting and stirring seas. I saw him freeing me from the
silences of the interior life."[22] As Ben Gove observes, Wojnarowicz, like
Genet, repositions romance by levering it away from its customary link
with monogamy.[23]

Two factors tend to complicate such visions. One is that hierarchy is not
so easily expelled. Dennis Altman declares: "The willingness to have sex
immediately, promiscuously, with people about whom one knows nothing
and from whom one demands only physical contact, can be seen as a sort
of Whitmanesque democracy, a desire to know and trust other men in a
type of brotherhood." However, as Leo Bersani points out, Altman admits
that "age and physical beauty set up their own hierarchies and barriers."[24]

Holleran insists on democracy in *Dancer from the Dance*. He sees in the
disco "a strange democracy whose only ticket of admission was physical
beauty—and not even that sometimes. All else was strictly classless." On
the dance floor, he adds, even beauty might not matter: "all of them mixed
together on that square of blond wood and danced, without looking at anyone else, for one another." "What a carnival of people."[25] The abundance of
anonymous contacts overwhelms the particularity of this or that partner.
There may be plenty of difference, but it doesn't make any difference.
Interestingly, effeminate boys are not excluded from Holleran's scene. For
White too, "Whitmanesque adhesiveness" does not preclude gendered
roles. He writes of polyandry (having more than one husband), and of a
partner who referred to himself as a "hubby," and of how he felt like a girl
alongside him.[26] These accounts are set in the mid-1970s. The development of the clone image (short hair, moustache, denim or leather) tended
to produce a repudiation or an effacement of gendered roles.

What is striking is that, insofar as they tend to erase hierarchies which
reinsert themselves, these legitimations of casual sex converge, strangely,
on *The Lost Language of Cranes*. Defenders of casual sex are evoking the
very bars and cruising grounds that Philip eschewed, but they share
nonetheless a suspicion of hierarchy. What have appeared to be the two
poles of gay experience are united in their anxious and inconclusive treatment of power in relationships.

Neil Bartlett presents the late 1970s moment of the clone as euphori-
cally inclusive: "It was a style that explicitly proposed a single culture. It
offered to embrace everybody, to erase all differences in a generous,

homogeneous, successful style. Commercially promoted on a mass scale, it seemed to absorb all the other, older styles." Not for nothing, Bartlett adds, was the biggest London discotheque opened under the name of "Heaven."[27] Even Kramer, despite his commitment to personal values in relationships and the generally caustic stance of *Faggots*, finally concedes and celebrates, for once, the indifference of the scene on Fire Island:

> The dancing's over for this night. Haven't we shared a night of nights! A night of fellowship. We have danced and partied and drugged and Meat Racked, and we have survived no sleep. Together. Together. Yes, we have braved and passaged all these rites together. Though we may not know each other's names nor will we necessarily speak when next we meet. The beach is filled with my friends.[28]

Sharing, fellowship, togetherness, friends—these terms are not far from Leavitt's, though they are adapted to Kramer's moment of self-abandonment, rather than a personal relationship.

Of course, the status of casual sex has been transformed by HIV and AIDS. Oscar Moore's *A Matter of Life and Sex* is one of many texts which accept a correlation between the delights of multiple and anonymous partners and the fate, as it appears in the novel, of infection and death.[29] William M. Hoffman in his play and film *As Is* makes Saul and Rich agree on the pleasures of "promiscuous sex"; they redefine it as "nondirective, noncommitted, non-authoritarian— / Free, wild, rampant—." But now sex even with your lover is too dangerous to attempt.[30] The most impressive antimonogamy texts attempt principled reassertions of multiple and anonymous partners in the face of AIDS. Thom Gunn in his poem "The Missing," in *The Man with Night Sweats*, reasserts a vision of unfettered sexual congress:

> Contact of friend led to another friend,
> Supple entwinement through the living mass
> Which for all that I knew might have no end,
> Image of an unlimited embrace.[31]

Again, difference evaporates into immeasurable multiplicity.

Bersani is the theorist of anonymous sexual relations (antirelational relations). He is sharply critical of commentators who domesticate sex by reinventing it as *redemptive*—as "less disturbing, less socially abrasive, less violent, more respectful of 'personhood' than it has been in a male-dominated, phallocentric culture." The broad indictment of male ascendancy, and of pornography in particular, by feminists such as Andrea Dworkin and Catherine A. MacKinnon, has in Bersani's view "had the immensely desirable effect of publicizing, of lucidly laying out for us, the inestimable value of sex as—at least in certain of its ineradicable aspects—anticommunal, antiegalitarian, antinurturing, antiloving."[32] Their exposé of the untamable nature of sex affords a reason not for banning pornography, but for encouraging it.

Yet, as Bersani pushes these ideas along, a familiar theme emerges. In an essay on Genet (which I discuss elsewhere), "an anti-monumental, anti-redemptive aesthetic" is discovered; it is endemic in homosexuality, Bersani believes. Within its orbit "an *identity* between the penetrator and the penetrated" occurs; "a fundamental sameness."[33] Bersani has driven his repudiation of authentic personhood in sex to the point where it makes everyone the same—identical in their anonymity and unrelatedness. Lately Bersani has theorized further his argument for the irrelevance of difference, through a reinterpretation of Aristophanes' fable of the divided creatures in Plato's *Symposium*. The missing portion, Bersani urges, is not the other, but a part of oneself. This is claimed for heterosexuals equally. What the lover lacks is not *the other*, as followers of Jacques Lacan in particular have supposed, but *"more of what he is."* This lack is based not on difference, therefore, "but rather on the *extensibility of sameness*."[34]

Across a wide spectrum of texts, and in diverse and ingenious ways, sameness is valorized and hierarchy is disallowed. Yet even, or especially, when the repudiation of hierarchy is associated with the highest aspirations, it is not easily banished. In later chapters I will explore the erotics of power in specific lived experience of gender, age, class, and race.

SEDUCTION AND IMPLANTATION

An argument about sexuality and power has to engage eventually with the psychoanalytic tradition. What has often troubled cultural materialists and other social constructionists is Freud's intermittent reliance on what he presents as universal factors—biological, phylogenetic (in the evolution of a race), primordial. In the wake of Darwin, such concepts tend to incorporate a murky, conservative view of human potential, in which sex is envisaged as designed for reproduction and gender roles are confined accordingly. For example, in Freud's "Wolfman" analysis we are told of a breakthrough at the point where the boy "discovered the vagina and the biological significance of masculine and feminine. He understood now that active was the same as masculine, while passive was the same as feminine."[35]

As I observe below, my argument that power difference informs sexuality consorts easily with sadomasochistic fantasies. But Freud, at least from time to time, prizes reproduction over perversion. He writes in *Three Essays on the Theory of Sexuality*: "The normal sexual aim is regarded as being the union of the genitals in the act known as copulation." Other practices, including fetishism, sadism, and masochism, are "the perversions"—that is, "sexual activities which either (a) *extend*, in an anatomical sense, beyond the regions of the body that are designed for sexual union, or (b) *linger* over the intermediate relations to the sexual object which should normally be traversed rapidly on the path towards the final sexual aim."[36] The "biological significance" of an element of male aggressiveness may "lie in the need for overcoming the resistance of the sexual object by means other than the process of wooing"; it becomes sadistic—perverse—when it is "independent and exaggerated" (71). However, this approach will not easily account for male masochism. Perhaps it is an instance of a principle: "Every active perversion is thus accompanied by its passive counterpart" (81). So "masochism is not the manifestation of a primary instinct, but originates from sadism which has been turned round upon the self."[37]

In " 'A Child Is Being Beaten,' " Freud holds that male masochists occupy a feminine position: "they invariably transfer themselves into the part of a woman; that is to say, their masochistic attitude coincides with a *feminine* one." This statement perhaps gestures toward the binary gendering that is associated with reproduction; Freud insists: "It makes no difference if in a fanciful embellishment of the masochistic scene they keep up the fiction that a mischievous boy, or page, or apprentice is going to be punished." But then, "confusingly enough," the chastiser also is a woman; Freud moves to another topic.[38] At other points Freud connects masochism to "the death drive," and "a fixation in childhood."[39] The last suggestion seems most plausible. To be sure, Freud offers other frameworks for thinking about masochism at other points in his writing. I have focused on his subsuming of power into reproduction because it occurs in major texts (the *Three Essays* were reprinted twenty-one times in ten languages between 1910 and 1938), and because it works against my sense that power differentials are intrinsic to sundry sexual identities and interactions, and not dependent on heteronormative interpretation. The priority of reproduction is still asserted by reputable thinkers. Luce Irigaray, for example, declares: "The human species is divided into *two genders* which ensure its production and reproduction. To wish to get rid of sexual difference is to call for a genocide more radical than any form of destruction there has ever been in History." It is a mistake, therefore, "to demand equality as women."[40]

Mainly since the publication of Jean Laplanche's *New Foundations for Psychoanalysis*, via a battery of conferences, translations, introductions, interpretations, and collections of essays, instigated and undertaken principally by John Fletcher, new theories have effected decisive revisions of Freud, and Lacan also, offering a new route beyond biologism.[41] Freud, along with Darwin, Marx, and Nietzsche, has often been credited with a *decentering* of man. Copernicus demonstrated that "man" is not at the center of the universe; these later thinkers have argued that he is not in charge of his own biology, history, and psychology. Laplanche declares this Freudian-Copernican revolution unfinished, and our dependence upon the other unacknowledged, so long as the infant is said to bring with him into the world fundamental drives:

> For if the individual is henceforth governed, in classical psychoanalytic theory, by the unknown drives of the unconscious, this "id"—however strange it is supposed to be—is nonetheless not an alien. It is supposed to dwell *at the center* of the individual, whom it governs in its own way, even if it has dethroned the ego. One sovereign in place of another, but well and truly installed in the keep of the castle.[42]

To address this problem, Laplanche reviews the "seduction theory," which Freud abandoned in 1897; this had understood neurotic symptoms as consequent upon the seduction or abuse which his patients reported from their childhood. Upon this abandonment, Freud posited the phases (oral–anal–phallic) of endogenous (growing from within) infantile sexuality, with its apparently biological sequencing.

Laplanche believes that passivity and seduction do constitute the individual's originary moment. The mother (or other primary caregiver) *does seduce the child into erotic pleasure*—not at all, however, in any sinister way, but as part of the routine parental ministrations without which the child would die. The feeding and handling of the infant exposes him or her to the caregiver's fantasy life, inviting cooperation, through strategies of translation and repression. Fletcher explicates:

> We are not talking here of abusive events. In Laplanche's sense seduction is ordinary. This leads him to talk of an *implantation* of stimulating, arousing and traumatizing non-verbal signifiers with their unconscious, enigmatic

significations: an implantation on the surface of the primitive body image or skin-ego of the infant. These are anchored or inscribed particularly in the erogenous zones as folds and openings in the body surface—mouth, anus, genitals.

Thus is effected "the primary mapping and zoning of the sexual body, indeed the very sexing of the body."[43] Martin Stanton asks: "Is there no input from the infant at all?" Laplanche replies that feeding—the initial demand—is interactive, but the sexual message that accompanies it is "a one-way action."

> From the beginning, one is active and the other is passive. But very quickly, the little human tries to turn this passivity into activity, that is, to make something of this message from the other. Still, there is this dissymmetry. This comes from the fact that the active one has more "knowledge," more unconscious fantasies than the passive infant.[44]

This way of explaining the development of individual psychic formations is notably compatible with my arguments about sexuality and power, in two main ways. First, the organization of fantasy in which the infant is involved is that of the mother (or other caregiver), and consequently already steeped in her tangle of scenarios. She, necessarily, has already her own personal take on the prevailing system of representation, fantasy, and unconscious desire, and this intrudes, also necessarily, upon the infant. Second, the infant's initial experience is of power imbalance. "The primary situation that gives rise to the sexual drive in the human being," Fletcher writes, "is one of a primary passivity and penetration by the other. It involves a breaking in that is characteristic of pain."[45] For what is undeniable in Laplanche's "situation of primal seduction" is both

> the wealth of its innate mechanisms of reciprocal communication between mother and child, and the profound *asymmetry* between the adult with an already formed unconscious, the bearer of unconsciously determined enigmatic signifiers or messages, and the new-born infant assigned a gender on the basis of adult perceptions of its anatomy but [as yet] without sexual fantasies.[46]

If, as I believe, Laplanche has evolved an important theory through which the power arrangements in our societies may be implanted in the infant, becoming the building blocks in the *bricolage* of our psychic life,

this should not be envisaged as an elementary mechanism of social con-
ditioning, producing automata incapable of independent agency. The
infant is subjected to extremely powerful inputs, but they are complex—
and it is the simplicity of a message that stifles agency, not its strength.
The transmissions in Laplanche's theory are fraught with untranslated,
resistant, and troubling remainders. Fletcher takes up Dominique Scarfone's argument that it is negation, repression, and enigma on the part of
the adult and her messages that provoke the infant "to translate, to
reprise and rework the enigmatic and exciting messages, to substitute its
own signifying sequences, fantasies, 'infantile sexual theories,' to interpret the blanks in the parental discourse, to sublimate by symbolising
otherwise."[47]

Further, the encounter may go wrong, implanting materials that resist
adequate symbolization. There is a "violent variant" of implantation, according to Laplanche: *intromission*. This is a blocking process which "short-cir-
cuits the differentiation of the agencies in the process of their formation,
and puts into the interior an element resistant to all metabolism," creating
the conditions for both the superego and psychosis.[48] Perhaps it is the gaps
and enigmas in the parental messages that create the space for the child to
interpret, translate, and fantasize, whereas when parental fantasies are
imposed, full on, translation is paralyzed—which may be why sexual abuse
in childhood is so destructive, impairing, and repetitive, from generation to
generation.

Of course, I am not equipped to evaluate theories of infant subjectivity.
In any event, Laplanche's insistence on the primacy of the caregiver issues
a reminder of the infant's experience of initial power disparity, while allowing space in which human beings might develop diverse and novel ways of
relating.

ARGUMENTS AND VISIONS

If hierarchies of sex and gender are both embedded in our psyches and a
sexual turn-on, attempts to thwart them must be both futile and austerely
abstemious. To be sure, power may be distributed irregularly between two
people, such that A is powerful in respect of p, whereas B is powerful in
respect of q. However, this does not mean that hierarchy evens out and
becomes irrelevant. More likely, quite intricate and engrossing negotiations
will be required to maintain the diverse claims; there will be more engagement with hierarchy, not less.

This is not to say that oppressions of gender, class, age, and race are either necessary or justified. We may campaign for radical transformations. Nor is it to say that it is acceptable to knock your partner around, or to manipulate him or her psychologically, or to use his or her relative poverty or general neediness to exert control. Nor is it to say that you should stay with a partner who abuses you in those ways. I write, I should say, as a relatively empowered person. I am white, male, salaried, and have published some books; I have some advantages of middle age (stability, security) and some of its disadvantages (likely to fall ill and die before long). It is perhaps easy for me to insist that power difference is sexy; my potential partner, if he is located on the more vulnerable side of those hierarchies, may be more exposed, psychologically, in his engagements.

The terms on which women might collude in hierarchies which derive from male-dominated ideologies have been effectively disputed in lesbian feminism. Sheila Jeffreys sets out from somewhere near the start of the present analysis: "Since the concept of difference or 'male-female polarity' is the organising principle of the heteropatriarchy it is not surprising that it should so profoundly have shaped the consciousness even of many lesbians."[49] However, Jeffreys contests any idea that lesbians should collaborate with it. She disagrees with women such as Amber Hollibaugh and Cherríe Moraga, who protest that feminist rejection of male dominance in heterosexuality has led to an ill-considered rejection of hierarchical relations between women. Hollibaugh opines: "what feminism did, in its fear of heterosexual control of fantasy, was to say that there was almost no fantasy safe to have, where you weren't going to have to give up power or take it. There's no sexual fantasy I can think of that doesn't include some aspect of that."[50] This is to say, Jeffreys replies,

> that we cannot build a sexuality which is about equality and mutuality. . . .
> The refusal to see any kind of sex without dominance and submission as possible, rules out the feminist adventure in the total transformation of sexuality with the object of eliminating sexual violence and the objectification of women, almost before it's begun.[51]

Moraga responds with her personal experience. She grew up with "the fantasy of capture, taking a woman"; her "identification was with the man, taking": that is how her sexuality works.[52]

In *Loving in the War Years*, Moraga relates these arguments to class and race:

What the white women's movement tried to convince me of is that lesbian sexuality was *naturally* different than heterosexual sexuality. That the desire to penetrate and be penetrated, to fill and be filled, would vanish. That retaining such desires was "reactionary," not "politically correct," "male identified." And somehow reaching sexual ecstasy with a woman lover would never involve any kind of power struggle.[53]

Judith Halberstam comments: "Chicana lesbians cannot suddenly be expected to cast off these sex roles in favour of a lesbian feminist egalitarianism."[54] Esther Newton and Shirley Walton are similarly skeptical. "Do away with masculinity and femininity and the residuum is egalitarian sexuality: open, honest, caring, and non-oppressive": that is the theory. However, "Power and sexual desire are deeply, perhaps intrinsically connected in ways we do not fully understand and just can't abolish," Newton and Walton contend. "It is true that men have more power than women in the sexual domain. But one cannot proceed directly from this fact to explain how sexuality works, any more than male domination of the art world, for example, explains aesthetic experience."[55]

It will be evident where the present study stands in relation to these arguments. Our sexual imaginaries probably are informed by hierarchies that are ultimately oppressive, but we have to negotiate within, through, and beyond that insight. It cannot be realistic to suppose that we might simply, through good intentions, sidestep the hierarchies of capitalism and male dominance. They inform our daily interactions, the language through which we come to consciousness, our psychic formations. Islands of individual serenity are a strategic aspiration for therapy, but finally we must be talking about damage limitation. Socialism in a single psyche must be a chimera.

What, then, of aspirations toward sex and gender liberation, and what prospects for the mutuality and harmony that have often been attached to sexual love in our cultures? Egalitarian impulses are not to be regarded as false, deluded, or partial. They too are produced within the system; where else could they come from? Often they are couched in terms afforded by the dominant, but this does not invalidate them. If the opportunities for containment of liberatory aspirations are large, so is the potential for idealism. For the cultural materialist, as well as critique, there is always the prospect of transformation. All the books discussed in this chapter witness to the vitality of reciprocity as an idea, even where they are marking the impediments that strew its path. Perhaps the most extreme instance of an unequal love relationship is between the commandant of a Nazi work camp and a boy inmate. Ursula Zilinsky makes this plausible in her novel *Middle Ground*. The commandant declares, even in this context, "I don't believe love is possible except between equals."[56]

Collaborative impulses certainly do figure in our sexual imaginaries. They have been important in heroic and romantic friendship; in some forms of romantic love; in partnerships founded in complementarity; in the element of interchangeability in some S/M relations. They have inspired our love poems. I have quoted Monette quoting Donne and Whitman. Philip Sidney's *Arcadia* (1580) features cross-dressing and same-sex passion. The singer of this song is a young man who says he overheard it sung by a young maid, so the effect is of a male addressing a male:

> My true love hath my heart, and I have his,
> By just exchange, one for the other given.

Yet this sonnet continues in a surprisingly violent manner:

> His heart his wound received from my sight:
> My heart was wounded, with his wounded heart,
> For as from me on him his hurt did light,
> So still methought in me his hurt did smart:
> Both equal hurt, in this change sought our bliss:
> My true love hath my heart, and I have his.[57]

The poem circles back to its initial declaration, reinstating reciprocity, but there's a lot of wounding and hurting in between, suggesting not just the convention of Cupid's arrows but also a social order where violent death might be the consequence of inappropriate loving.

Alfred Tennyson in *In Memoriam* (1850) sometimes celebrates the equality and reciprocity of the deceased Arthur and himself:

> I know that this was Life,—the track
> Whereon with equal feet we fared;
> And then, as now, the day prepared
> The daily burden for the back.
> . . . .
> Nor could I weary, heart or limb,
> When mighty Love would cleave in twain
> The lading of a single pain,
> And part it, giving half to him.

However, the poet more often dwells upon Arthur's superiority and inaccessibility:

> I vex my heart with fancies dim:
> He still outstript me in the race;
> It was but unity of place
> That made me dream I ranked with him.[58]

Now Alfred is left behind again, as the confident, privileged, and accomplished Arthur ascends into a more spacious life among the souls of the departed.

W. H. Auden allows that sexual passion may prompt an ideal vision in "Lay your sleeping head, my love" (1937). To lovers, "Soul and body have no bounds";

> Grave the vision Venus sends
> Of supernatural sympathy,
> Universal love and hope.

Yet for the boy with him he wishes that the "mortal world" will be enough, with all its mundane unevenness.[59] In another poem, "The More Loving One" (1955), Auden remarks that, while the language of love celebrates mutuality, it is unusual for two people's loves to match precisely:

> If equal affection cannot be,
> Let the more loving one be me. (282)

Evocations of ideal harmony may not be entirely unalloyed, then; they may smack of wishful thinking, tactics, and ideology; they may not sit easily with actual power differentials. Yet they do not have to be unalloyed to be important.

Although we tend to think of lesbians and gay men as subject to distinctively complex psychic, ethical, and political demands, the idea of egalitarian sex is far more problematic for heterosexuals. While same-sex partners may choose to engage with hierarchical imagery, the copresence of a man and a woman has to start from it (though other hierarchies of class, age, and race may undermine or counteract it, and perhaps put the woman in the dominant position). The most sustained quest for a viable feminist heterosexuality, from within current progressive thought, has been mounted by Lynne Segal, particularly in *Straight Sex*. She draws from

Naomi Segal the five elements of pleasure that may be said to characterize women's sexual desire:

purposeless playfulness;
a recovery of childhood feelings (or whatever consciousness can
    tolerate of their original polymorphous perversity);
a connection with nurturance;
games with power (especially the pleasure of feeling power over the
    powerful);
a narcissistic sense of completion through access to the body of
    another.[60]

While appreciating the elements of sharing, reassurance, and play in this sequence, we may notice also that it seems designed to accommodate and subdue hierarchy. The play has to be purposeless; only so much perversity must be recovered as consciousness can tolerate; the narcissism must not be merely self-regarding. "The pleasure of feeling power" is allowed only if you are generally the powerless one, and only by way of "games."

Lynne Segal's goal is an egalitarian containment which will both license and control the pleasures and dangers of hierarchy. It is a fine balance, though. For once you venture beyond mutual reassurance and a bit of play-ful slap-and-tickle, you get back into dominance and subordination. And unfortunately, Segal admits, men seem less amenable to routing their sense of male power through play. In fact, when Segal wants to assert the scope and vigor of fantasy against the puritanical antipornography stance of Dworkin and MacKinnon, she appeals not to heterosexual theorists but to the raunchy stance of Hollibaugh's and Pat Califia's lesbian feminist S/M genre (251). It is not easy to get companionate marriage and vigorous sexu-ality into the same frame.

An argument about dominance and subordination must finally confront the particular anxieties that cluster around the formalized role-play which we call "S/M," particularly when it entails the cultivation of scenarios from fascism and slavery. In my view it is a mistake to infer that power play nec-essarily involves distinctive gear, dedicated bars, and playrooms, and that in other contexts, conversely, the rest of us are egalitarian. Rather, S/M is continuous with other, less specific, hierarchical formations, such as I have been discussing. Consider John Rechy's attempt at quarantining S/M in *The Sexual Outlaw:* "I do cultivate a certain tough appearance because it attracts people sexually, and I do equate sex with power. But I know the dif-ference between that and the most negative aspect within the gay world—

S & M. . . . Pain and humiliation have nothing to do with love."[61] Rechy's distinction sounds less than secure.

Bersani discusses Foucault's attempt in an interview to distinguish the master-slave relation in S/M from actual power structures. S/M, Foucault said, is not "a reproduction, within the erotic relationship, of the structure of power. It is an acting out of power structures by a strategic game that is able to give sexual pleasure or bodily pleasure."[62] To be sure, there can be no simple "reproduction"; the S/M representation will indeed be "a strategic game." It will be oblique, displaced, allusive—even, perhaps, parodic. However, Bersani asks, "what is the game without the power structure that constitutes its strategies?"[63] Would erotic pleasure survive the evaporation of its ultimate allusion to a real-world model? Does the attraction of leather, say, stem from its texture and derivation from cattle, or would it not become less interesting if policemen and men with heavy manual jobs stopped wearing it? For a time, its residual associations would persist, but eventually it would become quaint.

Insofar as he regards sexuality as necessarily, in the circumstances in which we currently live, about power, Bersani's argument is congruent with that offered in the present study. His refusal to accept a consolatory story about the innocence of S/M also seems right. However, he derives this from Freudian principles and actively disputes Jeffrey Weeks's materialist suggestion that "the erotic acts as a crossover point for a number of tensions whose origins are elsewhere: of class, gender and racial location, of intergenerational conflict, moral acceptability and medical definition."[64]

My goal here is not to justify or dismiss S/M, but to observe its continuities with fantasies of dominance and subordination that are inevitable in our kinds of societies, and also with the everyday routines of sexual and interpersonal power, as they present themselves through the prevailing structures. The task, then, is to find ways of making hierarchy, in our sexual and personal relations, productive of pleasure and the other rewards of intimacy, and productive also of insights into the psychic economies through which we handle the triumphs and humiliations that the system bestows—while maintaining also the credibility and integrity of our political engagements. This is the project proposed by Claudia Card, who observes the influence of

roles of dominance and subordinance that characterize not only authoritarian adult-child relationships within the family or authoritarian religious relationships but, more generally, the norms of a patriarchal, misogynist society that is also riddled with homophobia, racism, anti-Semitism, and other forms of oppression. On this understanding, sadomasochistic desires have roots not simply in individual psychologies but in society at large; they are not mysterious givens but social constructions.[65]

Card's answer is to approach the issue on different levels. Interpersonally, we have to work with the idea of informed consent, despite its awkwardnesses. Politically, we have to oppose oppressive societal structures.

INSURRECTION

James Robert Baker's novel, *Tim and Pete*, explores the overlap between interpersonal hierarchies and those which sustain the state. The eponymous heroes believe in love and monogamy, at least in the time of AIDS. Spontaneous sex can be rewarding, Tim allows, but not the 1970s bathhouses:

> "it wasn't joyful. It seemed to bring out the worst in people. It wasn't sex as catharsis or redemption, but sex as a drug. A crazed, compulsive abuse of what sex can provide. Cynical and loveless. Sex as ego gratification, as ephemeral validation. Sex as a product, something you need to feel better about yourself for a while. A new shirt, a new car, a new fuck. Capitalism. I didn't like the music either."[66]

"Sleaze" is their term for cruising and occasional partners; however, they accuse each other of it continually, and it transpires that at least one of them has fucked at some time with almost everyone they meet.

Their quest for a renewal of their love takes them across Los Angeles, desolate and threatening after the riots of 1991, looking as if it were a sequence of film sets. "In fact, it was so deserted it almost felt like a set. The battered 1920s storefronts, the deep dusk blue of the sky, even the burned-out ruins, had a weird *designed* look, like a soundstage street for a Janet Jackson video. Or a 'gritty' background for a black-and-white Guess? ad" (92; Baker's emphasis). They view their situation through a filter of film and fantasy, as they reprise recent gay history. They love to improvise pornographic scenarios out of famous Hollywood films and clean-cut surf movies. However, there is a persistent political edge to their invention. "So we'd imagine, in the most extreme and lurid cinematic terms, the obliteration by gunfire of different right-wing people we disliked. . . . we could machine-gun George Will, for example, in Washington, and suck each other off in Mexico in the same sentence" (179; my elision). Pete heads up a post-punk rock band, and does a song called "What This Country Needs (Is a Baader-Meinhof Gang)." Tim has reservations: "I'd seen his point, that anything in art was permissible, that to depict something was not the same as to advocate it, let alone do it, and I felt that our fantasies, besides being fun, were a kind of harmless way of blowing off steam" (179). But suppose some people experience such a song as a rallying cry?

Pete's young friend Joey is involved with Glenn, who is forty-two; they have what Pete considers " 'an extremely fucked-up dynamic,' " a " 'possessive, obsessive dance-of-death thing' "—not formally S/M, but emotionally; deriving from Joey's childhood abuse. Tim calls it " 'a dad-and-lad scene' " (166). " 'I love Joey. We're both extremely fucked up and bad for each other, but I love him,' " Glenn says (226). It transpires that Glenn is leading a group plotting to assassinate ex-president Reagan. Initially, Glenn's interest in political terror was "on a kind of camp, ironic level" (199); this is familiar enough to poststructural critics, who have imagined that a purposeful gender-bending might seriously discomfort the system. Already in their paintings Glenn and Joey have drawn upon Tim and Pete's inventions, trying to break out of the customary boundaries of art; these paintings "were very much like some of the fantasies we used to spin" (179). Glenn tells Pete: " 'You've shaken us out of our catatonic grief with your inflammatory call to violence' " (221). Fantasies, and their expression, cannot be corralled into a safe world of art.

It may gradually dawn on the reader that there is a continuity rather than a contrast between Tim and Pete, as a couple, and Glenn and Joey. As I note in chapter 2, Tim and Pete present their relationship to themselves as free from hierarchies of class, age, and gender, but in practice these power differences afford them a guilty pleasure. A lesbian who gives them a lift advises that they might enjoy experimenting with dominance and submission (however, her vehemence destabilizes her own relationship). When Pete gives in and agrees to get back together with Tim, he signals this by singing "I Wanna Be Your Dog" (135–37). Having captured Tim and Pete, Glenn readily intuits the link between their current situation in a real political drama and the fantasies they have cultivated informally: " 'I'll bet my entire Colt pornography collection *you've* fantasized being stripped and restrained by a gang of rowdy outlaws' " (217). In fact Tim has admitted to this fantasy: " 'I thought about tying you up once. Like a western thing. But serial killers always tie up their victims. What if I snapped?' " (93). Power is everywhere in the system—in the nice guys as well as in the assassins and the president.

The most developed theory of countercultural art and the dramatic insurrectionary gesture derives from Guy Debord, Raoul Vaneigem, and the Situationist International group in the 1960s. It was influential in the May 1968 *événementes* in Paris, and the bombings of financial and governmental targets by the Angry Brigade in London in 1969–1971. The initial idea was to create the *situation* that would disrupt the rhythms of everyday life and the spectacle constructed by the state; it was insurrection at the level of representation. Because the state depends upon the spectacle of the commodified image, the revolutionary event may operate by reorienting those images. These ideas informed the underground press and counterculture of the 1960s and 1970s, and the work of prominent British dramatists such as Howard Brenton and David Edgar. For if power was theatrical, theater might be powerful. Leading artistic and musical figures in the punk movement professed familiarity with situationist thought.[67]

This is what Tim and Pete have been doing in their ad hoc appropriations of movies, Pete also in his music, and Glenn and Joey in their artwork. (It is interesting that people around the Angry Brigade, some of whom were Gay Liberation Front activists, called themselves "The Wild Bunch" and "Butch Cassidy and the Sundance Kid.")[68] ACT UP and Queer Nation are in this line of political thought but, according to Pete, they "don't go nearly far enough. . . . They should go into the Vatican, remove the fag art, and dynamite the place. Douse the pope with gasoline, set him on fire" (143; my elision). Glenn and Joey have made their pictures as transgressive as they can. The next step, as for the Situationists, is a counter-theater of momentous violence, intended not (as in traditional revolutions) to seize the apparatus of the state, but to undermine its spectacular facade by the radiant symbolism of the intervention. The most plausible instance of a positive effect from political violence in a modern state is perhaps the Black Panthers, who changed the self-awareness of African American people. " 'I miss the Black Panthers,' " Pete says. " 'At least they knew who the real enemy was.' " " 'Which is why they got wiped out,' " Tim replies (80).

Tim and Pete ends before the culminating act of violence which Glenn and Joey intend. Attention is switched to the fact that Pete's mother is there and would be killed. Of course, once she is factored in, the case for political violence is hard to sustain: nearly half the world is potentially somebody's mother. Finally Tim envisions the slaughter at the convention, translating it immediately into cinematic terms (*The Godfather*), and then imagining that he's "looking at a painting of Pete and me, as we were right now, the way Joey would have painted it" (256). You can't quarantine fantasy from political action. The question, still, is whether they can work productively together.

Actually I think *Tim and Pete* is about something else as well. One senses a less focused, more gestural sense of apocalyptic violence—for instance, in the references to Charles Manson. A strain in U.S. culture—both on the right and the left—has always been ready for apocalypse now; the conjunction of AIDS and the end of the millennium made it unavoidable.[69]

What is at work is less a political analysis than a community that is anguished and desperate. *Tim and Pete* is strewn with harrowing stories of official and personal disdain for people with AIDS. However, this is not just about the loss of lovers and friends and the threat of sickness and death: it is about social exclusion. There is one strategy running through Tim and Pete's numerous, impertinent appropriations of movie scenarios: at every point gay men are being inserted into recognized images of "America." (Pedro Almodóvar, conversely, is mentioned simply with respect; only American scenarios are appropriated.) Already these gay men have been rejected by their families. Now they are mourning "America." The president, once elected, is supposed to stand for all citizens. But George Bush the elder is quoted as admitting in 1987 that there was still a "giggle factor" in the government's approach to AIDS (9). Gay Americans find that their condition has excluded them from the nation. Centrally "American" images can be occupied by them only in a parodic or violent way.

They are, in one of David Wojnarowicz's titles, in the shadow of the American Dream. A leitmotiv in Wojnarowicz's *Close to the Knives* is that if only the president would pay attention to AIDS, we would begin to get somewhere with it. I find here a strange vein of surprise that gay rights have not been acknowledged; Wojnarowicz is shocked to read of a Supreme Court ruling that "only people who are heterosexual or married or who have families can expect these constitutional rights."[70] Lamenting the suicide of a friend, he asks: "Man, why did you do it? Why didn't you wait for the possibilities to reveal themselves in this shit country, on this planet?" (241). "America," surely, will come good in the end. I have remarked elsewhere this wish to believe in America, noting its role in the thought of Randy Shilts, Larry Kramer, Bruce Bawer, and Andrew Holleran.[71]

Andrew Sullivan is so keen to believe in "America" that he claims that it has actually discovered its true humanity by taking gay men to its bosom: "AIDS compelled a form of social integration that might have never taken place without its onslaught. Forced to choose between complete abandonment of the homosexual subculture and an awkward first encounter, America, for the most part, chose the latter."[72] This optimistic opinion can be corroborated only in the most fantastic and playful of texts. Social exclusion threatens the drag queens who stop off at a small town in *To Wong Foo, Thanks for Everything, Julie Newmar* (Beeban Kidron, 1995). "Look at 'em. Perverts!" exclaims the corrupt and homophobic sheriff. "When the Founding Fathers wrote the Declaration of Independence and the Constitution, and what have you, bringing in justice for all, they didn't mean them." He is proved wrong: the people in the film value the impact of drag queens on their society.

It is the epidemic that has released Glenn, Joey, and their friends. Like the men in the film *The Living End* (Gregg Araki, 1992), they are free because they believe they will die shortly anyway. "And there was a terrifying but profoundly seductive freedom in that. They could do anything now, anything they wanted to, anything at all" (*Tim and Pete*, 187). Glenn and Joey are free to engage in a range of sexual activities about which Tim and Pete are reluctant even to fantasize. Also, they are free for kamikaze sacrifices (180). So they enact what for other dissidents can only be fantasy. While gay men have not proved an insurrectionary force in the United States, others have. Mikey's idea of seizing a plane and crashing it into the building where the president will be is " 'a fantasy,' " Joey pronounces. " '*So what?*' Mikey said. 'Everything *starts* as a fantasy!' " (240; Baker's emphases).

In arguing that hierarchy is sexy, I am not saying that we should be abandoning politics, morality, and responsibility and plunging into reactionary and complacent relations which exploit oppressions of class, age, race, and gender. Thinking even for a moment about the reality of those oppressions should restore our commitment to fight them. Bersani, famously, evokes the anguish that may be triggered by the image of a man with his legs in the air.[73] But you would have to be truly perverted to find this more distressing than the image of a starving child.

If lesbians and gay men had in fact succeeded in wiping out power in relationships, all we would have to do is enjoy our egalitarian practice and let everyone else in on the secret. But that is far from the case. The prevailing sex/gender system, we have every reason to know, is geared to the production of hierarchy and, as part of that, to the production of anxious, unhappy, and violent people. It produces us and our psychic lives—straights and gays—and it is not going to leave us alone. Arguably, fantasy becomes specific at the points where it is most at odds, superficially at least, with reality. It is a liberal-bourgeois delusion to suppose that "private" space can be somehow innocent of and protected from the real world. The task is to find ways of engaging fantasy without hurting and disempowering other people.

We have to accept that crucial political commitments may fall out of alignment with our fantasies. As Judith Halberstam puts it, "while people may well invest in values like equality and reciprocity in their political lives, they may not want those same values dominating their sexual lives."[74] Bersani discovers a positive virtue in such misalignments: "Our fantasy investments are often countered by more consciously and more rationally elaborate modes of reaching out to others, such as liking or admiring people we don't desire. In that tension lies an important moral dimension of our political engagement."[75] A politics asserted over libidinal investments may be more considered, more authoritative.

If we don't acknowledge power differentials in our fantasies and our relationships, we don't begin to get a hold on exploitation—including that which we perpetrate ourselves. While the political priority of resisting actual oppressions must be maintained, power imbalances in lesbian and gay personal relations may be refigured as potentially rewarding, though inevitably troubling. We should be exploring ways to assess and recombine power, sexiness, responsibility, and love.

5

GENDER

Thus far I have tried to sketch a materialist theory of psychic life, drawing attention to the power hierarchies that dominate our relationships. While I have isolated gender, age, class, and race as the principal vectors of power, special confusions envelop the idea of gender.

HISTORY AND THEORY

The most disputed question in our historiography is whether there have always been lesbians and gay men, or whether we are a recent development—since the nineteenth century, according to Foucault, or, in some versions, since the Stonewall Riots of 1969. The former, universalizing position is taken by Rictor Norton and Terry Castle, who discover in the molly-house subculture and masquerading women of the eighteenth century a gay and lesbian history that is continuous with the present. Note, however, that these evidences of continuity depend upon gender identities.

Consider the mollies of the early eighteenth century, who set up clubs, cross-dressed, and took women's names. One contemporary account describes them as "so far degenerated from all masculine deportment, or manly exercises, that they rather fancy themselves women, imitating all the little vanities that custom has reconciled to the female sex, affecting to speak, walk, tattle, cur[t]sy, cry, scold, and mimic all manner of effeminacy."[1] This, surely, evokes a subculture organized around gender, not sexuality. According to Alan Bray, what "most scandalised contemporary journalists writing about the molly houses was the extravagant effeminacy and transvestism they could involve."[2] The focus was on people who felt themselves, or behaved as if they felt themselves, to be the "wrong" gender—not on people having, or desiring, same-sex relations. Nonetheless, Bray reads the mollies as "homosexual": "There was now a continuing culture to be fixed on and an extension of the area in which homosexuality could be expressed and therefore recognised; clothes, gestures, language, particular buildings and particular public places—all could be identified as having specifically homosexual connotations."[3] Norton makes the same elision.[4]

My argument is that most cultures give primacy either to gender identity or to object-choice. One of these terms tends to serve as the primary interpretive instrument; the other is incorporated as a subordinate, and consequently incoherent, subcategory. Of course, this does not mean that the subordinate discourse will be entirely untenable; social systems are always complex, comprising residual and emergent elements. But it will be more difficult to hold, for the individual and for others.

Terry Castle adduces the diaries of Anne Lister, composed between 1817 and 1824, in pursuit of her contention that the lesbian is not a recent invention. Lister and her partners refer to her repeatedly as masculine, a man, gentleman-like and having manly feelings, and to her female partners as Lister's wives or subject to her adulterous approaches. Lister fantasizes herself in men's clothes and as having a penis, and models herself on Lord Byron. For Castle, and Norton also, this is evidence that the lesbian identity existed before 1869.[5] However, as Judith Halberstam points out, it makes better sense to regard Lister as transgendered; she even rejected the label "sapphic," the contemporary term for sexual relations between women, insisting on her own masculinity.[6] The many eighteenth-century instances surveyed in Emma Donoghue's *Passions Between Women* indicate that women who desired other women were persistently discovered to be of irregular gender—hermaphrodite, male-identified, or cross-dressed. Even romantic friendships might be structured as husband and wife, or involve cross-dressing. Donoghue wonders "why a woman who loved women would want to pass as a husband."[7] The reason is that she was male-identified; her object-choice was a consequence of that. Castle, indeed, introducing her collection of lesbian writing, remarks how, from the eighteenth century to Krafft-Ebing and Havelock Ellis, "the wish to associate female homosexuality with physiological oddities such as distended genitalia or supposedly masculine features . . . seems inevitably part of a 'naive' or reflexive response to the lesbian idea."[8] She supposes that the lesbian idea is prior, and then misrepresented; I think (alleged) masculine features dominated thought and action in this period. Generally, on through the nineteenth century, George Chauncey Jr. has shown, gender was the prior category. "Investigators classified a woman as an invert because of her aggressive, 'masculine' sexual and social behavior, and the fact that her sexual object was homosexual was only the logical corollary of this inversion."[9]

Two distinct aspects of the sex/gender system are in play, then. One is structured in gender identity, and tends to look for signs of femininity in men and masculinity in women. The other is structured in object-choice, and depends upon sexual and/or emotional commitment to another person of the same gender. To be sure, they are bound to become tangled together; nonetheless, they are analytically separate, and by no means necessarily either homologous or in a permanent relation. Gayle Rubin, coming from feminism, reaches the same position; so does Eve Sedgwick.[10] John Fletcher declares:

> I want provisionally to hold apart, to separate at least analytically gender, sexuality and sexual difference, in order to interrupt the too easy assimilation of sexuality and the sexual into the question of sexual difference, male and female on the one hand, and the equally common and too ready assimilation of that sexual difference into the question of gender on the other.[11]

Yet opinion is not settled. Tamsin Wilton remarks: "The interlocutions between discourses of gender and the erotic manifest a complexity that I suggest indicates that they may not usefully be distinguished one from the other." William J. Spurlin makes a thorough case for this.[12] In his essay "How to Do the History of Male Homosexuality," the four premodern male traditions adduced by David Halperin (effeminacy; pederasty or "active" sodomy; friendship or male love; passivity or inversion) are derived empirically from particular times and places; they do not admit a primary distinction between gender identity and object-choice.[13]

The question with which I began, about continuity and rupture in lesbian and gay histories, is awkwardly posed, therefore: it runs together gender dysphoria and dissident object-choice. The confusion in these discussions may be traced to a reluctance to distinguish between desire-to-be and desire-for. Gender identity is a kind of desire-to-be, whereas object-choice is about desire-for. As I elaborated these categories in chapter 2, they involve two quite different kinds of dissidence. In model (rg), the relative gender model, the man constitutes a double affront to convention:

(rg) A man has: desire-to-be F   desire-for M

The man has a "wrong" gender identity and his object-choice is "wrong" as well, insofar as it is homosexual. Yet insofar as there is an "F" and an "M" in the model, he may be assimilated into a conventional binary formation. In model (c), the complementarity model, the dissidence is again in the object-choice (one male desires another), but without the offense of dissident gender identity and the consolation (as it is conventionally perceived) of a shadow of heterosexual desire:

(c) A man has: desire-to-be M   desire-for M

ORIGINS AND SPECIES

When these matters began to attract scientific inquiry, in the nineteenth century, the reigning theoretical construct was *degeneracy*. This was a product of Darwinism—a kind of reverse evolution; it was a vehicle for anxieties about class, imperialism, and European racial superiority. So far from differentiating gender identity and object-choice, degeneracy subsumed both of them, along with perversion generally, into a very broad concept of weakness, debauchery, madness, and criminality, resulting from an alleged hereditary corruption.[14]

It was in reaction against the crudeness of degeneracy as a construct that more patient and sympathetic theorists, now often called "sexologists," isolated *inversion*. They encountered self-confessed inverts who seemed admirable, and therefore attributed the condition to a congenital, but not necessarily pathological, abnormality. Both Havelock Ellis and Freud explicitly reject degeneracy as an explanation.[15] Ellis supposed that upon conception everyone might have 50 percent of male "germs" and 50 percent of female ones, and that in "the homosexual person" and "the psychosexual hermaphrodite" something interfered with the business of sorting out which were to predominate;[16] this is an elementary anticipation of Freud's idea of a universal original bisexuality. Whatever else psychoanalysis did, Foucault remarks, at least it opposed "the political and institutional effects of the perversion-heredity-degenerescence system."[17] Martin Scherzinger and Neville Hoad remark that development correlates with evolution in Freud's thought, and arrested development with degeneration.[18]

The sexologists' investigations generally started from the most conspicuous form of dissidence: "wrong" gender identity. They tended to suppose that "wrong" object-choice would correlate, but quickly ran into instances where this seemed not to be the case. One response, as Chauncey says, was to be more careful with one's terminology. "While 'sexual inversion' referred to an inversion in the full range of gender characteristics, 'homosexuality', precisely understood, referred only to the narrower issue of homosexual object-choice, and did not necessarily imply gender or sexual role inversion."[19] Halperin, in this vein, credits Ellis and Freud with the crucial discrimination: "That sexual object-choice might be wholly independent of such 'secondary' characteristics as masculinity or femininity."[20] Ellis and Freud do make this distinction. Notwithstanding, their accounts of object-choice reinstall gender identity as a typical component.

Ellis was aware of the potential for confusion. In *Sexual Inversion* (1897), he notes that Albert Moll has tidied up the terminology and recognizes only two terms: "psychosexual hermaphroditism and homosexuality." This, broadly, is the discrimination that I have been broaching: between gender dissidence and "an inclination [in a man] toward men."[21] In the second edition of *Sexual Inversion* (1901), Ellis clarifies his account of Moll's argument and remarks in a note that Moll now wants to reserve the term "inversion" for gender disturbance—for "those cases in which there is a complete turning around of the sexual instinct, the man feeling in every respect as a woman, the woman in every respect as a man." Ellis concedes that there is something to be said for Moll's distinction, but he prefers another. The term "homosexuality" he applies "to the phenomena generally," reserving "inversion" for "those cases in which the sexual attraction to the same sex seems to be deep-rooted and organic."[22] This is more than terminology: Moll proposed two discrete conditions, whereas Ellis is positing two levels of intensity.

So if inversion is a "deep-rooted and organic" condition, as opposed to "the phenomena generally," what are the signs of it? In practice, Ellis allows it to correspond to the presence of "wrong" gender characteristics. To be sure, he insists, the male invert need not be effeminate, he may just make a same-sex object-choice. Nonetheless,

> it must be said that there is a distinctly general, though not universal, tendency for sexual inverts to approach the feminine type. . . . Although the invert himself may stoutly affirm his masculinity, and although this femininity may not be very obvious, its wide prevalence may be asserted with considerable assurance, and by no means only among the small minority of inverts who take an exclusively passive *role*.[23]

In other words, the gender invert is the most complete type of homosexual. Object-choice is in a continuum with the model of "wrong" gender identity.

So with women: "In inverted women a certain subtle masculinity or boy-ishness is equally prevalent."[24]

The key Freudian text here, *Three Essays on the Theory of Sexuality* (1905), is far closer to Ellis than is often recognized. Freud places same-sex object-choice at the forefront of his analysis. But, so far from maintaining a differentiation, he continues: "People of this kind are described as having 'contrary sexual feelings,' or better, as being 'inverts,' and the fact is described as 'inversion.'"[25]

Like Ellis, Freud dismisses fanciful theories of innate inversion, and refutes the anatomical basis claimed in such theories. However, also like Ellis, Freud cannot forsake the thought that gender identity and object-choice might line up after all. He maintains this especially, though not only, in the case of women. "The position in the case of women is less ambiguous; for among them the active inverts exhibit masculine characteristics, both physical and mental, with peculiar frequency and look for femininity in their sexual objects—though here again a closer knowledge of the facts might reveal a greater variety" (57).

This indeterminacy persists in a note added to Freud's *Three Essays* in 1915: "Finally, it may be insisted that the concept of inversion in respect of the sexual object should be sharply distinguished from that of the occurrence in the subject of a mixture of sexual characters." Yet the ensuing sentence is equivocal once more: "In the relation between these two factors, too, a certain degree of reciprocal independence is unmistakably present" (57–58). So sexual object and gender identity are to be sharply distinguished; yet there is a residual, unspecified interaction. In a further note, added to the *Three Essays* in 1920, Freud tries a new tack. Following Sandor Ferenczi, he posits two types of male homosexual: "'subject homo-erotics,' who feel and behave like women, and 'object homo-erotics,' who are completely masculine and who have merely exchanged a female for a male object" (58). Only object homo-erotics, Ferenczi says, may be "influenced psychologically," whereas for subject homo-erotics there can be no question of "struggling against their inclination" (58). Once again, the real homosexual, the one who cannot be reached through analysis, is the one who wants to identify across the gender divide. Freud, while accepting Ferenczi's distinction, notes also that many people combine elements of both.

C. A. Tripp in his comprehensive survey of homosexuality, first published in 1975, dismisses psychoanalysis and declares, "Only in popular thinking are homosexuality and inversion synonymous."[26] However, prominent commentators of our own time have allowed confusion to persist. As

Sedgwick confirms, Foucault's invocation of "a personage, a past, a case history, and a childhood" is often invoked as charting the full emergence of a modern concept of sexuality.[27] However, Foucault says he is presenting "the nineteenth-century homosexual"—in fact, the invert. He specifies as the founding text Karl Westphal's article of 1870 on "contrary sexual sensations," in which the examples are a lesbian who dreamed she was a man, and an apparently heterosexual cross-dressing male prostitute. Indeed, "wrong" gender identity is central to the historical change registered by Foucault: "Homosexuality [L'homosexualité] appeared as one of the forms of sexuality when it was transposed from the practice of sodomy onto a kind of interior androgyny, a hermaphroditism of the soul." This change is characterized "less by a type of sexual relations [that is, less by object-choice] than by a quality of sexual sensibility, a certain way of inverting [d'intervertir] the masculine and the feminine in oneself."[28] Foucault is saying, in other words, that the modern homosexual is a blurred, composite figure, conceived in a confusion between object-choice and gender identity. Unfortunately, he does not explicate that confusion.

Gert Hekma, writing from the anthropological tradition, reviews the arguments of the classical inversion theorists (not including Freud), showing that their emphasis on inversion obscured object-choice, thus causing "additional problems and hesitations in coming out as homosexuals" for "more masculine boys." Nowadays, however, "the spectrum of gender possibilities has broadened to include different options" and "feminine styles" are "part of the diversity of the gay world."[29] Descriptively this is fair, though perhaps a bit eager to free the post-Liberation gay man from the stigma of effeminacy. But Hekma's judicious empiricism forgoes any attempt at a theory, either of gender or sexuality. There used to be a theory—inversion—but it was wrong; now we just have all kinds of people doing all kinds of things.

At the other extreme, Kaja Silverman's determination to retheorize these topics within psychoanalysis plunges her back into Oedipal conjecture and an assumption that gender identity is the key to homosexuality. After all, she avers, "human culture has to date shown itself to be stubbornly resistant to conceptualizing sexual positionality—and, more recently, object-choice—apart from the binary logic of gender."[30] Indeed it has. Silverman is not interested in separating out gender identity and object-choice; she believes that the gay man has to accept that "an identification with 'woman' constitutes the very basis of his identity, and/or the position from which he desires" (344). Lately, Silverman notes, some gay men have tended to appear masculine, but she isn't impressed: "It is by no means clear, anyway, that even the most committed practitioner of macho homosexuality can ever succeed in entirely extirpating the 'woman' within" (346). Even while abjuring "global pretensions," and acknowledging that her theory may account only for "certain kinds of male homosexuality," Silverman launches into her own reworking of the Oedipus complex as a mechanism for the acquisition of gender identity (346–47).

The most ambitious investigation of the thesis that the modern homosexual derives from the late nineteenth century is offered in Neil Bartlett's creative documentary, *Who Was That Man? A Present for Mr. Oscar Wilde*. Once, Bartlett says, he experienced his gayness "in complete isolation"; now he is "connected with other men's lives, men living in London with me. *Or with other dead Londoners*."[31] To establish this linkage, he ransacks nineteenth-century documents, especially around the Wilde scandal. An awkwardness, however, is that most of the available instances appear to involve effeminate men. This places them in specific discontinuity with contemporary gay subculture, the achievement of which, as Bartlett sees it, is to make us "handsome, *masculine*, demanding and unafraid of our pleasures" (219; my emphasis). The signals for gayness are historically variable, then: in the nineteenth century they centered upon effeminacy; today they are said to involve a relatively unremarkable masculinity.

Bartlett was writing in that period—which developed from the mid-1970s and held the field through the 1980s—when it was most difficult to appreciate gay femininity: in the heyday of the "clone" gay image. It was the time when Gregg Blachford and Jamie Gough could write, almost without reservation, of the masculinization of the gay world.[32] Dennis Altman observed: "The long-haired androgynous look of the early seventies was now found among straights, and the super-macho image of the Village People disco group seemed to typify the new style perfectly."[33] Richard Dyer, in an essay first published in 1981, confirms "the current 'masculinization' of the gay male style." However, he saw something else in the Village People: "all the stereotypes of ultramasculinity in a camped-up flauntingly gay way."[34] Even at this point, gay effeminacy has not gone away.

In fact by no means all Bartlett's contemporary gay Londoners were macho, but in *Who Was That Man?* he accepts the image. He himself wears Doctor Martins, 501 jeans, a check shirt, and a moustache: "I look like, or rather hope that I look like, a lot of other gay men" (205). Again, at the start of a section mainly transcribing nineteenth-century notions of effeminacy, he remarks how in his masculine gear he may pass as straight, while still being visible to other gay men (63). This is the image he presents on the BBC2 television program *The Late Show* (1993). There he urges upon gay men eclectic subcultural appropriation: the system scarcely acknowledges us, but we are piecing together our own lives. He offers his own outfit as an instance. Some might say that he is not entitled to wear it—he is not one of those "regular guys." But he has "earned the right," he says, through the (manly) confidence with which he carries it off.

Who Was That Man? makes much of the famous transvestites, Fanny Park and Stella Boulton, who often passed as young women until they were arrested in 1870. Bartlett sees them as demonstrating "the existence of our culture in London," though the charge was "being men and dressed in female attire" (143, 132). Significantly, he stops short of actually identifying with them: "I would applaud the men who wore them in their determined efforts to use their frocks to create public space for themselves," he says (137–38). Such a combination of affiliation and distance occurs again when Bartlett remarks: "I always enjoy asking a friend, in all drunken seriousness, *how's the wife?* We both know that there is no useful comparison between heterosexual marriage and the relationship being referred to." There is a point, though: "in using the word, I recall the house at 46 Fitzroy Street" where the police arrested a group of transvestites on August 12, 1894 (85; Bartlett's emphasis). The connection is awkward, but Bartlett believes it encodes a historical affirmation that is worth making.

Such strategic effeminacy has partly informed Bartlett's extravagant deployment of camp and drag in the theater, particularly in plays from that time, *A Vision of Love Revealed in Sleep* and *Sarrasine*. In an interview, Simon Fraser questions him: "But this is 1991. Is drag really important to gay men?" Bartlett's reply is not that lots of gay men are feminine really, but that drag is an emblematic part of the culture of British gay men: "Almost all the things that are now traditionally gay are very important for that fact alone, and they represent gay space. They are a cultural space which we can inhabit." The value lies in "seeing a gay entertainer in a room full of gay people, speaking a language that no one else could understand."[35] We do drag, then, not because we are really feminine, but because it's been one of our things; it is a matter of subcultural affiliation and respect.

In my view this is a fair proposition, but insofar as it subsumes gender dissonance into gayness it tends to marginalize men for whom femininity is the primary factor. In fact Bartlett's work, despite his apparent privileging of the macho image, has contributed significantly to the recovery of subcultures of effeminacy. As regards camp and drag in his stage work, he evidently has been intrigued by their theatrical potential. In Bartlett's novel *Ready to Catch Him Should He Fall*, Mother gets Boy into drag, but at an intense moment "his white-powdered female face and livid red lips were suddenly split open by a masculine grin of triumph."[36] This grotesque juxtaposition may remind us that drag is not about women, it is about gender boundaries; theater is not about display, but appearance and reality. Boy's triumph consists partly in the quality of his masquerade, partly in his maintenance of maleness. An ideology does not require the suppression of its other, but its productive management.

The Bar in *Ready to Catch Him* rehearses these issues. Boy is introduced as conspicuously masculine: "Keep him strong, keep him young, and, whatever his colouring, keep him gorgeous." The narrator invokes an allegorical figure of "Strength" (14–15). The Bar regulars appear to belong to another generation. Their culture is insistently feminine and centered upon gender identity. They have girls' names, camp talk, and a penchant for cross-dressing. Boy is not like them. At one point he is said to imagine leaving The Bar with a husband, but the narrator checks himself: "(Of course, Boy would never have used that word, *Husband*, that's my word. But then, I'm old-fashioned, I mean, we used to talk like that all the time. What word do you use, then?)" (49; Bartlett's emphasis). When Boy is being prepared to celebrate his union with O, he is dressed in drag, as a smalltown queen, and as a woman by Madame and Stella. However, he is also attired as a schoolboy, a soldier, and a black man. For the wedding Boy is not in drag; there is "no priest and no frock, this being an actual ceremony and not some party or parody" (207).

Yet, in practice, few of us want unremitting machismo. Bartlett remarks in *Who Was That Man?*: "I too often require of myself and my partners a female nature—sexually available, domestic, a surprisingly good cook and at all times attractively dressed—inhabiting a male exterior—sexually aggressive, potent, financially successful, socially acceptable" (63–64). In his attempt to reconcile the contradictory concurrence of (what he takes as) masculine and feminine norms, Bartlett comes unexpectedly close to the idea of Ulrichs and the sexologists: our souls may be partly female, but the male body is crucial.

Of course, not all gay men became clones; camp and drag continued to thrive; clone got described as a kind of drag. The position was not coherent, but it seemed to suffice, until the mid-1990s when transgender people, by declaring themselves, made the illogicality blatant. Lately, under the regime of Queer (regarded either as a political intervention or as a capitulation to capitalism), almost all styles are welcome. Augmenting the standard menu to "LGBTT" prompts a recognition that we still haven't sorted out the relations between sexual orientation and gender identity.

WHAT HAPPENED AT STONEWALL

Given the persistence of confusion over object-choice and gender identity in the thought of the most prestigious theorists of dissident sexuality, it is hardly surprising that gay men and lesbians have not readily clarified these matters. In the late nineteenth century some men, appealing to Walt Whitman, David and Jonathan, and the Theban Band, sought to establish that, so far from being effeminate, same-sex love might be quintessentially masculine. In Germany in the early twentieth century manly homosexuality was celebrated by the group around the journal *Der Eigene*. They abjured the notion that homosexuals were feminine in disposition, reasserting sexuality in chivalric love and the love of friends.[37] In terms of the models I have proposed, they posit males desiring other males, without relinquishing their masculine gender identities:

(c) A man has: desire-to-be M   desire-for M

They manifest a conventional gender identity alongside a dissident object-choice.

However, this was not the dominant ideology. In *Gay New York*, Chauncey has shown that until the 1930s men were not divided by object-choice, into "homosexuals" and "heterosexuals": this was not the primary axis of identification. A man displaying a committed feminine manner got called a fairy, but "the 'man' who responded to his solicitations—no matter how often—was not considered abnormal, a 'homosexual,' so long as he abided by the masculine gender conventions."[38] Donald Webster Cory, writing in 1951, cited a report from a U.S. sailor who believed that "the stranger who performed fellatio" was "homosexual," but not the man on whom it was performed. "The performer was a 'fairy.' The compliant sailor, not."[39] Still, between 1930 and 1960, gender dissidence is found by David K. Johnson and Allen Drexel to be the organizing principle of gay subculture in Chicago.[40] A similar story is told by Edmund White's friend Lou in *The Beautiful Room Is Empty*: homosexuals divide into boys, men, and vicious old queens. "The boy felt a natural affinity to girls, with whom he was always exchanging makeup tips. The man had once fucked girls but now had no further use for them." Tragically, "whoever succumbed to homosexual desire became immediately undesirable."[41] In Britain, John Marshall has shown, gender inversion remained the dominant paradigm on into the 1970s; it "effectively eliminated the need for a homosexual concept."[42]

This analysis has consequences for the mythology of Stonewall. Who, when we liberated ourselves, came out? Not the man who presented himself as inverted, effeminate; he was always visible. The ultimate instance is Quentin Crisp. He says in *The Naked Civil Servant* (1968) that people such as he "must, with every breath they draw, with every step they take, demonstrate that they are feminine."[43] Crisp was never *not-out*: continually he is propositioned, harassed, and beaten, on sight and by total strangers; employers and the army reject him out of hand. The distinction between manifest and closeted gay men is urged by Peter Wildeblood, writing with unprecedented boldness after his trial and conviction in 1954: "Everyone has seen the pathetically flamboyant pansy with the flapping wrists, the common butt of music-hall jokes and public-house stories." Such people, evidently, were not hiding. However, Wildeblood adds, "Most of us are not like that. We do our best to look like everyone else, and we usually succeed."[44] The object-choice men strive to distance themselves from the pansies. It is to these men, the ones who managed to look "like everyone else," that the 1970s offered a new identity.

The United States produces equivalent instances. Michael Bronski observes: while "most homosexuals could choose to 'pass,' the majority of homosexuals who formed this visible subculture were effeminate men, butch women, obvious queens, and the drags."[45] Kenneth Marlowe in a popular book of 1968, *The Male Homosexual*, distinguishes the "effeminate" and the "masculine" homosexual. The former, "because of his physical appearance, is sometimes labelled 'queer' from the start of his life"— everyone can see at once that he's different. Meanwhile, "the masculine homosexual," according to Marlowe, "is usually referred to as the latent homosexual, the closet queen."[46] Either way, he's not visible; hardly queer at all. Todd Butler, recalling New York in 1960, conjoins out-ness and effeminacy: "It was unusual for somebody to be fully 'out' and leading a gay lifestyle to be that butch. Usually, if you met somebody who was gay and butch, they were very uptight, closety types and very, very neurotic."[47] That sounds like Michael, Donald, and most of the men in Mart Crowley's *Boys in the Band*. Alan can hardly tell that he's crashed a gay party. But he knows about Emory: "Faggot, Fairy, pansy . . . queer, cocksucker! I'll kill you, you goddam little mincing, swish! You goddam freak! FREAK! FREAK!" Emory admits: "I've known what I was since I was four years old." "Everybody's always known it about *you*, Emory," Michael quips, unhelpfully.[48]

It is the straight-acting types who had a new opportunity: to come out. The 1970s are often presented as the birth of the modern gay man, his (self-)definition founded purposefully in object-choice, as a consequence of (partial) decriminalization in Britain, the Stonewall Riots, the founding of the Gay Liberation Front and other activist movements, and the burgeoning of a purposefully sexualized gay subcultural economy. The larger outcome was a reversal in the organization of the sex/gender system. *Homosexual, lesbian*, and *gay* got defined in terms of object-choice, and gender identity was subsumed, more or less uneasily, into that. Thus, for instance, we know that drag artistes are not invariably gay, but in practice tend to assume that they are; in *The Adventures of Priscilla, Queen of the Desert* (Stephan Elliott, 1994), everyone is shocked that Tick (Mitzi) is planning to return to his wife and child.

Lesbian awareness was complicated by other priorities in the women's movement; yet, here too, the attack on butch/femme styles and identities tended to validate object-choice rather than gender dissidence.

This has made better sense for many people, personally and politically. But, by the same token, people whose primary sense of themselves is strongly founded in gender dissidence—effeminate men, butch women, transvestites, transsexuals—have been marginalized. They have endured the dominance of a sex/gender model in which they hardly figure, or only as incidental, unintelligible, out of date, embarrassing. Leslie Feinberg in hir novel *Stone Butch Blues* shows butches being excluded by lesbians in the gay liberation movement.[49]

For many gay men, the post-Stonewall reliance on object-choice has afforded opportunity for a denial that effeminacy is a necessary part of gayness. Andrew Sullivan is notorious for his insistence that gays are "virtually normal"; for him this actually means *not effeminate*. Sullivan denies that he has ever experienced insecurity about this, though he recalls that when he avoided team sports at school a girl did ask him, "Are you sure you're not really a girl under there?"[50] Sissy boys are the problem, according to Sullivan. It is they who vindicate right-wingers, suffer identity conflict, and provoke explanations from psychologists. He is excited by the masculine tone of a gay party:

> While the slim and effeminate hovered at the margins, the center of the dance floor and the stage areas were dedicated to the most male archetypes, their muscles and arrogance like a magnet of self-contempt for the rest. But at the same time, it was hard also not to be struck, as I was the first time I saw it, by a genuine, brazen act of cultural defiance, a spectacle designed not only to exclude but to reclaim a gender, the ultimate response to a heterosexual order that denies gay men the masculinity that is also their own.[51]

This craven yearning to appease the sex/gender system that has marginalized us leads Sullivan to boost his manhood with injections of actual testosterone. Apparently this bestows a Nietzschean, Superman buzz: "What our increasing knowledge of testosterone suggests is a core understanding of what it is to be a man, for better and worse. It is about the ability to risk for good and bad; to act, to strut, to dare, to seize."[52] Somewhat defensively, Sullivan puts down gays who can't or won't normalize as "prone to adult dysfunction and pathology," and as "insecure gay adults" who "will always cling, to a greater or lesser extent, to the protections of gender mannerisms."[53]

Paul Monette takes a more thoughtful approach in *Halfway Home*. Tom has been assaulted as a child by his father and brother (Brian), both of whom see him as a sissy and a wimp. Still, in his mid-thirties, he is "a terrible sissy when it comes to crawling things."[54] He has internalized this view of himself; indeed, he has made it productive by leaving his hostile, smalltown, Irish/Italian-Catholic origins and becoming a performance artist in California (outside Malibu). His star turn has been his camp version of Christ on the cross, "Miss Jesus." As he faces death from AIDS, Tom's memories are reactivated when Brian appears, under pressure in a racketeering inquiry, with his wife (Susan) and son (Daniel).

This turns out to be the opportunity for Tom to revise his relations with manliness. This is accomplished initially through a bond with Daniel (who is seven), founded in Tom's awareness that his own childhood traumas are being reenacted in Daniel by the damaged Brian. Daniel evidently likes being with Tom—a man who is not going to become violent. As they walk together Daniel falls into step; Tom is gratified to be a model of manhood. He comes to realize that manliness is a precarious masquerade: "there was no special dispensation" in "the secret to being a man." It was not a natural gift, possessed by his father and brother and withheld from himself, but something continuously improvised and mimicked, "a waltz on the lip of the void" (199). This (relative) demystification of manliness frees up Tom's anxieties. He finds he is imitating Brian's "unconscious swagger," and thinks:

> This was how straight boys learnt to be men, mimicking and preening, stimulating the butch gene. As I trotted down in Brian's wake, I thought about Daniel following him and following me. Somewhere there had been a tradeoff, gentling my brother and toughening me. Brian stopped at the bottom of the stairs while I hovered a step above him, four inches taller now. And I prayed to the nothing I didn't believe in: *Let the kid have it both ways.* (238; Monette's emphasis)

Perhaps the next generation of men will be able to incorporate something of the sissy.

For this reader, the determination in *Halfway Home* to negotiate an acceptable form of manliness betrays a persisting anxiety. Brian doesn't give much ground; excessive hopes appear to be placed in alternative counseling sessions as a way of dealing with his violence toward Daniel. The brothers admit their youthful sexual activities together, though in Brian's case it appears to have been circumstantial and temporary (he was between girl-friends), whereas for Tom it was formative and continuing. " 'You know what I used to think?' " Brian asks. " 'That I made you gay. Like it was all my fault.' He spilled out a soft self-mocking laugh, and his fingers rustled my hair. 'Like I tempted you' " (177). This somewhat arrogant thought is not repudiated. The idea seems to be that the men, between them, engender, or anyway fos-ter, the gay boy; he is a by-product of their manly maneuvering, and hence not to be unfairly despised and condemned. There is little room in this for Susan, the wife and mother. As a nonmasculine influence she is barely effec-tive; her protectiveness toward her son leads Tom to compare her to Medea (121). Tom does have a supportive lesbian and gay family of choice, but they are edged to one side while patriarchal business is transacted (compare the emphasis on the brother in Larry Kramer's play *The Normal Heart*).

A feeling that Monette is protesting too much is strengthened when Tom manages to prove himself in more traditional fictive manner by dis-arming a gangster. So the gay sissy is allowed to run with the men, at least up to a point; and, correspondingly, the heteronormative system can be humanized, such that the gay man can love his birth family (as it seems he must), as well as his family of choice. The trouble is that reconciling ele-ments of the sissy with elements of the macho still leaves the true sissy exposed—and, for that matter, the true macho.

What *Halfway Home* does show is that manliness is learned. Again, in Joseph Hansen's novel, *Steps Going Down*, Cutler meets a young man. "The boy shakes hands limply, awkwardly, like a little kid who hasn't learned the knack. Or like a girl. Cutler's handshake is strong, manly. His mother made him practice. *A good, firm handshake makes people respect you.*"[55] Cutler's manly stance projects dominance; the young man may be correspondingly boyish, or even girlish. Masculinity is something boys acquire, if they are lucky. Hence a central dictum in queer theory, as enun-ciated especially by Judith Butler: *all* gender is performative. "Everyone is passing; some have an easier job of it than others," Kate Bornstein observes. Again: "Arnold Schwarzenegger does male drag perfectly, only he doesn't seem to have much of a sense of humor about it yet."[56]

THE RETURN OF THE SISSY

The triumphant revelation that the gruff-looking man in the hard hat speaks with a high-pitched voice, loves Bette Midler, and wants to be dominated in bed is repeated again and again in gay stories, as though it encapsulated a fatal truth. The persistence of gay male femininity, in the face of such discouragement, indicates that it is fulfilling some important functions in sexual dissidence. My larger thought here is that gender hierarchy is not something that gay men and lesbians have arbitrarily got stuck on: it involves one of the basic structuring ideologies in our societies and, like class and race, it is not going to go away.

What makes this topic so complex is the mobility, fluidity, ubiquity, and inexorability of gender typing. Historically, as I tried to show in *The Wilde Century*, effeminacy didn't always correlate with queerness; in the time of Shakespeare and Milton it meant paying too much attention to women. In the nineteenth century anarchists were termed effeminate, and Jews.[57] Still, today, all kinds of sensitivity, consideration, colorfulness, and exuberance may be stigmatized as failures in masculinity. Writers have often struggled to articulate sensitivity while denying effeminacy. In *A Streetcar Named Desire*, Blanche says her young husband had "a softness and tenderness which wasn't like a man's, although he wasn't the least bit effeminate-looking."[58] Probably many boys and men who exhibit femininity are mainly concerned to disaffiliate from the grosser aspects of conventional masculinity; they may simply be registering that a real man is not a very nice person.

These uncertainties about gender may be tracked in John Rechy's writing. In *City of Night* (1963), the narrator is a male hustler who self-consciously asserts his own macho performance, in contrast to the adoring johns and queens, without admitting his own gayness. This is a precarious stance; one of the narrator's clients rejects him when he leafs through a book: " 'really masculine men don't read!' "[59] However, the queens come into their own in the later, Mardi Gras chapters. Twenty years later, in *Bodies and Souls*, Rechy is looking for more positive potential in a reconciliation of masculine and feminine qualities. Billy and Stud are hustlers and presumptively not gay, but an affair develops between them. Stud's manliness is not at issue; he's not even gay, he says. Nor is Billy "effeminate"; he objects to being referred to as "she." Notwithstanding, Billy is said to be "beautiful," and Stud "couldn't think of anyone being that beautiful and not a girl." The narrator interprets: "Billy *was* beautiful. He had a slender blond body that turned golden instead of tan, eyes so misty at times they looked painted with water colors, and long eyelashes. It was true he was not effeminate—he was gracefully boyish, looking radiantly younger than his eighteen years."[60] As Stud begins to fall for Billy, he finds that "Billy's body was not softly formed; where had he got that idea? It was slim, yes—but very solid looking" (318). In fact, "he was becoming more masculine all the time" (323). So they are worthy of each other. Billy is represented as retaining, miraculously, both the feminine attributes that make him initially attractive, and the masculine attributes that make him an acceptable partner. Still Rechy is unable to get masculinity, femininity, and sexual attraction into the same frame without anxiety and contradiction.

In the purportedly documentary book *The Sexual Outlaw* (1977), Rechy's narrative voice assumes a purposeful gay liberationist stance. He asks whether gays are appreciating "their particular *and varied* beauty? From that of the transvestite to that of the bodybuilder? The young to the old? The effeminate to the masculine? The athletic to the intellectual?" He praises queens as "true hero-heroines of our time, exhibiting more courage for walking one single block in drag than a straight-looking gay to 'come out' on a comfy campus."[61] However, Ben Gove points out, the effeminate queens don't get much sex in *The Sexual Outlaw*; they are excluded from the masculine world of promiscuous cruising.[62] They appear what they are—left over in the post-Stonewall era which they helped to inaugurate.

Whether it is true that effeminate gays don't get much sex is unclear. Edmund White's writings do not support the idea that the destiny of the effeminate gay man is inevitably lonely. In *The Farewell Symphony*, he presents his desires as feminine—"I was so besotted by Kevin. I wanted to be his wife in the most straitlaced of marriages. I wanted to cook his breakfast and bear his babies. I wanted him to be my boy-husband, my baby-master."[63] However, Kevin is in love with the handsome Dennis. Nonetheless, White gets plenty of fun, friendship, and sex in diverse roles; *The Farewell Symphony* has been criticized for excessive reporting of tricks turned. The predicament of and opportunities for the feminine boy are displayed in Joseph Mills's Glasgow story, "Dreaming, Drag." We first see David with his best friend, Joan, a lesbian: he has orange hair, and is wearing a "working class housewife's coat."[64] He doesn't want to be a transsexual: he loves inhabiting the male body, and the male orgasm. On the other hand, he disidentifies with "the men in macho drag—gay or straight—who were in love with the male physique and all that went with it." He is uncomfortable when he realizes that, between these positions, there seems to be "no place for himself" (151).

David's manner had quite pleased Walter, now his ex-boyfriend: "He thought being with a camp guy made him more masculine, less gay. He was easing himself into a hetero relationship" (88). Walter can't stand the stigma of gayness. David gets into a fight and decides that his cuts and bruises suit better with a masculine style, so he attires himself in denim, with a leather jacket and studded belt. "Clothes make the man," he remarks (90). He falls heavily for Billy, who doesn't see him as camp; not that he's against camp, he thinks it very funny: " 'But I don't find it sexually attractive. I mean I like a man—otherwise why be here?' " (106). David deals with the mismatch by dressing himself in exactly the same clothes and dying his hair the same color as Billy. He finds himself elaborating contradictory fantasies about Billy and taking the "active" role in bed. However, Billy doesn't want a twin either. David goes back to feminine styles, abandoning " 'all that macho stuff. . . . Yes, we need to *complement* each other' " (117–18; my elision, Mills's emphasis). However, Billy is not convinced. He takes up with a man who has " 'the sort of Clark Kent, well-groomed executive look' " (123). David is left railing against " 'your little hierarchy of homosexuals . . . with the just-like-everyone-else-Walter type on top and the deviants like me on the bottom' " (130; my elision). He exclaims:

> "God what a freak. Billy's right. I would never go with someone as effeminate looking as me." . . . Handsome, masculine gay guys don't fall in love with camp gay guys. *Camp* gay guys don't fall in love with their own kind. . . . David had tried and tried again to be "normal," but he resigned himself to the fact that camp was normal for him most of the time, whatever the consequences. (138; my elisions)

However, it is not true that David doesn't attract men, and it is doubtful whether Billy's Clark Kent can turn into Superman. David remains irrepressible, like the divas he admires, and lives to fight another day.

In Leo Bersani's view, the matter is structural: as Quentin Crisp said, gay men are attracted sexually by machismo, not camp.[65] Bersani does admit that not all gays are the same, but he is committed to a Freudian supposition that sexuality must be reducible to a binary gender structure. This leaves gay men desiring from the position of the woman, while entertaining a simultaneous and contradictory wish to imitate "those desiring subjects with whom we have been officially identified: other men."[66] With heterosexual women, therefore, we have (reluctant) identity; with men only (respectful) imitation. As Patrick Paul Garlinger suggests, Bersani's celebration of the subversive impetus of the man with his legs in the air may be designed to manage the stigma of effeminacy.[67] While Bersani's organic model leads him ultimately to the idea of gay men as feminine and desiring the masculine, mine anticipates also a symmetry. If

A man has: desire-to-be F desire-for M

then it is at least plausible that there is a corresponding figure:

A man has: desire-to-be M desire-for F

In theory at least, there is a matching partner for almost all positions.

Social surveys indicate that there certainly are men who experience desire-for camp and cross-dressing men; Tim Bergling in his book *Sissyphobia* finds some; the "sissy boys" interviewed by Richard Green report sexual partners.[68] Gove concurs in respect of Miss Destiny in Rechy's *City of Night*, and mentions the films *Stonewall* (Nigel Finch, 1995) and *The Adventures of Priscilla, Queen of the Desert*.[69] Bernadette in the latter had a boyfriend who recently died (the boyfriend had a thing about transsexuals—"a sort of bent status symbol"); at the end Bernadette teams up with Bob. Divine and Our Lady of the Flowers attract masculine types in Genet's novel.[70] In the film comedy *To Die For* (Peter Mackenzie Litten, 1994), Simon loves and desires his camp partner Mark, in life and in death, but is blocked in the expression of his feelings by his relationship with his father. We are given to understand that Albin in *La Cage aux Folles* (Edouard Molinaro, 1978) and Albert in *The Birdcage* (Mike Nichols, 1996) have been beauties in their time.

Eddie is young, innocent, dreamy, and effeminate in *The Fruit Machine* (scripted by Frank Clarke, released on video in North America as *Wonderland*; Philip Saville, 1988). He watches musicals and romances on video with his mother, is given to what she calls "girly mannerisms," and is victimized by his father. He is plainly in love with his streetwise friend and protector, Michael, who regards himself as a straight rent boy and Eddie as a "best mate." They are both sixteen. When Eddie approaches the point of a declaration, Michael is embarrassed and shuts him up. Eddie claims them for femininity: they're "just a pair of little queenettes," he says. But Michael counters: "No we're not, we're lads, we're young men." Gove remarks the division between "gushy queen and defensive lad," and that the film assumes the latter to be the more sexy.[71] However, the viewer's sense of Eddie's erotic potential is probably enhanced when, after appearing somewhat awkward hitherto, he swims gracefully among dolphins. Michael finally admits his love when Eddie is dying.

In some of these instances, femininity may be attractive because of a conflation with boyishness. A choice of an older man between his wife and a camp boyfriend figures in John Hopkins's play *Find Your Way Home*.[72] However, this is not always so. An older feminine person may be protective (motherly), to either a masculine or a feminine boy. This happens in the film *Stonewall*, where Matty Dean, the new boy in town, is drawn both to the masculine, assimilationist Ethan, and the established drag queen, La Miranda.[73] In Harvey Fierstein's *Torch Song Trilogy*, camp drag-artiste Arnold is attractive both to Ed, who is older and so straight-acting that he insists on cultivating his affair with Laurel, and to Alan, who is a young model and hustler. Arnold is obscurely diffident about the relationship with Alan, and the text evades its outcome through the boy's violent death; we may conclude that fate is against such a liaison. Arnold goes on to foster and adopt a teenage gay boy, and the return of Ed, finally unable to resist Arnold, constitutes an explicit family of choice with Ed as father and Arnold as wife and mother. This secures an upbeat ending, though Arnold has to fight off his own homophobic mother, who assumes that his interest in the boy must be predatory (these homosexuals will stop at nothing). From a queer viewpoint, it is perhaps disappointing that Arnold's integrity depends on the implication that sexual love between a man of thirty and a boy of sixteen (now the age of consent in England) must, *by definition*, be out of the question.[74]

It would hardly be surprising if the attractions of male femininity were understated in our cultures. Richard Goldstein may, in many cases, be right: "butch is the face many gay men show to each other, but not the one they reveal to their lovers."[75] Gays may be reluctant to admit the attractions of being the feminine man, and the rewards of desiring him, but he is not without his admirers. Fergus vomits in *The Crying Game* (Neil Jordan, 1992) when he sees Dil's penis—the sign that the femininity that had attracted him is attached to a male body. Notwithstanding, Fergus is drawn to Dil. To keep him safe Fergus makes him look like a boy and hides him away; he says it's their honeymoon night, and surely a sexual act takes place (nothing less would placate Dil, and in the ensuing scene it is morning, Dil is asleep, and Fergus looks decidedly pensive). At the end, Dil visits Fergus in prison, along with the other wives and girlfriends though in more exuberant style. Dil's idea, for one, is that they are an ongoing couple: "I'm counting the days." "Stand By Your Man," the music comes up. To take care of Dil is in his nature, Fergus says.

In summary, if our dominant story encodes male femininity as misfortune, we have also a counter discourse, in which the feminine man may be a turn-on. The problem, I suspect, is not that he is unattractive, but that he has difficulty in establishing a belief in his own worth, in the face of the gross stigma that attaches in our societies to effeminacy. In *A Boy's Own Story*, Edmund observes that it is his own dislike of himself, endorsed by the prevailing ideology, that impedes his love life. "I see now that what I wanted was to be loved by men and to love them back but not to be a homosexual."[76] The narrator in White's later work, *The Farewell Symphony*, observes: "what the Stonewall uprising changed was not love so much as self-esteem, upon which mutual love depends."[77] In White's *The Married Man*, Austin attracts a partner who is masterful to the point of sustaining a conventionally sexual marriage.

While there may be a symmetry, whereby a man with desire-to-be F is matched by a man with desire-for F, the person in the subordinate position is likely to be the more vulnerable. He puts himself at the greater risk, psychologically, when he offers himself in a relationship. The problem—men with an element of dissident gender identity getting to feel good about themselves—still has a long way to go. James Kenneth Melson, informing his mother of his positive AIDS diagnosis, reassures her: " 'Mom, to me my sexual preference is only that. I'm not a fag, sissy or queen.' "[78] AIDS we can cope with, effeminacy is beyond the pale.

TRANSGENDER

The prospect of rewarding sexual encounters may not be the priority for gender-dissident people. Todd, age seventeen: "That's the basic problem. I want to be a woman *before* I want to have sexual relations with a man."[79] Trans people have good reason to distinguish desire-to-be and desire-for. "Gender identity for me answers the question of who I am. Sexual preference answers the question who do I want to be romantically or sexually involved with," Kate Bornstein declares.[80]

In other societies there are conventional roles for transgender people. The *fa'affines* of Samoa are apparently biological men who dress and largely live as women; they are recognized and reared as girls and appreciated as domestics and entertainers. Their sexual partners, they claim, are 99 percent of Samoan men. Some use them casually, some are ready for relationships. Young, articulate fa'affines have visited Australia and know that in other countries gay men sleep together. However, fa'affines don't have sex with each other; they are sisters; that would be two queens. They classify themselves as "women," and don't accept that the terms *gay, transvestite,* and *transsexual* fit them.[81] Again: *skesana* boys, in the single-sex context of mine-labor in South Africa, glory in their femininity and assume that their roles will be confirmed by their masculine partners:

> MARTIN: I think in a relationship the woman must attend to her man. Like a woman she must clean the house, and he must be treated like a man.
> THAMI: There must be a "man" and a "woman" in a relationship. A man must act mannish in his behaviour and his talks and walks. But a female must be queenish in every way.

The *skesana* (like a wife) gains protection and favors in a violent and uncertain system; also, Hugh McLean and the late Linda Ngcobo add, he "attains pleasure by flirting with power."[82]

There is no comparable framework for men in Britain and the United States for men who want to be women, but there is the amazing possibility, through medicine and psychiatry, of gender reassignment. In the face of the priority accorded to object-choice in our cultures, activists have put transgender on the agenda. Leslie Feinberg in *Stone Butch Blues* and Kate Bornstein in *Gender Outlaw* have published powerful and successful books based on their experience. Fiction on this theme includes *Trumpet* by Jackie Kay, *The Danish Girl* by David Ebershoff, and *James Miranda Barry* by Patricia Duncker. Barry is the subject also of Rachel Holmes's study, *Scanty Particulars*. We have the disconcerting photographs of Del LaGrace Volcano.[83] Films in general release include: *To Wong Foo, Thanks for Everything, Julie Newmar* (Beeban Kidron, 1995), *Different for Girls* (Richard Spence, 1996), and *Ma vie en rose* (Alain Berliner, 1997). I've already mentioned *The Crying Game*, and *The Adventures of Priscilla, Queen of the Desert*. Typically, these films depict transvestites and transsexuals enduring hostility and winning over ordinary, decent folk.

Academic studies have appeared, and the popular media are close behind. By early 1999, Polly Toynbee was writing in *Radio Times* (February 13–19) that "programme after programme seems to be obsessed with people of confused, indeterminate or wrong sex." She mentions a transsexual prostitute in the BBC1 series *Paddington Green*, a transsexual in Granada's soap opera *Coronation Street*, and a program in the BBC1 science series, *QED*. "There is a questioning and a redefining of sex roles going on and these cases are just the most extreme manifestations of a more general and diverse debate," Toynbee avers. Subsequently, Channel Four has presented a very positive, two-hour view of four female-to-male trans people in different circumstances (*Make Me a Man*: Katie Buchanan, 2002), and in 2003 broadcast an American documentary, *Sex Change*, showing the details of gender-reassignment surgery. Halberstam reports the interest of American talk shows in drag kings, but is disappointed by the sensational treatment.[84] To be sure, visibility is not necessarily power—otherwise, scantily clad young women draped across automobiles would be ruling the world.

The trans phenomenon challenges customary ideas about how gender and sexuality may interact. It is not just that a male-to-female transsexual may desire either a man or a woman, or both. When a person who has been assigned at birth a male gender experiences desire-for a male, *while declaring hirself to have desire-to-be a female*, it is impossible to say, definitively, whether that person has made a same-sex or a cross-sex object-choice. It depends on whether hir story about hirself is credited.

Transgender invites a reconsideration of *The Well of Loneliness*, which has traditionally been regarded as a classic account of "the mannish lesbian." Stephen does have desire-for other women, but her main anguish and affirmation resides in her desire-to-be male. " 'Do you think that I *could* be a man, supposing I thought very hard—or prayed?' " she asks her father.[85] Radclyffe Hall is drawing on ideas from the sexologists—she persuaded Ellis to write a preface. Jay Prosser suggests that Hall prefers Ellis, Ulrichs, and Krafft-Ebing to psychoanalysis, and also to the kinds of lesbian self-concept being developed by Natalie Barney and Renée Vivienne, because they focus more on the invert and thereby fit better with her own project.[86] Stephen's father has been reading the sexologists, and it produces in him the humane sympathy that Hall wanted in her own readers. However, it remains unclear how far Stephen's desire-to-be male is due to her upbringing (her father treats her like a boy and her mother rejects her), or congenital (in her physique, "her nature"; 29–30, 165). Both versions can be supported from the text.

While Stephen's condition is entirely mysterious to her mother and herself, all the neighbors can see it: "they feared her; it was fear that aroused their antagonism. In her they instinctively sensed an outlaw, and theirs was the task of policing nature" (123). What they see is aberrant gender. A hotel porter can discuss it with his wife: " 'Have you noticed her, Alice? A queer-looking girl, very tall, wears a collar and tie—you know, mannish. And she seems just to change her suit of an evening—puts on a dark one—never wears evening dress. . . . I dunno, there's something about her—anyhow I'm surprised she's got a young man.' " (181; my elision). This last inference is derived from the fact that Stephen is watching out for a special letter; it doesn't occur to the porter that she might be homosexual and looking for a letter from a woman. Stephen's condition is, at once, utterly opaque and devastatingly obvious, virtually inconceivable and cruelly policed. While she has to be ignorant in order to emphasize her bewilderment and perhaps her innocence, her transgression has to be communicated as the basis for her social rejection.

This rejection is grounded in her masculine appearance; her sex life is scarcely inferred. It is her body and clothes that are the offense, not her choice of partner; even the dog recognizes Stephen's maleness and longs for "that queer, intangible something about her that appealed to the canine manhood in him" (382). As Laura Doan has demonstrated, this failure to register sexual dissidence is plausible historically since, before *The Well*, boyish and mannish garb did not register any one, stable effect; if anything, they signified modernity. It was Hall's accomplishment to change this.[87]

Mary, on the other hand, is all right because she looks feminine. A fashionable hostess takes a great fancy to her, but sees in Stephen "only an unsexed creature of pose, whose cropped head and whose dress were pure affectation; a creature who aping the prerogatives of men, had lost all the charm and grace of a woman" (465). The fact that Stephen and Mary are both lesbians hardly figures. Halberstam remarks that *The Well* manifests an epistemology not of the closet (for Hall, like Crisp, was never not-out) but of the wardrobe: male clothing is fetishized as the badge of gender.[88] The tragedy is that Stephen is not allowed fully to inhabit that desire-to-be by becoming the master of Morton Hall and protector of hir partner.

So with the culminating affair with Mary. Stephen's initial doubt concerns whether she should respond to the innocent love of a younger woman who is not herself aware of inversion. (This dilemma recurs in Mary Renault's novel, *The Charioteer*.) The ensuing predicament, however, is that having accepted Mary's love Stephen declines to take her seriously. Stephen manages their joint affairs and gains success as a writer, but Mary has nothing to do. She has no work; she cannot go into Society, or to Stephen's family home; Stephen doesn't share her anxieties with her— hardly trusts her to go out by herself. In short, Stephen envisions herself and Mary on a husband-and-wife model, and hence their downfall. It is because they cannot play that game convincingly that Stephen pushes Mary into an opportune marriage. This was not the inevitable outcome for the invert: Hall herself seduced two women away from wedlock.

The confusions that invest *The Well*, we may suppose, were needed and desired. We should not be looking for the right reading, but observing how

this protean text has been deployed for diverse purposes by diverse con-
stituencies. Esther Newton highlights its importance in the mid-twentieth
century to women who valued the overt sexuality of the mannish lesbian as
pointing beyond the Victorian romantic friendship.[89] The dominant ideology, meanwhile, was ready to deploy gender dissidence to stigmatize
object-choice, and vice versa. Today *The Well* is still available to new con-
stituencies. While Prosser discovers there a depiction of transsexuality,
Halberstam finds a portrait of the "masculine woman."[90] Comparable arguments may be developed in respect of Gertrude Stein: "Though she's been
widely regarded as a lesbian, the fact is that she saw herself, in essence, as
a man," Jean E. Mills observes.[91]

" 'Is that a boy or a girl?' " people keep asking about young Jess in Leslie
Feinberg's *Stone Butch Blues*.[92] Like Neil Bartlett's Boy in *Ready to Catch
Him*, Jess finds hirself in a bar, where s/he is supported and appreciated as
a baby butch. The downside is vulnerability to raids and gross assaults by
the police. Jess, like other he-shes, works in a factory, but takes up with
Theresa, who has a clerical job in a university and knows about the Daughters of Bilitis, the *Ladder*, Stonewall, and lesbian and gay pride. However,
butches and femmes are not welcome among liberationist lesbians, and
Jess doesn't feel there is a place for her in the women's movement. It is no
simpler for Edna, a femme: " 'I know I'm not a straight woman, and lesbians
won't accept me as one of them. I don't know where to go to find the
butches I love or the other femmes. I feel completely misunderstood. I feel
like a ghost, too, Jess' " (214–15).

These new difficulties for the he-she are reverberations from the major
shift I have been discussing in this chapter—the moment when gender
identity is decisively superseded by object-choice as the key category for
understanding sexual dissidence. Like Crisp, these women appear to be
left over from the old conceptual regime, where gender dissidence was the
main factor. Jess in fact seems not to get much sex; everyone is too
exhausted just keeping going, and stone butches hate to be touched.

To resolve the indeterminacy Jess decides to begin hormone treatments
with a view to passing as a guy. Theresa cannot tolerate this: " 'I'm a femme,
Jess. I want to be with a butch. . . . I don't want to be with a man, Jess. I
won't do it' " (151; my elision). With the treatments, Jess passes as a man
quite effectively. Hir problem is that s/he now has no social context: intimacy threatens personal exposure and lovemaking seems meretricious.
S/he has to leave a job when hir gender history is revealed. S/he stops the
hormone treatment; "Whoever I was, I wanted to deal with it, I wanted to
live it again. I wanted to be able to explain my life, how the world looked

from behind my eyes" (224). Prosser is disappointed at Jess's turning back. It shows two things: that Jess is not at home in any version of hir body—radical indeterminacy is hir fate; and that society has difficulty accommodating a transsexual even when s/he is trying to regularize hir gender.

Transgender promises to unsettle established items on the agenda of queer theory and activism. The dialectic of passing versus coming out works differently for trans people, who confirm that they are indeed the person whom they believe themselves to be when they pass undetected in public. Drawing attention to their special gender characteristics defeats the purpose. However, it is difficult to build a movement when its members keep vanishing into the crowd. Sandy Stone has urged transsexuals, instead, to come out *as transsexual*, foregrounding thereby the constructedness of all gender categories. Stone actually has two main arguments. One is that passing forecloses "the possibility of authentic relationships."[93] This was Jess's problem: she felt unable to present hirself to other people—until she wrote the book, that is. The other is that by aspiring to be essentially a woman or essentially a man, the trans person colludes with the gender system that has oppressed hir in the first place; whereas refusing to pass calls into visibility and mistrust the criteria that delimit the binary sex/gender system.

That camp and drag may have potential to subvert the sex/gender system has often been proposed, most famously by Judith Butler, who seemed to suggest in *Gender Trouble* that "drag fully subverts the distinction between inner and outer psychic space and effectively mocks both the expressive model of gender and the notion of a true gender identity."[94] Butler's insistence that gender can never afford stable identities is surely right. However, there are two main problems with arguments that conceptual instability leads to insight.

First, such theory, which is a kind of poststructuralism, has supposed too readily that to demonstrate indeterminacy in a dominant construct is to expose its weakness and its vulnerability to subversion. In practice, gay pastiche and its excesses may be all too easily pigeonholed as illustrating that lesbians and gay men can only mimic true manliness and womanliness. Dominant ideologies are able to turn almost anything to their advantage; that is the sign of their dominance. Whether an instance is subversive or incorporative has to be assessed in its particular contexts. The Stonewall queens instigated gay liberation not because they were camp or wore drag—there was nothing new about that—but because they fought the police.

Second, many individuals are already having a difficult time with their gender identity, and don't want their mannerisms co-opted into a political argument. This point is made by Prosser, who emphasizes that many trans people experience their gender "precisely as a disorder, a physically embodied dis-ease or dysphoria that dis-locates the self from bodily home and to which sex reassignment *does* make all the difference." Transsexual passing is like gay coming out in one respect: it is not a once-and-for-all accomplishment: it may have to be renewed many times each day. Prosser calls for a "politics of home" which "would not disavow the value of belonging as the basis for livable identity."[95]

Belonging in the gender system is not the resolution that is offered in *Stone Butch Blues*. Jess reaches a stance of peace and productivity not by changing her body or her attire, but by finding other sex and gender dissidents in New York's West Village in the queer 1980s. Despite continuing horrific street violence, s/he finds acceptance and purpose in a new world of bookshops, drag queens, farmers' markets, Christmas, other ethnicities, AIDS campaigning, people who can talk about how they hurt and need, a gay rally where s/he feels able to speak about gender, and a future as a political activist. In a final dream Jess envisages a new world in which innumerable people of indeterminate gender are happy together. However, the message for the present seems to be: if you want to be different, find an alternative scene. Don't try to make your home in Middle America. The dangers are grimly confirmed in *The Brandon Teena Story* (Susan Musca and Greta Olafsdottir, 1998), and *Boys Don't Cry* (Kimberly Peirce, 1999).

BOYS WILL BE BOYS

Eve Sedgwick has warned against uncoupling homosexuality and effeminacy—"effeminophobia," she calls it. "After all, 'everyone already knows' that cross-dressing usually at least alludes to homosexuality": culturally they belong together. Further, the persecuted "effeminate boy" is left without the support of adult gays, who perhaps eschew him as an embarrassing remnant of their own childhood trauma.[96] Sedgwick is right to mistrust the motives of gay men who would jettison effeminacy, but the logical and experiential impetus of transgender has surely justified the isolating of gender identity as a category. A task now is to avoid any consequent marginalizing of yet other groups. Some butch/femme women have said to me that they experience, in the current emphasis on transsexuality, a de-legitimization—an imputation that butches are settling for a halfway position, as if they lacked the courage of their convictions.

Meanwhile, straight cultures today make their own stories out of our lives. A recent study of sexual bullying in an English secondary school finds that boys regarded as insufficiently masculine are called "gay" and "poof." However, they are *not* thereby supposed to be homosexual; the idea that real homosexuals might actually exist in the school is greeted with incredulity. "Nearly all the boys had knowledge of the existence of homosexuality but could not relate this knowledge to their school experience or people whom they might one day meet."[97] In this setting, "gay" signals only gender anomaly; the boys are using it to support their concern with male bonding.

The same case is put by the misogynist, homophobic, and popular white rapper, Eminem:

> "Faggot" to me doesn't necessarily mean "gay person." "Faggot" to me means "pussy," "cissy." If you're a man, be a man, know what I'm saying? That's the worst thing you can say to a man. It's like calling him a girl, whether he's gay or not. Growing up, me and my friends, "faggot" was a common word, like "you're being a fucking fag, man." Nobody really thought "gay person." I don't give a shit about gay men. If they wanna be gay, then that's their fucking business.[98]

In both these accounts, actual gay boys are invisible. The boy who suspects that he *is* gay is not just stigmatized; the compensations of gay belonging and subcultural resources are withheld from him. Wendy Wallace confirms that *gay* has become a general term of bullying abuse for any outsider in schools, while retaining the link with its homophobic roots. Ten-year-old Damilola Taylor was repeatedly taunted at school with the word "gay" before being killed in a knife attack.[99] In *The Laramie Project*, Moisés Kaufman's play about the death of Matthew Shepard, the murderer says Matthew looked "like a queer. Such a queer dude. . . . Yeah, like a fag, you know?"[100] We know.

In propounding a primary distinction between gender identity and object-choice, my goal is not to interfere in the lived experience of people; this is not a call to individuals to sort out who they want to be. Rather, I am hoping to contribute to a better analysis of what we have been doing. The case for retheorizing the extant combinations of gender identity and same-sex passion rests not on an attempt to tidy up desire, but on enabling diverse peoples to respect themselves and each other. If there have been tensions among sexual dissidents—caricatures, appropriations, repudiations—that is because we are accustomed to constructing sex/gender identities contradistinctively. Reassessing these processes may help us to rebuild a more elaborate dissident coalition, beyond binary organizations of difference. The rest of this book is about ways of reading sexuality that are not organized primarily around gender difference. Yet gender, we will see, proves remarkably persistent.

6

AGE

BOYS AND EMBARRASSMENT

In Armistead Maupin's novel *The Night Listener*, Gabriel is embarrassed about the age disparity between himself and his partner, Jess. Fifteen years is "not that big a difference," Gabriel says and, anyway, because they came out at roughly the same time they are "the same gay age." This idea offers to release them from the taint of age hierarchy and narcissism: "This meant we'd reached the same level in our personal growth . . . which was far more pertinent to our compatibility than our chronological difference."[1] Gabriel calls it "my marriage" (4).

However, hierarchy has not in fact been irrelevant; it has informed their sexual practice. Gabriel remarks that it was a big turn-on when Jess would gaze up at him "with slavish devotion. Or he'd work my nipples like a ravenous baby, murmuring, 'Sir, yessir, yessir,' until I came with a fury" (50). Actually Gabriel is too nice and cuddly for too much of that; an earlier relationship foundered because he was unable to play "The Great Dark Man" (80). Now Jess has left Gabriel, partly because he is not going to die soon of AIDS after all, partly because he has been getting into a rough, more manly, leather scene—shaving off his "baby-chick hair," growing a beard. Gabriel feels "old and disconnected" (51). Suddenly he sees Jess as "closer to middle age than to the soft-featured boy I'd fallen in love with" (211). A pattern emerges: previously Gabriel had a relationship with Wayne, who was at least ten years younger: "the grownup boy who had brought me childhood again." Gabriel confesses to "youthful longing": his ultimate pain is that he'll "never be strong enough, never be handsome enough, never be young enough, to really be a man among men" (132).

The age hierarchy of Gabriel and Jess correlates with class hierarchy, for Gabriel was already a celebrated gay broadcaster. Here too Gabriel has indulged in an element of disavowal. "Until now our friends had been largely mutual; we had cultivated them together as couples often do," he says; "Jess, after all, had been my satellite for ten years without complaint" (51). The unremarked discrepancy between "mutual" and "satellite" marks Gabriel's reluctance to acknowledge that his "marriage" has been founded in inequality.

This scenario is close to Maupin's own experience, as may be seen in a television interview in which he and Terry Anderson present themselves as the ideal couple, devoted to coping with Terry's anticipated death from AIDS.[2] Will and Jamie constitute a comparably symmetrical couple in Maupin's story, "Coming Home": they say the same things, laugh the same way, sound the same on the phone, speak of themselves as married. The age disparity is put at just five years, and Jamie has an independent occupation (coppersmith), whereas Jess manages Gabriel's affairs.[3] (Will and Jamie stories are claimed in *The Night Listener* as disguised autobiographical writing by Gabriel; 18). If, in retrospect at least, these versions of himself and his partners appear a tad manipulative and self-deceiving, in the novel Maupin confronts this thought, allowing us to see that the relationship had not really been equal and, indeed, had been experienced as lopsided and limiting by Terry/Jamie/Jess.

Gabriel's other main relationship in *The Night Listener* provokes another anxiety about age hierarchy. Pete, a thirteen-year-old who has been intensively abused and has AIDS, strikes up a phone dialogue, founded in his admiration for Gabriel's broadcasts. " 'I guess he sort of has a thing about me,' " Gabriel admits (39). Gabriel becomes equally involved; they get to use the terms "Son" and "Dad" (uppercase). Other people are suspicious, especially his reactionary father: " 'Well . . . you're a middle-aged man, and he's . . . well, people could get the wrong idea, that's all.' " This facilitates Gabriel's spirited defense: " 'The boy needs love. You don't have to be straight to do that' " (70–71; Maupin's pauses). Surely this is right, but its location in *The Night Listener* suggests Maupin's determination to establish that, even if he has to concede that his partnerships have been organized around hierarchies of age and class, this doesn't make him a pedophile. Yet he is prepared to acknowledge "a distinct resemblance" in his way of relating to Jess (lover) and Pete (quasi son; 182). As it transpires, he is protected by another doubt, as to whether there could actually be such a boy; perhaps he is an invention—the novel doesn't resolve this. These are awkward topics—the age of consent in several European countries is fourteen. *The Night Listener* discloses two embarrassments around age hierarchy: that it is immature and can't last, and that it is ultimately pedophilic. Gabriel, left alone at the end, questions the assumption that one must get a long-term relationship to lead a dignified and contented life. Perhaps the kind of partnership he can envisage will necessarily be immature; he might live better by himself.

I distinguished *gender difference* and *gender complementarity* in chapter 2. The former is founded in (relative) difference of gender; the latter is founded in similarity of gender, but characterized by difference within that. The gender complementarity model is founded in similarity of gender, but characterized by difference within that. In chapter 3, on fantasy, I showed how the two models may be substituted and conflated. Age constitutes one of the key hierarchies in the sex/gender system as it is lived in our societies. It is an inevitable factor in the first power structure that all of us experience: a child with adult caregivers. Without it the infant cannot survive and grow as a human creature. Age difference affords a hierarchy that may be used protectively. We should expect it to figure intensely in our psychic lives, and not to be confined to particular circumstances, such as same-sex communities or the coming-out process. The power distribution in the age/youth binary structure may seem less obvious than the others: notoriously, an older man can make a fool of himself over a young man, or a young woman. Notwithstanding, class for class and race for race, older people control far more wealth and institutional power than younger people. It is because this pattern may be disrupted in our societies by a premium upon youthful beauty that it gets so much attention.

Eve Sedgwick observes, shrewdly, that Wilde, who acquired after the trials the representative role of aesthetical, dandified, and effeminate queer, seems not to have thought of himself or his partners as inverted in gender:

> Wilde's own eros was most closely tuned to the note of the pederastic love in process of being superseded—and, we may as well therefore say, radically misrepresented—by the homo/hetero imposition. . . . his desires seem to have been structured intensely by the crossing of definitional lines—of age, milieu, initiatedness, and physique, most notably.[4]

What is surprising here is Sedgwick's rather sudden assertion that such "pederastic love [was] in process of being superseded." David Halperin not only takes this alleged supersession for granted, he sees little reason to regret it:

Although love, emotional intimacy, and tenderness are not necessarily absent from the [age-structured] relationship, the distribution of erotic passion and sexual pleasure is assumed to be more or less lopsided, with the older, "active" partner being the *subject* of desire and the recipient of the greater share of pleasure from a younger partner who figures as a sexual *object*, feels no comparable desire, and derives no comparable pleasure from the contact (unless he is an invert or pathic . . .). The junior partner's reward must therefore be measured out in currencies other than pleasure, such as praise, assistance, gifts, or money.[5]

This sounds to me at each point unnecessarily disapproving: in the marginalizing of intimacy in such a liaison, in the discrediting of the boy's desire, and in the assumption that genuine sexual pleasure is independent of factors such as praise and assistance. Halperin's emphases place him firmly within the dominant ideology, which prizes (purportedly) egalitarian relations. If, however, as I have suggested, age-disparate relationships are about loving versions of oneself—who one is, who one was, who one would like to be—they surely afford far-reaching potential for rewarding, interpersonal development.

Given their debt to Foucault, it is possible that Sedgwick and Halperin have been encouraged by a certain strand in his work to expect that models of sexuality will define, and be defined by, an epoch, characterized by distinct modes of thought, with change occurring through a sequence of large-scale epistemological shifts. Cultural materialists, drawing upon Raymond Williams, are more likely to stress uneven development, setting subordinate, residual, and emergent formations alongside dominant ones. These concepts allow that diverse models may be in play at any given time; we may identify one as dominant and another as subordinate or emergent.[6]

Age hierarchy must be profoundly embarrassing if even queer theorists want to distance themselves from it. Indeed, in today's metropolitan sex/gender system, it is freighted with implications of immaturity, narcissism, effeminacy, pedophilia, exploitation, and humiliation. These disturbing factors are founded in relations between age and youth in society at large, where younger people are more often credited with sexual attractiveness, whereas older people often have more economic, political, and social resources. Age hierarchy therefore invites stigmatization as merely instrumental on both sides, in contrast to the reciprocity attributed to age-matched relations. The disrespect accorded age-disparate relations is evident, Simon LeVay and Elisabeth Nonas remark, in the freedom other gay men feel to court the younger partner, while age-matched couples are accorded respectful space, and a hint of the sanctity of marriage.[7]

Indeed, such is the dominance of the egalitarian model that age disparity may actually appear more defensible when it is instrumental. By this I mean that it is more acceptable (slightly) for a youngster to allow it to be supposed that he is using an older man to find his way around the scene, or because he gets taken to the opera, than it is for him to declare that he is attracted and devoted to an older person. Correspondingly, it may be more suitable for the older man to be perceived as exploitative—on to a good thing—than for him to appear to take the boy seriously as a partner. It can work, Edmund White's narrator avers in *The Married Man*, if you get the chemistry right. Austin, unfortunately, "was incapable of picking out the talented tenth, the blessed exception, that nearly unique boy who admired experience and accomplishment more than an uncreased face and a tympanum-tight tummy. Nor could he spot that one guy in a hundred who was age-blind and didn't judge another man as a commodity."[8]

This chapter dwells upon the impediments in age difference; my habitual mode is critical, and inclined to discover difficulties. Notwithstanding, we have many invocations of the joys of age-disparate liaisons. Some of the deceptively diffident poems of Gregory Woods celebrate such liaisons, appealing sometimes to the gay tradition—Orpheus, Alexander, Whitman, Wilde, Rimbaud, Henry James. This untitled, twelve-line poem finds the poet on the island of Sirmio (I deduce), where the ancient Roman lyricist had a villa:

> Under where Catullus
> toyed with reality
> in his cushioned saloons
>
> a decorum of very
> reasonable cabins
> oversees the bathers.
>
> But we beyond the rocks,
> a slippery broker
> of boyhood and I
>
> with water up trunks down
> to our knees, negotiate
> the space between our ages.[9]

Catullus's ancient, luxurious villa was above; the modern, decent cabins are below, as if policing the beach scene. But the poet and his boy have located a third place, beyond the rocks. The imagery has a financial edge; perhaps money is being discussed. Yet the scenario is not primarily about money; the boy is slippery because of his wet skin, not dishonesty, and their trunks are down, not their futures. It is age disparity and sexual attraction that are being negotiated, as they once were by Catullus and his boys. One way or another, we will find a space.

ADJUSTMENTS

I discussed Paul Monette's novel *Halfway Home* in chapter 5. Tom, the narrator, forges a great relationship with his nephew, Daniel, a classic desire-to-be: "I noticed how he set his pace to mine as we walked across to the store. I would have done anything for him just then, for he made me feel like I was a fellow to be emulated, as he studied his way to becoming a man" (139). Monette makes the boy as young as he can, given the kind of sensitivity and awareness that he wants him to have, and thus unavailable for sexual advances (he is seven). Nonetheless, Tom is fearful that he will be perceived as corrupting Daniel. He comes upon him doing a jigsaw puzzle he has found in the house: the picture is of Michelangelo's statue of David. Tom is terrified that Daniel's parents might enter and suppose that it was his idea. (Indeed, Susan is very suspicious and aggressive.) "Instantly I knew, sitting like a giant beside this little boy, what I was really afraid of. That Daniel would turn out gay, and they would blame me and curse my infected ghost." And this was "the old self-hatred": "Because what I really meant was that I didn't *want* him to be gay, to run that gauntlet of misery and solitude. Where the hell was all my pride that had marched in a hundred parades?"[10] Meanwhile Tom, against his expectations, reorients his own age allegiance. He falls in love with Gray, the older man who has been quietly protecting him. "His being fifty had no downside; he was simply a full-grown man. And lying there lazily under the comforter, I took the most wanton joy in being the younger one" (156).

In Jack Dickson's Glasgow thriller, *Oddfellows*, Joe (aged thirty-one) is in turn the younger and the older partner. He feels indebted to Billy, who gave him a job and a place to live when he was thrown out of the army. Billy is a club owner, engaged in endless negotiations with other entrepreneurs, and with the police (over drugs and murder). He demands brutal sexual episodes, but this power play suits Joe, whose fantasy investments center upon being humiliated and beaten in the army. He is less happy when Billy behaves as if he owns him. He gives him an expensive watch, and insists that he give up work, and hence his financial independence; "The gold strap on his wrist suddenly felt very tight."[11] Billy orders Joe around and strikes him in public. Even more distressing is a growing awareness that Billy is violently abusing youngsters. Joe leaves, but Billy doesn't like being thwarted and the outcome is violent.

Joe is specially sensitive to the treatment of boys because of his strong feeling for his nephew, Sean, who is fifteen—even as Joe was drawn to Sean's father (now dead). It becomes clear that Sean is gay and devoted to Joe, while Joe finds himself moved sexually by Sean's boyish body. Eventually, in the final episode of the book, they declare their love. However, they cannot pursue the relationship, Joe insists. They are too close; Sean has to sort things out for himself; he needs another kid to explore himself with; Joe would be holding him back. The combination of brother, father, and lover all rolled into one is "An ideal, a fantasy . . . not made for the real world, a world in which Sean had to learn to function" (301; Dickson's pause).

Joe tells himself that Sean deserves the truth, but he lies when he tells him that he doesn't want to be the boy's lover: " 'Ah'll be here fur ye, but ah'll no' be part o' yer life . . . ah don't want tae be.' Amongst all the lies he'd ever told himself, that was the hardest" (Dickson's pause). We understand that Joe is disguising his feelings and putting Sean off for his own good. "From somewhere deep inside Joe found the strength to say what he knew he had to" (302). Why does he have to? Because of normative assumptions about youth, maturity, and their proper development; whether these matters might be different for gay boys is not considered. Joe accedes to conventional notions of equality and manhood. He is going to move in with Andy, who is of a similar age and background: " 'maybe mates ur the maist important thing. Maybe ah'll love him as a mate, maybe as somewan ah want tae spend the resta ma life wi' ' " (302). Also, Joe confirms his rejection of Sean by an appeal to manliness: he asks him whether he is a wee boy with a crush on his uncle, or a man? "As one pair of blue eyes stared deep into another, silent agreement passed between two men. Men. Not a kid and a man" (302–303). Despite this sudden maturation, Sean remains off limits for sexual love.

With Sean as well as with Billy, Joe has to reject the hierarchical option—the one because it is too close, the other because it betrays any possibility of closeness—despite passionate involvement. Or perhaps because of it. There is, after all, a tradition of gay renunciation. In *The Well of Loneliness* (1928), Stephen introduces Mary to lesbian experience and subculture, but finally pushes her out into marriage. In Mary Renault's *The Charioteer* (1953), Laurie has to reject the innocent Andrew in order to allow him the opportunity to grow out of his queerness.

The dangers of age-disparate liaisons are stressed again in Simon Lovat's psychological thriller, *Disorder and Chaos*. Here gays generally have a hard time, except the couple, Derek and Bob. They wear each other's clothes, or identical denim outfits; Keith calls them "The Bookends." He "notices how similar they look now. Twin haircuts, twin mustaches, twin forced jollity in their glinting eyes. Or is it simply that he's forgotten how much they operate as a two-cylinder machine, now that he sees so much less of them?"[12] " 'We don't take the clone thing seriously,' says Bob" (25). The Bookends admonish Keith about his liking for youngsters: " 'These age gaps are a disaster area. . . . What you need is someone who has finished growing up. Someone who threw away their L plates years ago' " (15; my elision). Keith does come to accept that his liaisons follow a doomed pattern, as his dependence upon Nick, a disturbed, devious, and dishonest sixteen-year-old, degenerates. Buying clothes, for instance: " 'I'm not a doll, or a kid,' Nick had said, flying into an instant rage. 'It'd make me feel under control, under your thumb' " (133). Keith's infatuation leads him to prison. Upon release, he appears to forsake any sex life, as he generates a new obsession, with the infant whom he believes to be his son (he has donated sperm to a lesbian couple). He decides to abduct the boy; he will be very gentle with him, "take care of him, spoil him, love him" (225). As in the treatments of Monette and Maupin, there is an ominous though unspecified overlap between sexual and filial emotions.

Meanwhile Lenny, who is married, has been suppressing his gayness. He is helped along by an experienced man, though he remains cowed by his senior partner in dentistry. He uses contact advertisements; most of the replies are from married men, and Lenny is inclined to reject them; but he too is married, so what can he expect? Like Owen in *The Lost Language of Cranes*, he sensibly looks for someone like himself. Lenny is suddenly freed from conventional obligations by the strange behavior of his daughter, Monica. She proves highly tolerant of his gayness, but this is perhaps part of her general weirdness. She is into black magic and, it transpires, has a fatal fixation upon serial killer Myra Hindley. Lenny's concluding reflections apparently point the moral: "subterfuge, half-truths, and lies" create "disorder and chaos" (249)—referring to the title of the book. On this criterion, only Derek and Bob match up. It's a dangerous world, Lovat seems to be saying, and other kinds of liaison are asking for trouble.

MENTORING

The social system wants its young people socialized, so that they can contribute to the workforce and the rearing of the next generation. For the most part, though, it does not want them socialized into gay subculture. Even for the ancient Greeks, Foucault points out, this was a tricky matter. "Because if there were no problem, they would speak of this kind of love in the same terms as love between men and women. The problem was that they couldn't accept that a young boy who was supposed to become a free citizen could be dominated and used as an object for someone's pleasure."[13] The interface between these two desiderata, which are often located in the same individuals and institutions, is probably more heavily policed since gay liberation than it was before.

A gay man may justify to himself and others his sexual attentions to boys by dwelling upon the emotional and practical support he is providing. David Leeming in his biography of James Baldwin writes of him as obliged by a "puritanical streak" to "deny the merely carnal" by placing himself as "a father figure, financial sponsor, and teacher for a much younger individual." So with a North African "street boy" Baldwin insisted almost immediately on "formalizing the relationship on somewhat paternalistic grounds, by meeting the boy's family."[14] Compare *The Swimming-Pool Library*, where Charles maintains a paternalist idea of his role as colonial administrator. Will is less convinced: "I wanted to save Arthur. At least, I think that's what I wanted to do to him. It was a strange conviction I had, that I could somehow make these boys' lives better, as by a kind of patronage— especially as it never worked out that way."[15] Keith in Lovat's *Disorder and Chaos* tells himself that he is helping Nick to get himself together. "He knows it's a delusion but it holds up, providing he does not scrutinize it too much."[16]

Uncles and nephews, I notice, are a recurring feature. Here the man has mentoring status already, perhaps along with some incestuous thrill. They occur in *Halfway Home*, *Oddfellows*, and *Wasted* by Aiden Shaw; Edmund in *The Farewell Symphony* gets to look after his attractive nephew, though he's not gay. In Larry Kramer's *Faggots*, Richard has an anxiety attack when he is accosted in a club by his nephew, Wyatt. They compare sizes—Wyatt is well-endowed—they hasten "to join each other in family togetherness." Wyatt should be " 'overcome with Jewish guilt,' " Richard objects. But Wyatt thinks Richard " 'really should get some help.' "[17] Again: when Luke leaves home and comes to London to be gay, he naturally calls on his gay uncle Martin—so *This Island's Mine* by Philip Osment. However, in this virtuous Gay Sweatshop theater company play there is no embarrassing familial romance: it is assumed that uncle and nephew will each find a partner of his own age.[18]

A gay man may be confident enough to combine his official and his sub-cultural mentoring. George in Christopher Isherwood's novel *A Single Man* is coming to terms with the death of his partner, Jim, in a traffic accident. The emphasis is on their equal partnership, but we may deduce that Jim was the younger, as Isherwood's lovers always were ("he treats his exclusive interest in very young men as entirely natural," Paul Robinson remarks).[19] Now George is feeling old. In Tennyson's poem "Tithonus," which he expounds to his students, he is both Eos, the lover of boys, and Tithonus, the repulsively aging former boy.

Nonetheless, George is looking around for a new partner. Kenny, one of his students, seems to have conceived a special interest in him. In a bar George experiences with Kenny something like a Platonic dialogue, a "symbolic encounter"; Kenny appears "beautiful. *Radiant with rapport.*"[20] Kenny likes authority; he thinks respect and friendship are most likely between males of different ages; it pleases him to call George "Sir" (133). They swim in the ocean and the rapport becomes physical. Moving indoors, to George's home, calls forth a return of responsibility: he refuses Kenny's invitation to shower together. However, the conversation becomes

> positively flirty, on both sides. Kenny's blanket, under the relaxing influence of the talk and beer, has slipped, baring an arm and a shoulder and turning itself into a classical Greek garment, the chlamys worn by a young disciple— the favourite, surely—of some philosopher. At this moment he is utterly, dangerously charming. (143)

Inveighing against a society which prefers "flirtation instead of fucking," George finds himself uttering a sexual proposition. Kenny "grins, dazzlingly," but George passes out (150). We will never know what the enigmatic Kenny might have done.

The Platonic dialogues which George invokes are a characteristic focus for the official and sexual roles of the mentor. Socrates' strategy is to tease the boy with talk of love, while maintaining the idea that the teacher is on a higher plane, above physical expression. Even if the boy is keen, as Alcibiades is in the *Symposium*, it may be beneath the Socratic teacher's dignity to respond. Plato has been a conduit for same-sex passion and, simultaneously, a way of disavowing any such concern. Platonic ideas of intense friendship were made available in the Renaissance by Marsilio Ficino, revived in the eighteenth century by Johann Winckelmann, and deployed in the formative stages of modern gay self-construction by Walter Pater. These are the terms for Wilde's famous speech from the dock on the love that dare not speak its name: it is David and Jonathan, Plato, Michelangelo, and Shakespeare; "It is that deep, spiritual affection that is as pure as it is perfect. . . . It is beautiful, it is fine, it is the noblest form of affection."[21] Unfortunately for Wilde, this exalted vision seemed not to embrace the casual sexual and financial liaisons of which he was accused.

In *Death in Venice*, Aschenbach's growing infatuation with Tadzio is accompanied by quotations from the *Phaedrus*, which keep floating into Aschenbach's head. As Jonathan Dollimore shows, Mann is on Freudian territory: the ambivalent innocence of the Socratic dialogue is exposed as sublimation.[22] At a key moment in Mary Renault's novel *The Charioteer*, Laurie approaches and then evades self-disclosure when he shows the innocent Andrew his copy of Plato's *Phaedrus*. " 'I haven't read this one,' " Andrew says. " 'I thought it was the *Phaedo* for a minute, we did that at school.' " The *Phaedo* was a safe text, the *Phaedrus* not. " 'What's it about?' " Andrew asks, allowing Laurie a second chance to reveal or conceal himself: " 'Well, primarily, it's about the laws of rhetoric.' "[23] There were acceptable and unacceptable Platonic texts, and acceptable and unacceptable ways of addressing them.

A striking deployment of the ambiguity of Plato is effected by Allan Bloom, whose best-selling book *The Closing of the American Mind* chimed in with a reactionary turn in literary and cultural education in the United States in the late 1980s. Bloom's distinctive pitch is a yearning for a relationship between the teacher and student such as he believes Socrates shared with the young male aristocrats of Athens. Since the 1960s, he believes, sexual relations have been routinized and corrupted by Freudianism, the decline of the leisure class, and the women's and gay liberation movements. Socrates had the right idea: "The longing for his conversations with which he infected his companions, and which was intensified after his death and has endured throughout the centuries, proved him to have been both the neediest and most grasping of lovers, and the richest and most giving of beloveds."[24] Such relationships work best, in Bloom's account, with upper-class students—"they have money and hence leisure and can appreciate the beautiful and useless" (279).

Surprisingly (it is the surprising part of the book), Bloom allows the sexual teasing to become manifest. The survival of Socratic relations is most likely with students who

have not settled the sexual problem, who are still young, even look young for
their age. . . . A youngster whose sexual longings consciously or unconsciously inform his studies has a very different set of experiences from one
in whom such motives are not active. A trip to Florence or to Athens is one
thing for a young man who hopes to meet his Beatrice on the Ponte Santa
Trinità or his Socrates in the Agora, and quite another for one who goes without such aching need. (134; my elision)

In other words, the unformed young man is likely to fall either for a nice
young lady from Smith, or for his male professor in the classroom. Bloom
again courts sexual interpretation when he writes that his students "wanted
to find out what happened to Glaucon during his wonderful night with
Socrates" (332). Perhaps we should go back to sublimation, a "naive and
good-natured" freshman suggests; "I was charmed by the lad's candor but
could not regard him as a serious candidate for culture" (234). Bloom cannot get sexuality properly into, or out of, his classes.

Further light is thrown upon Bloom's stance in the novel which his old
friend Saul Bellow based on his life and ideas, *Ravelstein*. The narrator is a
journalist, straight; he has known Abe for a good while and Abe wants him
to write his biography. The novel recalls meetings at which they discuss
this, Abe's death from AIDS-related illness, and the narrator's own sickness
and difficulty in writing. In the course of these lucubrations the narrator
has in effect written the biography.

Abe "was considered, to use a term from the past, an invert. Not a 'gay.'
He despised campy homosexuality and took a very low view of 'gay pride.'"[25]
His apartment scarcely hints at his sexual preference: "One had no reason,
in any respect, to suspect him of irregularities of the commoner sort—the
outlandish seductive behaviors of old-fashioned gay men. He couldn't bear
the fluttering of effeminate men" (99). He is upset when a nurse may be
overheard saying that it's time for his AZT. Nonetheless, "He was doomed
to die because of his irregular sexual ways," the narrator declares. "About
these he was entirely frank with me, with all his close friends" (160). Not
much of the sexuality gets into the novel, though; "There were times when
I simply didn't know what to make of his confidences," the narrator confesses (160).

Like Bloom in *The Closing of the American Mind*, Abe depends heavily
on Aristophanes' speech in Plato's *Symposium*, about how each of us pines
for his or her other half, to restore an original complete whole (24).
Whether Abe's maneuverings sometimes led to a sexual liaison is not indicated. His sexual feelings have increased, he tells the narrator, and " 'some

of these kids have a singular sympathy with you' " (143). The stronger
impression, in Bellow's novel, is that Abe has romantic-paternal relations
with his students while cultivating less exalted sexual relations in other
quarters. When he needs a check made out to cash so that his companion
will not know of it, the narrator supposes that this is a payoff for some sexual indiscretion (143).

There is a further force in Abe's life, one not avowed in *The Closing of
the American Mind*: Nikki, his "companion" (5). "He would sometimes
lower his voice in speaking of Nikki, to say that there was no intimacy
between them. 'More father and son'" (69); presumably this was not so initially. Nikki is from Singapore, in his early thirties and "boyish still" (5). The
narrator is notably ill at ease around him.

> Nobody questioned the strength of Nikki's attachment to Abe. Nikki was
> perfectly direct—direct, by nature, a handsome, smooth-skinned, black-
> haired, Oriental, graceful, boyish man. He had an exotic conception of him-
> self. I don't mean that he put on airs. He was never anything but natural.
> This protégé of Abe's, I thought—or used to think—was somewhat spoiled.
> I was wrong, there, too. Brought up like a prince, yes. Even before the
> famous book that sold a million copies was written, Nikki was better dressed
> than the Prince of Wales. (68)

Nikki was attached, direct, and natural; but he did like to spend money. A
suspicion is floated, that he is on the scrounge and Abe is something of a
dupe. The narrator carefully distances himself from Abe's high opinion of
Nikki's talents: "in Nikki, Abe saw a brilliant young man who had every
right to assert himself." As well as clothes, Nikki gets a BMW car: " 'He
feels he should have something outstanding and entirely his own,' " Abe
explains; " 'It's only natural' " (71, 74).

The gay reader need not share the narrator's prejudice against Nikki.
The narrator's wife is also much younger—one of Abe's former students, in
fact—but her credentials and her motives are not interrogated, and nor are
the narrator's. Nikki returns from Geneva when Abe is ill, and abandons his
studies to look after him. His devotion when Abe is in hospital is exemplary.
We might recognize here a successful mentoring partnership, beyond the
artificial teasing with the students.

Of course, this is a notable example of the conflation of roles: Nikki's
position is as much to do with his race as his age. "He had his own kind
of princely Asiatic mildness, but if you were to offend him Nikki would
tear your head off," the narrator remarks (145). Damn'd inscrutable, these

orientals; never know where you are with them. There is an arrogance and condescension in the attitude of the older men:

> Nikki was training in a Swiss hotel school. I can't say more than that because I'm not the ideal person to recall the minute particulars but Nikki was an accredited maître d.' He was ready to go into fits of laughter when he modeled the cutaway coat of his trade for Abe and me, and put on his professional dignities. (18–19)

Nikki is expected to mock his own ambitions for the amusement of his backers; I suppose the cutaway coat allowed him to display his bottom. I don't know whether to be angry at this debasing of Nikki, or to rejoice in his resourcefulness. Yet perhaps his display is no more demeaning than Bloom cavorting intellectually for his upper-class students, who know that their father and the military-industrial complex are paying for all this.

Eve Sedgwick studied with Bloom, though there is no indication that he gave special attention even to such an exceptional woman. What Bloom has produced, Sedgwick says, is "an ingenuously faithful and candid representation of . . . the stimulation and glamorization of the energies of male-male desire" in teaching the humanities. It is an eloquent analysis of "the prestige, magnetism, vulnerability, self-alienation, co-optability, and perhaps ultimately the potential for a certain defiance that adhere in the canonical culture of the closet."[26] That is well put. However, we don't need to assume that the erotics of teaching can thrive only in the closet. The fully-out teacher is relegitimated with the fully-out student; everyone knows the score. Now the teacher may exchange glances with a grown-up boy or girl, without fearing or hoping that they are going to be seduced in ignorance, or against their will.

An air of desperation often lurks around mentoring in modern times, starting with Wilde and Bosie. Disappointment may be avoided at the price of death. Thomas Mann's *Death in Venice* is retraced in Gilbert Adair's novel *Love and Death on Long Island* (filmed by Richard Kwietniowski in 1997): the established author Giles De'Ath, a reclusive widower, becomes obsessed with a young actor in a trashy film. He tells his agent he is developing a new theme: the discovery of beauty where no one ever thought of looking for it. He dies. Lecturer Ivo is, in effect, killed twice when his affair with a student collapses in Barbara Vine's psychosexual thriller *No Night Is Too Long* (adapted for BBC television with a screenplay by Kevin Elyot in 2002). In Isherwood's *A Single Man*, mortality disrupts a potential relationship before its enigmatic promise can be explored. Patricia Duncker in *Hallucinating Foucault* makes the charismatic great author die before the continuance of his liaison with a student can be tested.[27] Edmund White in *The Married Man* shows Austin's care for Julien, who is half his age, cut off by AIDS. The love affair between Tonio, a dancer, and Jack, a therapist, is tormented and energized by Tonio's impending death in the film *Alive and Kicking* (Jim Sharman, 1996; screenplay by Martin Sherman).

THE MEN AND THE BOYS

The strong presence of the coming-out story in gay fiction is very understandable: gay people are born into largely hostile social contexts, and finding their way to an alternative home base is rarely easy. Guides and initiators tend to be important. However, the structure of narcissistic complementarity especially invites a crossover between desire-for and desire-to-be. The boy's desire-for the man may well be involved with a desire-to-be the man, leading him to wish to *graduate out* of boyhood. Eric in Baldwin's *Another Country* is disconcerted when Yves says he wants to make his future in New York. " 'I can find my way. Do you really think that I want to be protected by you for ever? . . . it cannot go on for ever, I also am a *man* . . . my youth. It cannot last forever.' " Eric "knew what Yves meant and he knew that what Yves said was true."[28] In many coming-out stories age hierarchy is presented as a tactical convenience. A satisfactory outcome usually implies the boy's release from such artificial supports, and his readiness for rewarding sexual relations on the egalitarian model. The mentor must, by definition, be cast off. One classic instance is Baldwin's *Giovanni's Room* (1956): David finds himself at the expense of Giovanni's life. Another is Joe Orton and Kenneth Halliwell.

In Kenneth Martin's 1950s novel *Aubade*, Paul, who has just finished high school, is pleased when he is taken up by Gary, who is a graduate from medical school, securely middle class, with a car. Paul's desire-for Gary is tied up with desire-to-be him: "He's exactly the way I'd like to be when I'm his age, thought Paul."[29] Nonetheless, when Gary declares his love and tries to kiss him Paul flees in terror. Eventually Paul acknowledges his own passion, but the summer is over and the guide must be discarded. Paul puts it all down to experience: " 'It was part of growing up, wasn't it?' " (155). Gary has a definition of the homosexual which excludes Paul and himself:

"Do you know what homosexuality is? It's wanting to fiddle with every little boy you see. It's standing on the pier waiting for the next boatload of sailors to come in. It's giving women an inferiority complex. It's standing taking peeks in a man's toilet. I'm not like that, Paul. I love you, I love you." (128)

So no nasty queers need apply. The typical coming-out novel is strewn with repudiations not only of the mentor but of other "bad" types whom the boy brushes with but fortunately evades—effeminate bitchy queens, fearful closet types, disgusting (tearoom) cottagers, often any organized gay scene at all. The emergence of Laurie in Renault's *The Charioteer* depends on such exclusions. I showed in chapter 4 how Philip in *The Lost Language of Cranes* rejects the closeted secrecy of his father, the old-style Wildean mannerisms of Derek and Geoffrey, pornographic movies, cruising, and bars with back rooms. Eventually he settles down with Brad, an old school friend who is of the same age, class, race, and educational background.

Such repudiations are sanctioned as necessary to the process of self-discovery, as the young man sheds the accretions of an oppressed history and steps out into the bright sunshine of an accomplished gay freedom. Charles, a minor character in Timothy Ireland's novel *Who Lies Inside*, wears makeup and dresses flamboyantly in the local pub; he gets beaten up. This enables the emergent young Martin to feel revulsion and pity: "He always gave me the creeps somehow," says our young hero.[30] Charles fails Martin when he turns to him for help. Eventually Martin finds love with Richard, an attractive boy from his own class at school whom he has been enticing and rejecting since the start. Martin is still anxious about being "homosexual," but Richard (who has himself benefited from experience with an older man) reassures him that there is no need for labels, since they are all persons.

In *Coming Out*, an East German film directed by Heiner Carow (1988), Philipp, a schoolteacher, allows himself to be drawn into a relationship with Tanja, a colleague, and marries her when she becomes pregnant. However, he is in denial about an earlier queer episode, and has found his way to a gay bar (he was just wanting to buy cigarettes, he says). Pretending that he is unattached, Philipp allows a romantic gay boy, Matthias, to fall in love with him. Tanja and Matthias find out about each other and Philipp loses both of them. He is left to cruise an alienated scene. Asked by his mother why he must be this way, Philipp declares that it is nature, and he would be wrong to pretend and lie to himself. This thought is tardy, however, the harm to Matthias is already done. The film tends to suggest that gays must be lonely and unhappy, but it shows also that people should take more care with each other.

The selfishness of the neophyte is sharply analyzed again in Guy Willard's novel *Mirrors of Narcissus* (discussed also in chapter 3). Guy has been dismissive of middle-aged men who pursue boys, but eventually he responds when propositioned by a well-preserved professor, Harry Golden:

> He was old enough to be my father, yet I found him strangely attractive. Occasionally, when I thought about him, my feelings for him were distinctly sexual—perhaps inevitable, given his intelligence and strong character. I'd always been drawn to dominant types. Though he was past his prime as far as looks were concerned, his personality almost made physical attractiveness seem unimportant. And there was the seductive thought of his power—he was a full professor while I was just a freshman boy.[31]

The disparity in their ages has advantages, Guy finds. It frees him from competitive impulses and shame, and from "the need to adopt a tough, masculine facade. Instinctively I knew he wouldn't see my desire as a sign of weakness" (160). In a typical conflation of roles, Guy reads his submission as feminine: "Within the protective clasp of his big strong arms, pressed chest-to-chest in an intimate hug, I felt the stirrings of a tender submission. The secret little girl inside of me came alive and blossomed, gloriously" (162). He feels "exalted," but Golden is now redundant; he appears "helpless and weak" without his glasses, and has no further part in Guy's story (164). Thus fortified, Guy feels able to embrace his homosexuality, to abandon his girlfriend, and to force his attentions upon his friend.

While the situations of lesbians are quite distinct—for instance, there seems to be less of a premium on youth—the thrills and spills of the coming-out process may be similar. In Jill Posener's classic Gay Sweatshop play, *Any Woman Can*, predatory and stereotyped older lesbians are the problem for the bright and determined Ginny, rather than straight society. Rising from the ashes of her former selves, she discards the nervous and the exploitative and, through her own dramatic coming out, becomes an effective model for other women.[32] Jeanette, in Jeanette Winterson's *Oranges Are Not the Only Fruit*, is supported by several women in her contorted Christian community and responds with affection and respect. However, Miss Jewsbury, who has seduced her, is rejected. "I don't know why I didn't thank her, or even say goodbye."[33]

If boys ultimately have time on their side, men generally have control of representation. From Shakespeare's *Sonnets* through J. R. Ackerley's *We Think the World of You* (1960) to *The Swimming-Pool Library*, we get the story predominantly from the viewpoint of the older man. This replicates the situation of the male suitor and the idealized female object of his attentions, in the classic heterosexual love lyric from Dante and Petrarch through to the present. A prime reason why we don't get the boy's story is that by the time he is in a position to write it, certainly publish it, he has become a man. The story he then writes, even if it is presented as if through the eyes of the youngster, is likely to manifest the viewpoint of experience.

Even in fiction written ostensibly out of the perceptions of the younger person, we may in fact be getting an adult's fantasy. In P-P Hartnett's *I Want to Fuck You*, Handa San (PE teacher) and Takeo (schoolboy, thirteen) are drawn sexually to each other. In one chapter Handa San's thoughts are indicated:

> Handa San wasn't the only teacher in the school who didn't want to think of himself as a *paedophile* or *ephebophile*. He hoped the shivering attention he paid Takeo was just a phase he was going through. After all, he consoled himself, he didn't actually want to fuck the boy, get the boy on his knees or anything like that. He liked his students, was genuinely interested in their variety of character and outlook.[34]

That is a plausible representation of Handa San's thought. Compare this passage, from a chapter focusing on young Takeo:

> Takeo dragged shirt and vest over his ears together and folded them as a complex on the back of his homework chair. These warm clothes gave off a fragrance many would buy if bottled. Over that same chair Takeo layered his socks, smoothed flat into two-dimensional neatness. Finally, he undid the belt of his trousers, wriggling out of them with extravagant movements of hips and behind. He slithered out of his pants exposing his total, subtle naked body to the paired full length mirrors on the inside of the wardrobe door. (54–55)

The first sentence there could be Takeo's account of himself; so could the third. But the sentence in between—"These warm clothes gave off a fragrance many would buy if bottled"—is the perception of experience, not innocence. The narrator invites a voyeuristic interest in how Takeo takes off his trousers; it is not only the mirrors that have Takeo under surveillance. In short, the narrator is close to Handa San.

The anonymously published novel *The Scarlet Pansy* offers other examples. Again, it may appear at first sight that the viewpoint of the novice is represented, but actually the appeal is to the experienced reader. The young protagonist is revolted by the approaches of older homosexual men: "Randall turned this episode over in his mind. Was he always to be pursued by some man? Then the only hope of escape was the cultivation of the utmost reserve." The narrator seems to have entered Randall's viewpoint. However, the passage continues: "Quite unconsciously he was laying the foundation for one of the greatest charms of any person. He suppressed himself; a faint smile took the place of laughter, and thus he forever escaped that prevalent bane, the society grin."[35] The author has the experienced view, and invites the reader to share it.

The appropriative power of these narrators mimics the personal advantage of the experienced man. If the boy's desire-for the man is destabilized by his desire-to-be the man, the feeling of the man for the boy may be complicated by a desire-to-be him. We may suspect, indeed, that interest in coming-out stories has less to do with succoring oppressed youth and asserting gay rights, than with the fantasies of older writers and readers, who may be moved by an unstable conflation of desire-for and desire-to-be such a boy. Edmund White has recognized this. In the preface to *A Boy's Own Story*, he positions his present, writing self against his younger self: "If I'd hated myself as a boy and adolescent, I now felt an affection for the miserable kid I'd once been, a retrospective kindliness one might call 'the pederasty of autobiography.' "[36] Again, in the novel, White's narrator finds he has come to like the fifteen-year-old he once was, "even desire him"; it is a "retrospection three parts sentimental and one part erotic" (158).

In *The Folding Star*, Alan Hollinghurst makes a narrative virtue out of the young man's silence and distance. Edward, aged thirty-two, experiences a sexual infatuation with a mysterious youngster whom he is supposed to be teaching—Luc, age seventeen. He spies upon Luc and his young friends; he systematically steals his underwear. " 'He thinks of me as a friend,' " Edward avers. " 'How on earth would you know what he thinks. You haven't got a clue what goes on inside his head,' " Luc's young friend Sibylle retorts (370). The reader is no better informed; Luc's behavior is surprising at every turn, and not fully explained even at the end of the book. The folding star of the title evokes Milton's "Lycidas": " 'It's when you know you've got to put the sheep all safely in the fold' " (247). However (as in *The Swimming-Pool Library*), this pastoral impulse is accompanied, for Edward, by sexual pursuit: he is the wolf as much as the shepherd.

The local saint is Narcissus, though Edward says he doesn't " ' believe in the narcissist theory of gay attraction; I've always loved it with people who are different from me' " (156). However, as I argued in chapter 2, in narcissistic desire a man loves not so much himself as an idealized displacement of himself—what he is, what he was, what he would like to be, someone who was once part of himself. Edward acknowledges such an impulse when he wonders whether in placing no-longer-fashionable poems before Luc he is betraying an "impulse to keep him back with me in a shared childhood" (115). His determination to script Luc as having gay interests positions Luc as replicating Edward's own youthful sex life.

The central theme appears to be the fatal power of sexual fascination. As Edward's quest for the boy moves to a conclusion, so does the story of Paul, the museum curator. He recalls how as a boy during the German Occupation he had a liaison with a young man, not realizing that he was in the fascist militia. Thinking of Jewish children hidden away during the war years, Paul ruminates: " 'Personally I wouldn't want to place so much trust in a frightened or bereaved teenager—but what could they do when it was their only chance?' " (386). Again: a youngster " 'picks up an older person's life and then—he is distracted, self-absorbed, over-zealous, or perhaps quite unreflecting, he's no idea what he's doing—lets it drop' " (414). Perilous creatures, these boys.

VISIONS AND ACCOMMODATIONS

I choose to close this chapter with positive views of its themes. In *A Fairly Honourable Defeat*, published in 1970, Iris Murdoch explores some of the pitfalls that beset age hierarchy. Rupert and Hilda are married.[37] Simon, Rupert's young brother, after sowing some wild oats, has settled into coupledom with Axel, Rupert's old friend. Simon is twenty-nine, Axel forty-two. In an initial, notably complacent conversation, Hilda displays casual liberal prejudices. Perhaps Simon is not really homosexual, queers are always a bit sly, they don't like being reminded of normal relationships or happy marriages, queer friendships are so unstable, Simon is so much younger. Rupert disputes such generalizations. Axel bullies Simon, Hilda thinks; " 'Some people like to be bullied,' " Rupert responds; the novel is a study in the abuse of and retrieval of dominance and subordination. " 'Thank heavens our relationship is democratic,' " Hilda declares—complacently, as it transpires (15–18).

Simon does look queer, he cheerfully acknowledges (198); he is in charge of interior decoration at their flat. It is out of character, friends agree, for him not to like opera because he's such a feminine person, as may be observed in his decor. Rupert and Hilda's son, Peter, jeers at Simon for being more female than Shakespeare's fairies. (Peter is very insecure.)

Axel is straight-acting to the point of total inscrutability, even to Simon in their early meetings. He complains at Simon's aftershave lotion—" 'Try to remember you're male, not female, will you?' " Axel won't have any "camp" (in quotation marks) or *risqué* jokes (36). When they first drew together, Axel hesitated because he believed himself to be naturally monogamous, whereas Simon "was by nature frivolous, inconstant, evasive, impulsive, irrational, shallow" (202). Actually, Simon is seeking someone to give his heart to; "Yet he enjoyed some of his adventures and liked the jokey parochial atmosphere of the gay bars which he had been used to frequent" (37). Sometimes Simon himself fears he may be too trivial a person for Axel. His declarative outbursts only provoke Axel to withdraw. For Simon, "There was at every moment total vulnerability. There was a dangerous thrilling trembling inner circuit of the soul" (39). He suggests that they are like Apollo and Marsyas.

In fact Axel is chronically jealous and insecure; it is surprising that Simon doesn't quite realize this, and lose respect for him. He won't let Simon learn to drive, tries to stop him drinking and becoming exuberant at parties. He accuses Simon of being irrational, but enjoys putting him through the drama of accusation, reproach, and separation. Then he commands him to be independent. " 'You mustn't let me influence you so much, dear boy' " (87).

Enter Julius, another old friend of Rupert. He worked on biological warfare for the United States, but gave it up because he became bored. (Eventually it emerges that he was in Belsen; he considers himself an instrument of justice.) He denies that goodness is important: "'we know what moves people, dear Rupert. Fears, passions of all kinds. The desire for power, for instance. Few questions are more important than: who is the boss?'" "'Though of course some people prefer to be bossed!' " " 'Yes, yes. It's all a question of choosing one's technique' " (225).

Julius is a dedicated controller: he experiments with people and it gives him the pleasure of confirming his amoral principles. The other disturber of the peace is Morgan, Hilda's sister, who is even more dangerous because out of control. Julius makes a wager with Morgan that he can get Simon away from Axel. The "fairly honourable defeat" of the title is Julius's failure to part Axel and Simon while managing to maneuver Rupert and Morgan into an affair, with purloined letters and Iago-like insinuations.

Julius traps Simon into moments of complicity and small lapses in total candor; he plays on Simon's fear that Axel will see him through Julius's eyes: "Axel would suddenly see how flimsy Simon was, how unsophisticated, how lacking in cleverness and wit, how hopelessly ignorant about important things such as Mozart and truth functions and the balance of payments" (77). Julius, alternately flirting and commanding, exploits Simon's tendency to be dominated—effortlessly because, unlike Axel, he has little at stake. Simon is frightened by his attraction to Julius. "But then, thought Simon, I have never really been able to distinguish between fear and sexual desire" (160).

Julius predicts a sorry end for Simon's partnership with Axel:

> "You choose at present to give in. But every time you give in you notice it. Later perhaps you will make Axel's life a misery. Then gradually the balance will tilt. You will get tired of being Axel's lapdog. You are not at all monogamous really, my dear Simon. You miss your adventures, you know you do. And you will find out one day that you want to play Axel to some little Simon. The passage of time brings about these shifts automatically, especially in relationships of your kind." (269–70)

These are perhaps characteristic pitfalls of age hierarchy. However, the narration suggests that they need not be fatal.

Simon eventually tells Axel all about Julius. Axel confesses that he was miserable when he thought he would have to end their affair; he admits that his reserve has kept Simon insecure, that he is guilty of a failure of love and trust. Simon appreciates that Axel does love and need him. " 'A little bullying between lovers needn't matter. But I've always withheld a bit of myself,' " Axel admits (434). The important distinction, in Murdoch's view, is between fumbling good will and the destructiveness of Julius and Morgan. The pattern remains, but it is interpreted with trust. At the end Simon seems justified in feeling "the warm anticipation of a new happiness" (437).

Murdoch's account is surprisingly modern; clones, AIDS, queer, and lifestyle lie between us and *A Fairly Honourable Defeat*, but she comes through with a valuable analysis. Perhaps this is because she is not troubled by the age-disparate liaison as such: she takes its potential for granted, and is thus free to pursue wider and deeper psychological and ethical dimensions. Compare other mid-century fictions—Stephen Spender's *The Temple*, Angus Wilson's *Hemlock and After*, Barbara Pym's *A Glass of Blessings*, the film *Victim* (Basil Dearden, 1961). In *We Think the World of You*, Ackerley's protagonist does his best to keep things going with his boyfriend, but finds he gets on better with the dog.

The most striking affirmation of age-disparity occurs in Neil Bartlett's *Ready to Catch Him Should He Fall*. Bartlett doesn't shrink from awkward aspects of the theme. He invites readers to occupy the position of the man, and to share in the constitution of the ideal boy. Perhaps the narrator's description is wrong for some readers: "do go back, and amend my description of Boy so that he is, is some way, if you see what I mean, your type. Make him fit the bill; imagine for him the attributes that you require."[38] At the same time, the image will derive from and belong to the subculture. Boy is destined to discover himself in a historic gay identity, self-consciously bestowed by Madame, who owns The Bar, and her clientele. He needs "application, study, repetition, diligent imitation and sincere admiration of his peers" (33). He is the figure we (men) all hold in our imaginations. He is in a line with Chance Wayne played by Paul Newman, Alec Scudder in *Maurice*, Boy Barrett in *Victim*, Bosie Douglas—drawn purposefully by Bartlett from several generations. The idea of Boy is a ratification of gay history, and hence of gay existence.

There is no question that Boy, in assuming this identity, is doing what he wants to do, though he is only nineteen (at the time of publication the gay age of consent was twenty-one in England). He is already exhausted with questing for The Bar; already imagining sexual practices that men might pursue together. He only ever goes home with older men. "One thing Boy never said, the line of [Paul] Newman's he would never have used, was *don't call me Boy*. He loved to be called Boy" (13). It is a position of honor, not of inferiority. He wants one thing more than to be one of the men in The Bar: "to be reassured that he might somehow remain a boy for ever" (38). (I discuss the gendering of Boy and The Bar in chapter 5.)

O is The Older Man—forty-five at least. No celibate, but very self-contained; "you never saw him following anyone, gazing after someone or persuading them to come home with him. Asked exactly how O took people home, you'd have to say that O just summoned his men to him somehow" (68). O's stance toward Boy is protective (hence the title of the novel), but sex between them is violent—though Boy does bruise easily. "I should say here that Boy never once wanted O to stop, and that he was used to sometimes being frightened by what O wanted to do, and by what he made Boy himself feel that he wanted to do, things he hadn't ever known that he wanted to do" (141–42). As in other novels we have considered, and especially in Paul Russell's *Boys of Life* (discussed in chapter 7) and Duncker's *Hallucinating Foucault*, innovative and fierce power play in bed is prized by the boy as evidence of the man's general commitment to life and particular appreciation of the boy.

What follows this intense courtship is less remarkable. Boy and O affirm their relationship in a version of the conventional marriage ceremony. Some of The Bar people are offended by this; it is the one point in the novel at which there is any subcultural dissent. Boy and O form "The model couple in the model flat, Boy at home all day with the appliances and O out to work" (225). For Murdoch, the key question is about how men adapt their fantasy desires and personae to the business of getting along together. This is admitted in *Ready to Catch Him*: "what really matters is what happens when two people try to hold things together" (309). Boy "spends the evening or night with a younger man sometimes now, a man younger than himself, a boy really" (309). We are not told quite how this is managed. Is Boy's desire-to-be O translating into a desire-for a boy of his own? Will O meet a new Boy? Are the differences between O and Boy fading away, leaving an egalitarian couple?

Reviewing *Ready to Catch Him*, Adam Mars-Jones criticized its endorsement of The Bar and its insistence on the special, poetic quality of gay sex; they correlate, Mars-Jones says, with a separatist as opposed to an assimilationist aesthetic. He contests the idea that "it is by exhaustively exploring their fantasies that gay people best prepare themselves to take their place in the world."[39] This is surely somewhat abrupt; it is hard to imagine a commentator writing in the *Independent* that black people should not investigate and value their histories. Bartlett has justified the introspective stance of the novel as an attempt to consolidate gay subculture in a context where AIDS was taking the lives of friends and legitimating homophobic assaults. "You couldn't walk down the street or open a newspaper without flinching, because there would be some new graffito about AIDS—on the wall or as a headline in the best selling newspaper."[40] This is not all, however. Although we prefer to regard our fantasies as private, the public iconography of art, advertising, and pornography demonstrates conclusively that they are acquired through a collaborative process. The Bar is a metaphor for the communal mechanisms through which we negotiate desire-for and desire-to-be. "I apologize," says the narrator, "if this description of Boy sounds to you like some fantasy and not a real person" (15). Bartlett's aesthetic is all about peak experiences, moments at which fantasy miraculously catches up with actuality. Boy is indeed a fantasy, a luminous evocation of all the boys who have been loved since Antinous enchanted the Emperor Hadrian in A.D. 120.

7

CLASS

Difference in disposable assets is happily acknowledged in the Pet Shop Boys' "Rent." The song is offered from the point of view of a kept boy. Financial status is not effaced: "You bring me food, I need it, you give me love, I feed it." To the contrary, it is claimed as integral with love:

> Now look at the two of us, in sympathy with everything we see
> I never want anything, it's easy, you buy whatever I need
> Look at my hopes, look at my dreams, the currency we've spent
> I love you, you pay my rent. I love you, you pay my rent.

Their sympathy is founded in shared consumption, rendered the more passionate and pleasurable by the fact that there is no hesitation about commitment. "I love you. / You pay the rent": no syntax. It is not "I love you, therefore you pay the rent." Nor is it "I love you because you pay the rent." The personal feeling and the provision of security occur together. The currency they have spent is both money and psychic investment. The liaison works; as well as sympathy there is "sometimes ecstasy."

One of Eve Sedgwick's pregnant remarks is that many dimensions of sexual choice appear not to have a "distinctive, explicit definitional connection with gender; indeed, some dimensions of sexuality might be tied, not to gender, but *instead* to differences or similarities of class or race." Sex, in other words, may be organized around hierarchies other than gender; "to assume the distinctiveness of the *intimacy* between sexuality and gender might well risk assuming too much about the definitional *separability* of either of them from determinations of, say, class or race."[1] In earlier chapters I located the cross-class liaison as a version of the complementarity model, in which sameness of gender is complicated by other differences. Our experience of class evokes intense idealizations and enduring humiliations. I am taking "class" approximately, as comprising hierarchies of wealth, income, status, educational attainment, and cultural sophistication, along with their markers in attire, decor, and general lifestyle. While I disagree with Trotskyists, who proclaim the ineluctable priority of class struggle, I believe that class difference is everywhere in our psychic lives, as it is in our social system.[2]

TURNING ON TO CLASS

The Wilde trials, I and others have suggested, were crucial in establishing the stereotype of the queer man which dominated until gay liberation in the 1970s.[3] At the trials, the entire, vaguely disconcerting nexus of effeminacy, leisure, idleness, immorality, luxury, insouciance, decadence, and aestheticism, which Wilde was perceived, variously, as instantiating, was transformed into a brilliantly precise image. The principal twentieth-century stereotype entered our cultures: not just the homosexual, as the lawyers and medics would have it, but the queer. A comparable effect was produced for lesbianism by the prosecution of Radclyffe Hall's *Well of Loneliness* in 1929.

Wilde's effeminate manner was linked as much to class as to gender. Already by the end of the eighteenth century, the aristocracy was positioned as feminized. The newly dominant middle class justified itself through an ideology of work, manly purity, purpose, and responsibility. The leisure-class male was identified, correspondingly, with effeminate idleness and immorality; his options were to repudiate this identification, or to embrace it. Wilde affected a feminine stance in order to claim a class position, while exercising the male authority of accomplishment in public life; the combination of these strategies evidently made him impressive to the boys whose acquaintance he cultivated.

The Wildean, cultured gent and his bit of rough trade became the dominant image of the queer for the twentieth century, up until the 1970s. It was less an individual experience than a subcultural myth.[4] As Foucault puts it, "it was in the 'bourgeois' or 'aristocratic' family" that sexuality was "first problematized," whereas "the working classes managed for a long time to escape the deployment of 'sexuality.'" He disputes the idea that the surveillance of sexuality was inflicted upon the lower orders by the ruling classes: "Rather it appears to me that they first tried it on themselves."[5] The lower-class partner might be presented as a secretary or manservant; John Addington Symonds did this, so did Somerset Maugham and Nöel Coward. Otherwise, it was difficult for two men to live together; Terence Rattigan installed his lovers in nearby apartments. (Of course, that cost money.) When she lectured in the United States, Gertrude Stein presented Alice B. Toklas as her secretary.

In the United States also, it was upper-class men who first got the idea of "being a homosexual." George Chauncey Jr. shows that working-class men, particularly those linked to "masculine" milieux—sailors, laborers, hoboes, and other transient workers—might engage in same-sex activity across class without having to categorize themselves as "queer."[6] After all, they might be, or might appear to be, motivated largely by social deference and financial advantage; probably they were married. As Murray Healy observes, this is not to say that there were no working-class pubs, cruising grounds, or gay identity; rather that these resources were rare, and other options more available, more visible, more attractive.[7]

This way of regarding cross-class relations was not confined to homosexuals: to a striking extent it replicated wider class and sex/gender patterns. It was in practice almost acceptable for an upper-class man to have as a mistress, or to have casual sex with, a female of a lower class (typically a servant, a shopgirl, or a secretary), or to employ a sex-worker; it was almost expected. What he was not supposed to do was foul up his own social stratum by forming extramarital liaisons with women whom he might meet there. Freud actually imagined this as a universal trait. In an essay "On the Universal Tendency to Debasement in the Sphere of Love," he posits that a man—any man—has difficulty in combining "the *affectionate* and the *sensual* current."[8] He can't satisfy his desires with a woman he respects; hence "his need for a debased sexual object, a woman who is ethically inferior, to whom he need attribute no aesthetic scruples, who does not know him in his other social relations and cannot judge him in them" (254).

The cross-class queer liaison worked similarly. It is often remarked that some of the objection to Wilde's behavior was that he had crossed class barriers. For example, he was questioned about Alphonse Conway: did Wilde buy him a suit "In order that he might look more like an equal?"[9] The furor over *Lady Chatterley's Lover* was similarly framed. Famously, prosecuting counsel asked the jury whether they would want their wives or servants to read the book.[10] Actually, the offense was not that Wilde had cultivated cross-class liaisons, but that he had openly paraded them—as Lawrence did in fiction. The more disgraceful connection was between Wilde and

Douglas; this was too sensitive to be addressed in court. The crucial opposition was not between heterosexuality and homosexuality, then, but between legitimate and illegitimate relations, defined in terms of class.

It is clear that, for many people who expressed their sexualities in this way, the cross-class liaison was not just a convenience: it was a turn-on. For many middle- and upper-class men, lower-class people were sexy *as such*. For most middle-class men, after all, servants had tendered the principal physical, affective, and intimate support in infancy. In the 1850s, Arthur Munby, a lawyer and civil servant, established a liaison with Hannah Cullwick, a servant; the impetus for each of them is clear in their diaries. They developed his lustful overseeing of her, scrubbing the floor on her knees, into a scenario in which she got herself dirty and undertook rough, slavish tasks and manners for his pleasure. Peter Stallybrass and Allon White comment: "The opposition of working-class maid and upper-class male, then, depended upon a physical and social separation which was constitutive of desire." As they note, Freud's "Wolfman" retrieves an intense early experience involving a maid in a scrubbing posture.[11] Hannah was not just a figure of "lowness," however: she was also a figure of comfort and power. Her diaries indicate clearly that she is entirely happy with her subordinate position. She is both glad and sorry when Munby says that he almost tells a friend about them: "glad 'cause it show'd that M. does love me, & sorry 'cause I don't want to disgrace him & I canna bear for anyone to think I want to be anything but what I am to him. And so I want no one to know." She is not aspiring to change class; she likes her work and is proud of it: "But tho' I'm never so happy as when I'm with him or working for *him*, yet I want to be still a servant & working so as to be independent & get my own living."[12] At Munby's behest they do marry, but Hannah feels it has "little to do with our *love* & our union" (252; Cullwick's emphases).

The mysteries of lower-class life may hold a fascination for the middle-class man. Crime thrillers, from *The Heart in Exile* by Rodney Garland (1953) through *Skinflick* by Joseph Hansen (1979) to *Doing Business* by Jeremy Beadle (1990), have depended on the middle-class man being sucked into a mysterious underworld of rent boys, hustlers, and beach bums. He mediates the lower orders to presumptively middle-class readers.

The happy ending to Garland's *Heart in Exile* is secured when the protagonist, a psychiatrist, finds after a period of loneliness and gloomy exploration of queer subculture that he is drawn to his manservant.

I confess that the attraction was much stronger when I saw him doing the sort of work I would never had dreamed of asking him to do. When my charwoman left, he insisted on scrubbing the kitchen floor, kneeling on the rubber mat, bending over the mop in his singlet. One saw the servant's humility in the attitude. But one also saw the broad shoulders, the arched back with the freckled skin under the rebellious hair, and he would look up as I entered and give me a beautiful smile of his brown dog eyes and white teeth.[13]

The excitement here appears to arise from a coalescence of subordination and strength. On the one hand, Jeffrey Weeks comments, we are seeing "a form of sexual colonialism, a view of the lower classes as a source of 'trade.' On the other we may have a sentimental rejection of one's own class values and a belief in reconciliation through sexual contact."[14]

Stephen Spender tells in his autobiography how in the mid-1930s he took up with a young man whom he calls Jimmy Younger: "I asked him to live in my flat and work for me."[15] The contrast in their background, Spender more or less admits, was not just an inconvenience; it was exciting:

> For the differences of class and interest between Jimmy and me certainly did provide some element of mystery which corresponded almost to a difference of sex. I was in love, as it were, with his background, his soldiering, his working-class home. Nothing moved me more than to hear him tell stories of the Cardiff streets, of Tiger Bay. . . . At such moments, too, I was very close to certain emotions awakened in childhood by the workers, who to us seemed at the same time coarse, unclean, and yet with something about them of forbidden fruit, and also of warm-heartedness which suddenly flashed across the cold gulf of class, secret and unspoken. (158–59; my elision)

There were tensions, however. Jimmy "was accustomed to be treated rough, and he expected that I would behave like his past employers. When I did not do so he was disconcerted and felt that in some way I was gaining power over him as no one had done before." He said, " 'You are very nice to me, but I feel that I am becoming your property' " (151).

As in the Pet Shop Boys' "Rent," it seems plain that the lower-class person may gain more than a meal ticket: there is a romance about the affluent, an aura about the powerful, that may make them sexy. However, indignation and resentment are equally likely: a role reversal (such as I discussed in chapter 3) might place the lower-class man in control. That is the theme of Robin Maugham's novella, *The Servant*, filmed by Joseph Losey in 1963.

Contemporary viewers are invited to recognize a liaison from the 1960s in John Maybury's film about the painter Francis Bacon, *Love Is the Devil*

(1998). George (Daniel Craig) arrives in Francis's studio through the skylight, as a burglar, looking notably proletarian in a donkey jacket. "Come to bed, and you can have whatever you want," says Francis (Derek Jacobi). George's first question when we see them in bed is: "You actually make money out of painting?" He's pleased when Francis says he may use him as a subject; he allows Francis to buy him new clothes. George is ill at ease among Francis's posh-bohemian friends, however. They have common ground in boxing, but George's old East End friends despise his new connections. They warn him that he will be used and dropped. Sexually, Francis likes to be submissive, to relinquish control; in the relationship he holds all the cards (this is a typical reversal of class roles).

Francis gets bored with George, who, having no occupation or space of his own, becomes importunate, obstreperous, maudlin, suicidal. Francis tells himself that his work leaves him no room for relationships; that he is powerless to protect George from his dreams. He apologizes for him to his friends. His impatience and unkindness are defended as the artist's necessary response to his demons. Francis takes George as subject; the pictures in which he figures are especially admired, but Francis can't tolerate him in the studio. Friends warn him that George needs help, but he can't be bothered. George takes pills and alcohol while Francis is feted. George's body seems to grow and fade, miasmically, in and out of the artworks (now famous and immensely valuable) that he has made possible.

THE PERSISTENCE OF CLASS

It is a pleasant trope of conservatives that class is no longer significant in our societies. At the same time, the gap between the rich and the poor is wider than ever in Britain and the United States.

It might be thought that the idealized relationship between two boys of the same age, who live in adjacent flats on a working-class estate, in a play designed explicitly to contribute to the campaign for an equal age of consent, would be free of class hierarchy. However, Jonathan Harvey in his play *Beautiful Thing* makes Jamie's mother upwardly mobile (she is promoted to manage a pub) whereas Ste's father is definitely rough (drunken and violent). Jamie's care matches Ste's endurance. Further, in familiar ways, class correlates with gender: Ste is good at football, whereas Jamie reads about soap stars in his mother's magazine.[16] (Note, however, that, unlike earlier coming-out narratives, *Beautiful Thing* does give a positive role to gay institutions—such as the magazine *Gay Times*, and a gay pub.)

While it seems appropriate to elaborate the concept of class so as to register social, educational, economic, and political inequalities, this need not entail any abandonment of a more traditional Marxist sense of class as about economic, political, and social control. In the last analysis, all power is about command over the means to life. If we have neglected that thought in metropolitan contexts, it is because we have been immensely fortunate in the second half of the twentieth century, to the point where many of us have stopped worrying about food and shelter, and centered our anxieties upon the attainment of a new update of our sound system. Nonetheless, the intense commitments that we call "love" may, ultimately, be intricately mediated versions of a will to survive, ontologically as well as materially. This may lead us into interpersonal opportunities which seem to afford a reassuring exercise of our own power. Equally, it may draw us into the orbit of people who appear to be powerful and may protect us.

The importance of class is indicated in an abiding image in gay pornography and popular fiction: the maintenance man who comes into your house to fix the plumbing and ends up in the shower with you. A thoughtful version of this scenario—told from the viewpoint of the working man— is offered by Jay Quinn in his story, "The Kitchen Table." Phil regards himself as straight, and has been in prison; he is employed by Trace to work with him on his house. As they share their exertions, Phil finds he is increasingly drawn into sexual fantasies about Trace (they are the same age and both presumptively white). "He noticed how his upper arms and thighs hardened from an office worker's slack fullness to the firmness suited to their new function."[17] Hitherto, Phil has been hostile to gays who have approached him, but generally he takes things as they come; he is scarcely troubled by his attraction to Trace. They develop a physical rapport. Unusually for an American story, class difference is made explicit. When a building inspector is not satisfied with Phil's work, he nonetheless defends Phil against Trace. When it comes down to it, Trace observes, " 'A working man'll side with one of his own kind over somebody in a three-piece suit every time' " (188). Despite his business habits of decision and command, a photograph of Trace and his deceased lover shows Trace as the one who is held, supportively, from behind: "Trace was relaxed into the man's broad chest, held lovingly by his large hand on his bare stomach" (199). This is evidently the role demarcation Trace and Phil will now assume. They have a relationship of mutual respect, in which Trace's bourgeois introversion is matched by Phil's work-a-day steadiness.

To be sure, class difference may be only relative. The English novel that seems designed to set aside traditional hierarchies, representing a partnership between two ordinary blokes, is Tom Wakefield's *Mates*. Cyril and Len meet up in the army in 1954 and stay together for a lifetime. Cyril is pleased that their fellow soldiers don't regard them as conventional queers. He is afraid they will somehow intuit his sexuality.

> They nodded to him as they usually did, and he nodded back. It was a relief to find out that he didn't look any different. He turned to look at Len. His friend Len didn't lisp, wear scent or make-up. That's what he was supposed to do, according to all the newspapers of the day. So what if he did? Sod them, sod them all. No, not all of them. The tea-lady was all right.[18]

Cyril doesn't envisage that he might himself wear scent; Len may be relatively feminine, but neither of them cultivates an upper-class, Wildean manner.

Yet even this relationship is framed in terms of class. The six weeks of basic training make them appear equal, but hierarchy reappears when they receive different postings because Cyril has good examination results whereas Len, though bookish, is unambitious. Cyril is more confident socially and sexually; he takes up with a local group of artistic and professional men; becomes a head teacher. Len remains a conscientious clerk and does the cooking and the shopping. Finally, Len is unable to assert himself when Cyril dies, and gets pushed out of their home by Cyril's businessman brother.

Class may figure largely a matter of cultural capital. Austin in Edmund White's *The Married Man* is a successful American writer living in Paris; as such he has both money (earned) and prestige. He is taken with Julien partly because of his status and aura as minor aristocracy. Austin writes about the furniture of upper-class families and as a boy daydreamed of finding that his mother or father was descended from Huguenot nobility. Apparently it is in such elevated circles that Austin can best be himself: "Only in upper-class French life had Austin found the exact shade of inclusion he had craved for. Perhaps it was natural in a society where a king had been surrounded by cute boys, his *mignons*, and in which the brother of Louis XIV, '*Monsieur*,' had maintained an all-male shadow court."[19] Julien entertains Austin with fantastic tales of his eccentric family; when he doesn't want to talk about something he will "smile and turn his head slightly to one side with a sort of royal unreachability" (129). Austin is charmed. After Julien's death, at the end of the book, Austin and the reader learn that all this was fantasy and bluff: Julien comes from a peasant family. Whether French people were deceived by him, or cared very much, is not disclosed.

The history, albeit dimly perceived in recent years, of preliberation liaisons as typically cross-class and exploitative, has led lesbian and gay people to repudiate or understate the influence of class in our affairs. Gender, race, and sexuality have seemed the more promising banners under which to unite. Sally Munt describes how commitment to lesbian feminism made her feel that talking about class "was to be labelled a spoiler, a guilt-tripper, a Manichean thinker, a fifth columnist."[20] As Munt adds, the occlusion of class has been more powerful in the United States, where Marxism has become hard to think about. A collection of essays reasserting the value of Marxism to Shakespeare studies begins by repudiating any supposed priority of class, as opposed to race and gender; the collection makes almost no further mention of class at all.[21] The same thing happens in Ken Plummer's collection, *Modern Homosexualities*, Leslie J. Moran points out.[22]

An intriguing interaction between different kinds of capital is described by Carol M. Ward in her account of a two-year relationship between Rita Mae Brown and Martina Navratilova in 1979–1981. It might be thought that the tennis player possessed considerable financial and cultural capital. However, Brown was strongly aware of her own status as a successful novelist and intellectual. She saw Navratilova as "a nice young girl in a limiting profession; where you can make a lot of money but know very little."[23] Correspondingly, Navratilova felt that her career as a sportswoman was being held in low esteem. She wanted to learn from Brown—to read books, visit museums, and talk about politics—but not at the price of her own self-valuation. According to Navratilova, the relationship broke up because Brown's attitude undermined her ambitions in tennis: she became ambivalent about her own aims. Brown believes that the relationship foundered when Navratilova took up with basketball star Nancy Lieberman; Navratilova says Lieberman was only coaching her—helping her to recover her will to win. After a violent breakup, the two women became friends.

Dorothy Allison's experience leads her to believe that class is highly active among Americans, in the constitution of both sexualities and political attitudes. She relates her masochistic desires, and her use of dildos and leather, to abuse by her stepfather, and to the white trash culture in which she grew up; she tells a fictionalized version of the story in *Bastard Out of Carolina*.[24] "What I know for sure is that class, gender, sexual preference, and prejudice—racial, ethnic, and religious—form an intricate lattice that restricts and shapes our lives, and that resistance to hatred is not a simple act," she says. Hence the hostility of middle-class feminists and lesbians toward her practices. They are uncomfortable with her butch, working-class partners: "The kind of woman I am attracted to is invariably the kind of woman who embarrasses respectably middle-class, politically aware lesbian feminists." The task, Allison says, is "to understand how we internalize the myths of our society even as we resist them."[25]

In fact, probably because of general pressures toward embourgeoisement in personal relationships and the particular effects of the targeting of the pink economy, we have scarcely sought to imagine a subculture in which class would be truly a matter of indifference. Instead, we have complacently supposed that gay people will become, almost by definition, middle class—in lifestyle and aspirations, if not in background and income.

Class hierarchy may be obscured through processes of substitution and conflation which make it easy to read class as gender or age difference. Texts which I discuss in other chapters as structured by gender, age, and race usually include a significant element of class difference—so Maupin, *The Night Listener*; Dickson, *Oddfellows*; Hall, *The Well of Loneliness*; Baker, *Tim and Pete*; Feinberg, *Stone Butch Blues*; Monette, *Halfway Home*; Hollinghurst, *The Swimming-Pool Library*. When Malone in Andrew Holleran's *Dancer from the Dance* is living with Frankie, they begin to look like each other (they dress similarly), "like all homosexual lovers"—except for "that unmistakable difference": race. (They are from Irish and Italian families.) "When they lay tangled in each other's limbs by day or night, the pale, golden form, and the swarthy, dark-eyed, one, the northern and southern race joined at last.[26] In fact what is clear, but unmarked, is that their class and educational backgrounds are entirely dissimilar—Malone went to Yale Law School whereas Frankie labors, maintaining the subway system. This is far more relevant than race as such; when the romance wears off they have little to talk about, so they quarrel and part.

Class is not secondary. If a gay man gets off on wearing the gear of a construction worker, or desiring someone else who does that, it is not helpful to read this as a gender phenomenon and translate it into his relations with his father. It is more reasonable to recognize that there is a historical figure—the construction worker. If he appears sexy and dominant—tough, highly skilled, and inured to danger—it is because behind the fantasy lies an actuality in which there is hard, difficult, and perilous labor, probably worsened by stressful working conditions and management resistance to unionization. If he appears sexy and ready to serve, it is because he cannot afford to risk dismissal. It is in such a world that the middle-class gay man invests, financially and psychologically, in real estate and decor.

The corollary of the centrality of class in gay affairs has been intense evocations of man-to-man equality. The apostle of the liaison that transcends class, in the United States especially, has been Walt Whitman. David Bergman shows how the gay critic F. O. Matthiessen, drawing partly on Edward Carpenter, established Whitman as a poet of organic unity who believed that personal fulfillment might be continuous with social unity.[27] Whitman's reputation as the model for an ideology of opportunity, democracy, and rights, crosses, perhaps too easily, into gay culture as an ideal of comradely, manly, sexual democracy. A memoir of Mark Bingham, for instance, presents him as a regular guy, a rugby player and business executive; a former lover recalls how, when Bingham was coming out, he would read him Whitman. The reason for the memoir is that Bingham died on the hijacked 9/11 plane that missed its target. Surely he must have been one of the passengers who rushed the hijackers; attention to Whitman certifies his heroic potential.[28] In fact, Whitman's adhesive partners were lower class and younger, and his life and work may be seen as displaying damaging hints of effeminacy.[29]

In practice, democracy and freedom have immense difficulty evading the demands of wealth and beauty. Money was never absent from the elaborate cruising opportunities of the 1970s. The idea that a kind of democracy flourished on Fire Island is evoked but then given further twists in Ethan Mordden's story, "And Eric Said He'd Come":

> For here we find gay stripped to its essentials. The beautiful are more fully exposed here, the trolls more cast out than anywhere else—thus their pride and passion. The beguiling but often irrelevant data of talent and intelligence that can seem enticing in the city are internal contradictions in a place without an opera house or a library. Only money and charm count. Professional advantages are worthless, for, in a bathing suit, all men have the same vocation. Yet there are distinctions of rank. Those who rent are the proletariat, those who own houses are the bourgeoisie, and houseboys form the aristocracy.[30]

At first it appears that only sex appeal counts; then we learn that money matters after all; indeed, the island has its own version of the class system.

James Kenneth Melson had a mixed experience of the prestigious Studio 54 disco, he says in his autobiography. He proved that a boy from Ohio could gain entrance just by looking good. Once inside, there was no problem: "the atmosphere was devoid of the pretenses, the 'attitude,' that prevailed among those left standing outside. Everyone could let his hair down; royalty would dance with rock stars, Eurotrash with debutantes, and pro athletes with the likes of Disco Sally and Rollerena, two of the notables of the 'outrageous' category."[31] Better still, this democratic atmosphere seemed to facilitate Melson's quest to seek out the most wealthy and influential men. However, they expected him to comply with their sexual demands, and attempts to pursue upper-class acquaintances beyond the club scene and the bedroom left him rapidly and comprehensively snubbed. He found qualifications and a job on Wall Street a better route to success.

The implicit underpinning for the Whitmanesque, gay egalitarian ideology is supplied by the concept of "America." As Steven Epstein observes, the appeal is to "the rules of the modern American pluralist myth, which portrays a harmonious competition among distinct social groups."[32] On this basis, lesbians and gay men have constituted themselves as something like an ethnic group claiming rights. How far that pluralistic myth is to be trusted is a question far wider than queer politics: it is about how much we should expect from the institutions through which capitalism and heteropatriarchy are reproduced.

Pete in Baker's *Tim and Pete* offers an explanation for and reaffirmation of the general idealism and the aspiration to transcend class that gay men have associated with a "Whitmanic" feeling. Pete relates it to " 'a lot of people feeling good about themselves for the first time in their lives. That was the best time, really, the early gay lib days. There was a bohemian spirit, you know. In a sense it was still the sixties.' "[33] The image may still be potent. Whitman would have been at home in the semimystical gatherings of the Radical Faeries in 1990, Paul Monette avers.[34]

WHO SPEAKS?

Phil in "The Kitchen Table" and Melson in his autobiography tell their stories from the viewpoint of the relatively lower-class man. Generally, as we see elsewhere in this book, the feelings of the partner in the subordinate position are less well documented. For instance, we can only speculate about the subsequent sex lives of the boys who featured in Wilde's trials. The unusual factor in Munby's household is that we have Hannah Cullwick's diaries.

Neal Drinnan's *Glove Puppet* ingeniously refocuses the perils of the cross-class liaison. The novel is written from the viewpoint of Johnny, also called Vaslav, who is now twenty; he interprets his early life, promising the reader some lurid details. Johnny comes from a classically deprived background: he has never known his father, his mother is a sex worker and a drug addict. When she dies suddenly on a railway station he is scooped up by Shamash, a gay ballet dancer whose son has recently died, and taken to Australia. There, at the age of seven, he is named Vaslav and passed off as Shamash's son. He lives happily and luxuriously, and adopts the concepts and values of an artistic, bohemian community. From the age of eleven he finds that his feelings of filial affection for Shamash are complicated by an intense sexual awareness. Shamash tries to damp this down, but at age fourteen Vaslav encourages Ashley, Shamash's partner, to seduce him. When Vaslav is sixteen, he and Shamash become lovers.

As we saw with age hierarchy, purported accounts of sexual experience from the subordinate viewpoint may offer to titillate the reader, even while inviting condemnation on the ground of exploitation. This process is actually incorporated into *Glove Puppet*, for Johnny/Vaslav indicates that he expects to make a lot of money from his book. "People love sex freaks, trash fucks, dirty young beauty; fresh filth-statutory rape-date rape, boy pussy surprise."[35] The reader has been warned—or is it enticed?

An adult having sex with a boy of fourteen is presented as the moral issue of *Glove Puppet*. Although it is clear that Vaslav was hell-bent on gaining sexual experience, he maintains consistently that Ashley was wrong to exploit him. However, another vein of thought in the book suggests that, in one way or another, Johnny was always bound to be bad, sooner or later and whoever he was with, because of his class origins. Hence his relatively early development: "hormonally I developed early in that white trashy way that really was my genetic inheritance" (72). His enjoyment of Shamash's lifestyle is complicated by his assumption that really he is Johnny, the rough boy on the make, bad by definition.

> He [Johnny] was winking at me from where he slouched by the garbage dump in the council estate. In my mind's eye he was making lewd gestures just like those trashy boys in the porn movies, his hand outlining the erection in his torn jeans, his other hand fingering his mouth for saliva, for lube. He was mustering his strength, weighing his sex because that's all he had to sell, that was his only ticket out of the council estate and at that stage his only ambition. (115)

This enticing but threatening creature has only one object in view: a ticket out. Any signs of untainted love and trust are merely deceptive. Johnny "could never be tamed or cultured. He was like his mother, hardly a person at all, just someone to do stuff to, something to fuck," like a boy in a pornographic magazine (80).

When the narration of the novel catches up with present time, Vaslav is entrenched in sauna, pornographic, drug, and sex-worker scenes; he is depressed and has tried to take his own life; yet he is surviving. Shamash has confessed to sodomizing his own son and is in prison. This is on the supposition that Shamash is Vaslav's father; the reader knows better. The issue is not incest, nor even underage sex (in most metropolitan countries sex at sixteen is legal), but the destructive intrusion of the lower-class boy. The reader may or may not choose to accept Vaslav's repeated claims that the truth of gay life is revealed in his corrupt but thrilling story: "We might frighten ourselves, us fags, but we are what we are and we do experience some extraordinary sensations in our endless pursuit of whatever it is we are looking for—momentary oblivion or eternal rest" (173).

A powerful novel which takes seriously the potential and the predicament of being the lower-class and younger lover is Paul Russell's *Boys of Life*. Tony is seduced as a sixteen-year-old in Owen, Kentucky, by Carlos, a bohemian, avant-garde filmmaker who is passing through. Carlos is charismatic, worldly wise, and very good at sex; he gives Tony the whiskey he craves, and promises him a role in a film. Despite or because of his rural innocence, Tony already has same-sex experience. His initial response to Carlos is a combination of fascination and trepidation. Thereafter, all the sex is marvelous. Writing about the first fuck still breaks Tony up, ten years later: "suddenly I was so upset about everything, I couldn't stand it. I started crying, sobbing like some crazy drunk to think how that's all gone, nothing like that's ever going to happen again and the only thing I can do is try and remember it."[36] The sexual absorption appears reciprocal, though Carlos is not interested in being fucked. "I guess you could say he was greedy with me, but I didn't care one bit once he started in on me" (72). Carlos's exercise of power is sexy.

So, according to the narration, offered as Tony's retrospective account, it could not fairly be alleged that Tony was seduced into sexual experience which he did not want. In fact, the problem is the other way around: Tony is totally infatuated. In New York he spends the days waiting for Carlos to come home—"I'd hear him tramping up the stairs. He never knew how happy I was to see him come in that door" (62). Nor has Carlos detained Tony from heterosexual experience. He doesn't think of himself initially as queer or gay, and he does look at girls in the street—though they tend to be of boyish appearance. "Maybe it was knowing somewhere inside me I really was a queer that made me look at those women the way I did; maybe I was saying good-bye to something, even though I didn't know that's what I was doing" (64–65).

When he is abandoned by Carlos, and bored with making movies and cruising the bars, Tony allows Monica (who is somewhat boyish) to fall in love with him, take him down to Tennessee, and marry him. So eventually he picks up where he might have been if he'd just stayed among his own class in Owen—"finally back on track" (219). However, he doesn't find Monica or Tennessee sexy or interesting.

After two months in New York, Tony intuits that Carlos has no real interest in his personal development. "I grew up on Carlos right then—not that I ever thought he was going to get me through stuff, but I do think I hooked up with him back in Owen because I could see I needed some kind of help. And now that fell apart" (91). He accuses Carlos of using him. It is at this point that Carlos cements Tony's attachment by starting work on the movie with him as star. What hurts Tony crucially is the discovery that he is neither the first nor the last of Carlos's boys. Tony's dawning realization that he has been displaced and he and Carlos will never fuck together again is very painful to read. Carlos claims later that he intended to set Tony free: " 'I wanted you to learn that you wanted to go away. . . . I sent you away, I let you grow up' " (295; my elision). However, it sounds like special pleading. Carlos does this with everyone, we learn; it is how he works as an artist. He needs to break his performers to get them to realize their potential for the camera.

Tony, when he is angry, accuses Carlos of being manipulative and exploitative. However, a thought running through the narration is that people generally do what they want to do; if it had not been Carlos for Tony, it would have been somebody else. This thought governs Carlos's film technique, which relies upon improvisation to the point where the performers' fantasies emerge. Tony is adamant that the sexual practices in the films were the decisions of the actors, not under compulsion or hypnosis (177, 179). This is perhaps all very well, but if each person is responsible for his own actions, consent must be informed. When Seth tells Tony about Carlos's other boys he adds: " 'I just think people have got a right to know certain things. So they can make their own decisions, if you know what I mean. But to do that they've got to know what's what' " (150).

These questions are sharpened toward the end of the novel, as Carlos pushes his experiments with sex and power to new limits. It is disclosed that Carlos has seduced also Tony's younger brother, Ted, and that they pursued the reality of art and the freedom of the actor into increasingly violent and finally fatal courses. Carlos repeats the libertarian motif of the book: people do what they want to do, it takes two to fuck. Now Tony challenges this. "I hated this man. I hated how he stepped into my life and ruined everything he touched and then just walked out without ever look-ing back" (301).

A recurring topic, on the other hand, is where Tony might have been otherwise. Mainly through people he meets around Carlos, he becomes politically aware and personally sensitive, in ways that, he says, could not have developed in Owen, Kentucky. " 'Carlos lifted me out of all that' " (117). Intellectually, imaginatively, and morally, Tony becomes superior to the sys-tem that is going to incarcerate him indefinitely. His defense lawyer argued that Carlos was a monster; Tony is writing to set the record straight. The problem, according to *Boys of Life*, is not class or age hierarchy, and cer-tainly not the sex that goes along with them. It is Carlos's insatiable appetite for new partners, and his fluency in devising theories to justify it.

HUSTLING

Richard von Krafft-Ebing, *Psychopathia Sexualis*, case number 146: "I felt myself drawn exclusively towards powerful, youthful and entirely mascu-line individuals. . . . Since my desires are limited to persons of the lower social order, I could always find someone who could be had for money."[37]

In *Bruiser* by Richard House, Paul, an anxious Englishman, is attracted by the readiness of Adrian, a young waiter, to gratify him sexually while he pays the bills. "Despite moments of tenderness between us, it's my money that keeps him with me," he admits to himself.[38] However, this arrange-ment is satisfactory for Paul: it gives him a new confidence to express him-self sexually. He forsakes his bourgeois caution and sets out to drive from Chicago to Mexico, without proper papers, banking arrangements, or travel information, and terrified by the thought that Adrian is HIV-positive. The boy, removed from his accustomed context and subject to Paul's priorities, becomes bored and captious. His erratic and enigmatic behavior initially intrigues Paul, but then increasingly undermines his sense of prudence, order, and purpose. If initially Paul was exploiting Adrian's dependency, he becomes his caregiver, trapped by the boy's insufficiency and his own mid-dle-class sense of responsibility. "He looks like an old man, his face puffy, cheeks and jawline swollen; it is hard to understand how it all came to this" (170). Surprisingly, the novel ends with them together, escaping other com-mitments as they had wanted.

The outcome is less fortunate in *Steps Going Down* by Joseph Hansen. Darryl Cutler has always lived off older men, and now is waiting for the death of his lover/employer. When he falls for a casual pickup, Chick

Pelletier, he meets his match in vanity, selfishness, and brutality. Chick is already being kept by an older partner, and has a girlfriend as well. He demands that Cutler get him a starring part in a film, and spends his money copiously as a way of compensating for his dependence. He abuses Cutler verbally and physically. But Cutler is infatuated, and is drawn further into fraud and murder. When Chick leaves him Cutler attracts the devotion of Eduardo, a Mexican delivery boy, but Chick tips off the immigration service. "Find some nice guy with a job and a bank account, someone your own age" (74), an acquaintance warns him.[39] That seems to be the moral.

The hustler is sometimes a romanticized figure in gay writing. Mike (River Phoenix), blessed with beauty but not quite able to function by himself, spends time in a supportive group of street boys in *My Own Private Idaho* (Gus Van Sant, 1991). This is a consolation also in Pai Hsienyung's novel, *Crystal Boys*. Phil Andros meets all kinds of interesting people as he peddles himself around Chicago and San Francisco; indeed, he finds that he is himself already a legendary figure.[40] The clients are respectful, given to swapping literary quotes, and many are so sexy themselves that it is unclear why they need a hustler's services. The cops are sexy as well in their uniforms, and happy to join in. Unsurprisingly, such celebration of the hustler occurs toward the pornographic end of the spectrum of writing. As I argued in chapter 4, the function of pornography is to present images of sexual relations that are otherwise impermissible, or barely permissible. Phil Andros's adventures propose a liberty and a success that most of us can only fantasize about. To be sure, if hustling were truly so rewarding we would all be doing it; but we may like to imagine that it may be so.

Hustlers are likely exponents of the value of multiple and anonymous relations, and may well be explicit about the overwhelming of difference that they enact. Phil Andros's collection *Below the Belt and Other Stories* is dedicated to "Twelve Johns, eleven Dons, four Kennys, nine Jims, two Ikes, three Sams, two Scotts, four Garys, four Roberts, one Dean, and lots of other good guys too numerous to mention" (v). Porn star Scott O'Hara writes in his memoir, *Autopornography*, of a particular sexual encounter:

> I can't say much about that night, except that it was the most perfect night in my memory. What makes one particular night stand out so, from among the hundreds of nights of good sex that I've had? Cynically, I have to say that it's largely due to the fact that I never saw Colm again. We never had a chance to become familiarly contemptible (or is that contemptibly familiar?) toward each other.[41]

What made Colm special was his anonymity.

John Rechy's narrator in *City of Night* presents a more acerbic view of the scores (clients), hustlers, and queens. He finds his way from Texas to Times Square: "like a possessive lover—or like a powerful drug—it lured me. FASCINATION! I stopped working. . . . And I returned, dazzled, to this street. The giant sign winked its welcome: FASCINATION!"[42] He resists attempts to settle him, either as a lover or as an employee. The seductions of the scene are continuous with the dangers: "Life is lived on the brink of panic on the streets" (150)—panic generated by the vice squad, and by the prospect of finding that you are no longer young and desirable. The narrator's relation to all this is ambivalent. The others are presented as trapped in the scene, whereas the narrator, even while working it, is an observer. Which we are to take as the dominant image is unclear.

Eventually the narrator is almost persuaded by a client, Jeremy, to admit that really he wants to be loved, and has been using the passing of money as a repeated, because unsatisfactory, reassurance that he is wanted. Money will not be irrelevant, of course: Jeremy is offering full support in New York. However, this would require the narrator not just to trust himself in someone else's hands, but to admit that his response to gay sex is personal and not merely professional—that he is gay. He decides that love is a myth to which he should not surrender (after all, Jeremy has not found it himself); he prefers the reality of the "grinding streets" (370). There is no suggestion that he has been damaged, any more than anyone else in a godless world.

Hugo in Oscar Moore's *A Matter of Life and Sex* is attracted by the romance of hustling:

> He wanted to be let into the game, to join in the tawdry spectacle, dressed up with tinsel and a smile, sinister and all-knowing, feigning naivety, feigning experience, battered by fate and by pimps, teetering on the brink of the gutter and drugs, living in a nightlife world of sex, violence and cash in the hand.[43]

He is from a suburban background and goes to university, but exploiting his sexual attractions seems more fun. However, the streets have changed and there is no "fraternity of hustlers" such as he has read of in fiction. The scene is managed through an agency and is in hotel bedrooms. Initially, Hugo enjoys being attractive and skillful, but constant faking destroys his spontaneity. He makes no friends, and fails to find a sugar daddy or to meet a celebrity. Part of the lore of hustling is that you insist on your limits, what you will and will not do, and avoid dangerous situations. However, Hugo is forced. This happens also in *Close to the Knives*, David Wojnarowicz's novel. Both protagonists tell their stories with their deaths from AIDS in view.

AIDS and other sexually transmitted diseases apart, it is not obvious that the employment of sex workers is doing much *distinctive* harm to anyone—by this, I mean much harm that is not already endemic in the lower-paid, unregulated regions of market capitalism. The exploitation and humiliation is hardly less if you are working in a manufacturing sweatshop, and there may be a better prospect of the occasional thrill. Donald J. West in his study, *Male Prostitution*, finds a pattern of social malaise among the boys, but concludes that "they would have been problem personalities in any event and that involvement in street work was incidental to the disaster-laden course of their lives."[44] The exchange of sexual favors for money is, perhaps, less a perversion of egalitarian, companionable relations, than a counterpart of them.

Notwithstanding, sex that is paid for is firmly signaled as second-rate in much of our fiction. In Michael Arditti's much admired novel *Easter*, readers learn to dislike the Archdeacon; he is hostile to the sincere, conscientious, and troubled vicar and curate. So when we find that on Good Friday he conducts a masochistic scenario centered upon himself as Christ and artfully elaborating the biblical narrative, we are hardly surprised. The corruption that we intuited is exposed. Ronan, the young man who is paid to flog and humiliate the Archdeacon, is supplied by Harry, a typically sinister professional, who was corrupted when a church server; Ronan is black, inexperienced, and has no money. " 'Do you think I want [to] do this? I'm telling you I'm skint, man. I'm going mad stuck in three rooms with my mum and sisters.' " He embodies a normative perspective upon the Archdeacon's doings. "Ronan no longer knows what to think. Nothing Harry said has prepared him for such perversity." To the Archdeacon, he's one of Pilate's thugs. " 'You see the broken, bruised, bloody body in front of you; so what do you want to do to it?' " " 'Cover it up?' " Ronan suggests, artlessly. " 'No, you fool: flog it! Don't you know the gospel story?' "[45] When the Archdeacon ejaculates with a cry of " 'It is finished,' " Ronan rebels: " 'You're completely round the twist. . . . I'm not staying here' " (339; my elision). It is left to the Archdeacon's mother, in an unscripted conflation of Mary Magdalene and Mary the mother of Jesus, to get him down from the cross.

Yet is this all so contemptible? If it is not your thing then it will appear weird, but other people's fixations are always like that. Of course, it is hypocritical of the Archdeacon to use the imagery of religion, in the face of its traditional doctrines of abstinence, for sexual excitement. But if fantasy is dependent on a supply of provocative materials from the power structures in which we live, as I have been arguing, it will feature substitutions and reversals of authoritative imagery (such as that of Christianity). Must it be that fantasies featuring heterosexuals in the missionary position and trying for a baby are authentic, while more adventurous scenarios are ridiculous or evil? To whose advantage is that? Should we not, in fact, be wary of satire as a form (on the cover of my edition, Muriel Spark says, "Arditti writes about Western Christianity with pungency and satirical frankness")? Does satire not, often, insinuate a taken-for-granted set of normative assumptions?

HOUSE PARTIES

A versatile location for the cross-class liaison is the weekend house party. Here the upper-class man will feel at home, and probably keen to show off the sexy man he has captured. The lower-class partner will feel like an outsider and ill at ease, so their relationship will be tested. At the same time, the outsider may offer a challenge to the other occupants, drawing attention to their own deceptions and insecurities. The class intruder is a wild card; he doesn't know the rules, you don't know what he might do (the plays of Harold Pinter are ultimately about this).[46] The outcome, typically, finds some couples fading in commitment and others growing. Most often the outsider is cast off—illustrating the dominance of intraclass pressure over sheer sexiness.

In *Love! Valour! Compassion!*, Terrence McNally's play (filmed by Joe Mantello in 1997), everyone in the house responds to the attractions of Ramon, a young dancer of Puerto Rican origin and little education, whom John has brought with him to a gathering of old friends involved in the making of stage musicals. His strangeness is immediately registered: "A Third World boyfriend. So John Jeckyll has gone PC."[47] They discuss funding for the arts, and the need for a Diaghilev; but he would expect sexual favors. The only thing an artist should do for free is make love, Ramon declares. John, who is not a happy man, feels sidelined, and tries clumsily to assert his proprietary rights. "Can we go upstairs and fuck?" he demands. "I didn't appreciate that fucking remark in front of your friends," Ramon complains later (29). The situation is delicate, he reminds John: "Look, I'm sort of out of my element this weekend. . . . You're all old friends. You work together. You have a company. I'm just somebody you brought with you" (33; my elision). Notwithstanding, John corrects Ramon's vocabulary and calls him "Chiquita" in front of the others. We learn later that John's sexuality is fixated upon a master-and-servant scenario, deriving from an early experience with an Irish boy who worked for his father.

However, Ramon is already asserting his independence by setting out to seduce Bobby, who is blind and the partner of Gregory who owns the house. This leads to the breakup of John and Ramon, and eventually of Gregory and Bobby. However, it is when he accepts that it is Ramon who must dance the work that he can write but no longer perform that Gregory is released from his work block. Not all affairs are doomed to fail. Arthur and Perry reaffirm their fourteen-year relationship; but they are class-matched—an accountant and a lawyer. Buzz and James, both of whom are living with AIDS, fall in love. The action is finally overshadowed by AIDS, which is said to be a genocide, destroying gay life. Actually, *Love! Valour! Compassion!* displays the subculture as disconcertingly resilient.

Lyle takes Robert to meet his old friends John and Marian, in Peter Cameron's novel *The Weekend*. Lyle lives in a Brownstone house he has inherited from Tony (who was a travel writer), and has written a successful book on painting. Lyle was a visiting speaker and Robert was employed to drive him to the airport: that is how they met. Robert is a struggling young artist and a waiter in an Indian restaurant (he doesn't get on with his father, who is Indian, lives in Delhi, and makes money manufacturing counterfeit sportswear). Lyle is able to offer Robert a studio; he is attracted by his malleability—"'He listens to people; he really listens.'"[48] Robert listens mainly to Lyle:

> He found almost everything about Lyle sexy: his body, his mind, his talk, the way he climbed stairs, the way his fingers gripped a fork, blushing with tension, the way he smelled and tasted, the impossibly soft way his back and neck and shoulders congregated, the spot there, the crux of him, naked and lickable. (127)

Robert perceives Lyle as powerful, not in this or that respect, but generally, through his entire person; even his points of softness and vulnerability are powerful. Unfortunately, Lyle doesn't have much wisdom.

John and Marian (not "Mary-Anne," she insists) are too wealthy to have to work. They are old friends of Lyle, Tony was John's half brother, and he died of AIDS; so a lot is at stake when Lyle brings Robert to visit on the anniversary of Tony's death. John does his best to absent himself; under Marian's scrutiny, Robert appears not to belong. When he says "'We've just lay about all afternoon,'" Marian wants to correct him. "*Lain* about," she wants to say (103); when Lyle has a black eye from walking into a tree, John asks if Robert has hit him; his white shirt is presumed to be one he wears as a waiter. The symptomatic incident is at dinner, when Robert pulls a grape from the bunch, unaware that there are special scissors for grapes (they had belonged to Marian's grandmother). Laura, who is Italian and raunchy, takes Robert's part: " 'Oh, don't tame him!' Laura suddenly cried. 'Let him eat grapes with his fingers if he wants! Let us all be free of these stupid affectations!' " (180). Robert, who has overheard Marian saying that she doesn't like him, feels that Lyle is siding against him and leaves abruptly for the city.

Neither Cameron nor his characters quite say that class is the issue. " 'He's all wrong for Lyle,' " Marian declares (156); " 'we are not well suited,' " Lyle accepts (235). On the defensive, Lyle denies that the feeling between Robert and himself can properly be called love: " 'If you loved me—if what you feel is love—love would be a very cheap and common thing' " (189). However determined the effacement, these are class terms. My sense is that Robert offered a challenge which the others failed to meet. It is unclear, at the end, whether Lyle and he can rescue anything.

The stranger is already within the gates in Alan Hollinghurst's novel *The Spell*. Justin used to be with Alex but is now with Robin; he invites Alex down to Robin's house in the country. Alex is a civil servant and Robin is an architect who tidies up country houses; both have a lot more money and status, and are far more established in the world than the somewhat younger men to whom they are attracted. These are principally Justin, who wants to be an actor; Danny, who is Robin's son but works as gallery attendant; and Terry, the local factotum with an eye for the main chance (a cross between Alec Scudder in Forster's *Maurice* and Ron Wrigley in Angus Wilson's *Hemlock and After*). In a sequence of episodes alternating between London and weekends at Robin's house, Alex becomes accustomed to Justin's defection and falls for Danny, who becomes bored and leaves him.

Justin has a starkly instrumental idea of relationships. " 'You're like me, darling, you need someone older to look after you,' " he tells Danny. " 'I know Alex is rather shy and sensitive, but he's got plenty of money and a comfortable house and a sports car—and in bed . . . well—.' "[49] Actually, it emerges, being kept is not very good for Justin. He is bored all day, and finds himself unable to get interested in housework (which, of course, would confirm his subservient status). At one point Robin's approach affects him "like a secretary briefly disarranged by an importunate boss" (124). Danny maintains his own flat and gets a job so as not to be "a kept boy"; however, it is only casual work (141). Both Justin and Danny feel justified in undertaking flings with other, similarly placed young men. Justin tells himself "how outrageous it was of Robin to leave him locked up here, like a slave, a mistress with no life of her own" (93). Terry is available: " 'I can slip in through the back gate,' " he says (48).

The answer, it appears, is to avoid relations of manifest, one-way dependence. Robin and Justin get onto a better footing eventually: the trigger is Justin's inheriting money of his own, so that he is no longer beholden. Alex takes up with Nick, who is of similar background and interests to himself and slightly older. The (relatively) egalitarian liaison wins out, then, though Alex finds that the spell of Danny lingers.

8

RACE

HUMILIATIONS AND AFFIRMATIONS

Hierarchies of gender, age, and class afford a range of attractive scenarios for sexual power play. Age difference, for instance, may plug into fathers and sons, and teachers and pupils; these may be entirely amiable relations, though they may also afford scope for the enactment of violent and exploitative fantasies. The scenarios that race sustains are centrally and indelibly embedded in slavery, colonialism, apartheid, and servitude; they reference actual practices of torture and ill-treatment of such extremity that they have been outlawed in many countries. Historically, even benevolent relations between white people and people of color have characteristically involved condescension and stereotyping. It is still hard to think of intimate relations between black and white men without invoking a heritage of dominance and subordination.

In an encyclopedia article on "Black Gay Americans," Ward Houser posits a range of responses to this heritage, often involving role substitutions, reversals, and loops. For some it seems appropriate for a white male to take a "female" role in a mixed-race liaison, because this may compensate for the historic dominance of white men. Others, "being more comfortable in the submissive role, generalize from their experience of whites as holding the major power positions of American society to perceive white males as particularly sexually powerful, and so are attracted to them." Correspondingly, some whites may "feel more comfortable dominating" effeminate black gays, whereas others are drawn to more "macho" black men because they are supposed to be more virile. (We might hesitate there at the expression "feel more comfortable." A good deal of the published evidence suggests that such preferences may be passionately driven; as I observe in chapter 3, fantasy is as likely to involve compulsion as freedom.) Even those who are not much affected by those hierarchical factors, Houser says, are likely to be involved in "the attractiveness of the 'different,' curiosity, class differences, rebellion against social custom, or a belief that race should not be a factor in discriminating between potential sexual partners."[1]

There is no reason to suppose that gay men and lesbians will be unusually progressive about other disadvantaged groups. In the 1970s and 1980s, Puerto Ricans seem to have been regarded in a notably functional light on the New York gay scene. In *The Farewell Symphony* Edmund White remarks casually, of a man he sleeps with: "he was himself bewitched by Puerto Ricans, as who was not"; the question is so rhetorical that it doesn't get a question mark. Midwestern boys, in particular, are said to find Puerto Ricans exotic.[2] In Andrew Holleran's *Dancer from the Dance*, Puerto Rican boys are ubiquitous, beautiful, and said to have "big cocks."[3] They unload boxes at a store, exterminate roaches, and carry messages; they play handball in empty lots; they are never within the social orbit of the narrator and his friends. Malone "loved those boys, as did I, to be among them was enough; he was in thrall to them, he was in the thrall of Puerto Ricans" (188). Again: "My dick would straighten out like a divining rod, forcing me to follow more than twenty blocks in fruitless pursuit" when a Puerto Rican passes, we are told in David B. Feinberg's *Eighty-Sixed*.[4] There is no sense that these enthusiasms might be personally and politically problematic; no concern about how it might feel to be the object of such casual attentions.

To be sure, sexual attraction frequently involves objectification. But race supplies the most ready-made, and hence the most crude, repertoire—and all no more than *skin deep*. In Lyle Glazier's story, "Chester," the narrator, who prefers black men, remarks of a partner: "I thought he had no formal education, no book learning, no academic interest in literature, music, the fine arts. I erased our difference. I was engulfed by his brown warmth. He was pure sexuality—gentle, placid, as open to love as the earth is open to the sun. I loved his brown against my white."[5] The narrator tries to make his partner a blank, erasing every attribute but two: sex and skin color—and finally just skin color. Further, racial differences are usually permanent. As Rhonda Cobham remarks, the youth in ancient Greece was expected to accept homosexual advances while a boy, on the assumption that this was an interim stage before he became himself a citizen. But you don't grow out of racial subordination, even if you change class (in the language of race, you remain a "boy").[6] Indeed, the white mentor may feel threatened at the prospect of his black protégé rising in the social scale. In Paul Thomas Cahill's story, "The Reunion," Rodger (white) has left Julius (black) because he couldn't cope with his being successful: " 'I couldn't be in charge, couldn't take care of you as I thought I was expected to, not when we were . . . equals.' "[7]

James Baldwin in *Another Country* depicts Rufus as driven to violence, despair, and suicide by his inability to handle the racial milieu in which he is trapped. Rufus's sister Ida is tougher, at the cost of total separation: " 'If any *one* white person gets through to you, it kind of destroys your—singlemindedess. They say that love and hate are very close together. Well, that's a fact.' "[8] Black Panther Eldridge Cleaver, in his notorious attack on Baldwin in *Soul on Ice*, alleged that *Another Country* displays "the most grueling, agonizing, total hatred of the blacks, particularly of [Baldwin] himself, and the most shameful, fanatical, fawning, sycophantic love of the whites." In Cleaver's view, "many Negro homosexuals, acquiescing in this racial death wish, are outraged and frustrated because in their sickness they are unable to have a baby by the white man."[9] Actually, *Another Country* is not incompatible with Cleaver's hostile analysis: it amounts to an extended demonstration that cross-racial affairs are irretrievably doomed, because of hang-ups such as Cleaver posits—and, anyway, are scarcely tolerated by people in New York (let alone the South). The good sex, in Baldwin's novel, is between white men. Notwithstanding, Huey Newton, another Panther, envisaged an alliance between the black, feminist, and gay movements, and labeled Cleaver himself a repressed homosexual.[10] These concerns are still politically active in the United States around Minister Louis Farrakhan and the Nation of Islam.

There may be scarcely less objectification when the conjuncture of sexuality and race is offered as the ground of spectacular harmony. In the films *My Beautiful Laundrette* (Stephen Frears, 1985) and *The Wedding Banquet* (Ang Lee, 1993), a miraculously egalitarian, racially blind gay relationship is presented as a magical opportunity for the overthrow of (merely) cultural misunderstanding. The boys in *My Beautiful Laundrette* inhabit a world in which "Asian" and "skinhead" are the most antipathetic terms, but between the two of them race is unremarkable. In *The Wedding Banquet*, Wai-Tung's Taiwanese family produces intense cultural disruption in the relationship of Wai-Tung and Simon, but the two principals appear ideally harmonious in every other respect, and totally unaware of any complication in the conjunction of sexuality and racial difference. Racial blindness appears comparably in Marshall Moore's story "Everybody Loves the Musée d'Orsay." In this instance a Sino/American couple are living happily in Malaysia, when the American mother and the demands of family intrude clumsily upon them. Again, race itself appears to be merely incidental for the two men.[11] *The Crying Game* (Neil Jordan, 1992) presents transvestism as the big shock, while making racial difference of little account between Fergus and Dil.[12] This instance is complicated by the fact that the white man, Fergus, is Irish—of a subjugated people—whereas Jodi, who is black and from Antigua (formally independent) has signed up to fight for the imperial power. The simply English person is Dil, who is of mixed race.

IMPERIAL RESIDUES

The alleged inadequacies of colonial subjects position them as the inferiors that witness to European superiority. Fiction indicates that colonial Europeans spent a good part of their time producing anxious, self-justifying stories about the relationship between the natives and themselves. If colonial fiction "can demonstrate that the barbarism of the native is irrevocable, or at least very deeply ingrained, then the European's attempt to civilize him can continue indefinitely, the exploitation of his resources can proceed without hindrance, and the European can persist in enjoying a position of moral superiority," Abdul JanMohamed observes.[13]

In the midst of apartheid, South Africa produced stories exploring the rewards and difficulties of black-white liaisons. David's initial defining experience, at the start of John Sandys's novel *Against the Tide*, is on the beach, with "a golden-brown gypsy boy with dark, curly hair."[14] David is in his late twenties and can't settle in England after World War II, personally or to an occupation; there are said to be more opportunities in South Africa. On arrival there he immediately gets invited to a party of same-sex "Coloureds." They have "dark-skinned shining bodies, beautiful to behold, muscular, deep-chested, narrow-hipped, long-legged" (58); they are "young, virile, gentle and uninhibited, with music in their souls and laughter in their hearts" (61). However, David is quickly told that mixing is not tolerated. He despises the local white men he sees at gay parties, and the married couple who take him in and try to seduce him.

David becomes a commercial traveler; it is love at first sight when he is assigned a Zulu driver. "Ugi was the golden-brown gypsy boy and he was in love. He asked God to bless them both" (82). Ugi, we learn, fell in love immediately with David. Their meetings are dangerous and desperate. David is distraught when he learns that Ugi has a wife and children. However, Ugi introduces him to Guy, another white man with a black lover, who explains that marriage is required by local custom. Guy draws David into a circle of clandestine black-white couples, but even here he dislikes the whites.

"'Why do they refer to a grown man—a husband and a father as 'boy'?'" David demands (126). Nonetheless, his relationship with Ugi depends on difference. "Ugi gave a wide smile. 'Me happy to be David's boy,' he said proudly'" (126–27). Ugi uses the name given to him by white employers; David himself thinks of him as "this beautiful child" (87). Ugi apparently has a preference for male lovers: he thinks of himself, in the idiom of his people, as a "woman-man" (140).

However, Ugi has educated himself and gives David the best advice on how to establish himself financially. He sees a market opportunity, making and selling lampshades; he becomes the creative force in the business. Compare Alice Walker's *The Color Purple*, where Shug and Celie secure their future by setting up a business making pants: it appears that small-scale capitalist development is the key to security, advancement, and affluence. David and Ugi pay no attention to the political situation, and consequently are taken by surprise when business confidence is destroyed by the Sharpeville Massacre. Eventually they are driven from South Africa, but their love survives and they will start again in England.

In *Against the Tide*, the South African political situation figures mainly as threatening David's personal and business affairs. In Stephen Gray's *Time of Our Darkness*, the personal bears a political message. This novel is set in South Africa during the school boycott which led eventually to the release of Nelson Mandela and the end of white rule. Pete has a fading gay relationship with André, who is Afrikaans and an airline pilot. Pete is a teacher at a private school and well aware of the rule, "never to lay a hand in amorous expectation on a pupil."[15] Disley, the token scholarship black student in the class, age thirteen, arrives at his house, evidently in need of support. The boy seduces Pete, and they become lovers. Like Ugi, Disley has an independent understanding of sex between men—he knows already about single-sex hostels, mine compounds, André (Pete's partner), and André's pickup.

In the metropolitan, egalitarian mode, *Time of Our Darkness* is inclined to play down the sexual significance of hierarchy between Pete and Disley. "We were more than equal in the dark," Pete declares, referring, I suppose, to genital endowment (78). He does not admit to any special thrill from age and class difference, and appears not to have entertained any prior idea of sex with black Africans.

I was brought up not to touch black skin. Black skin was unhealthy, scaly like a reptile's, gave you TB. A whole country has been divided on that prejudice. When I was a child my mother pulled me out of the reach of the nanny, feeding me herself, bathing me. When I was at primary school we'd run down the corridor, make a circle around the cleaner on her hands and knees, reassemble, not having touched black flesh. (138).

For Pete, skin color is a revelation rather than an abiding fascination. "Do I need to describe the sensation that I experienced as the blackness went out of Disley's skin for me and I felt the person beneath. [Again, there is no question mark.] All of him" (138). In this passage Disley's skin is sexy not because it is black, but because, for Pete, it is no longer that. In a typically egalitarian gesture, Pete erases the blackness of Disley's skin and finds "the person beneath. All of him." Even in such an extreme situation, difference is said to be unimportant.

Yet, contradictorily, Pete does proceed to find positive value in Disley's skin. He imagines a visit from the police:

Let the man in the raincoat come. I had a few things to tell him: about black skin, about how it felt, the texture, the grain. And about loss. And about deprivation and humiliation. I was sick with it, as my white, police-supporting countrymen were, but they were sick with their aversion for black skin. (138)

Now we have positive qualities of texture and grain; Disley's skin is relevant after all, it does contribute to an erotics of difference.

According to Gray, in an interview, the age difference in his novel is symbolic. His idea was that "the entire impetus of the uprising in South Africa in the mid-1980s, during which children assumed the role of adults and adults became, to say the least, vindictively childish, should be acted out literally."[16] The message is that the country has been plunged into turmoil by a pointless phobia, and that children, by refusing to learn Afrikaans in schools, are leading the revolt. Actually, black skin has its own attractions and the children are wise. For the time being—the time of darkness—the system wins: Disley achieves not a gay relationship but martyrdom in the cause of his people.

Evidently, South Africans have not finished with this scenario. A more gloomy version appears in "A Son's Story" by Tony Peake.[17] Paul (white) is having a loving sexual relationship with young Memphis (black), who looks after the garden, and whom Paul is coaching in English literature. The relationship is destroyed when a grossly violent dispute between ANC and

Inkatha factions draws Memphis back to his family home. In his distress, and perhaps resentment, Memphis tears up all the literary books. Unfortunately, we learn nothing more precise about his feelings, since he is given almost nothing to say. This is partly because the action is seen from the viewpoint of an English visitor, a born-again Christian—a rather easy target.

A traditional skill of the fiction writer is entering into unfamiliar consciousnesses. Yet Sandys in *Against the Tide* makes little attempt to explain Ugi's thoughts to the reader. We don't know what the two men talk about when they are together, except business and how beautiful and sexy each finds the other. When David (upset by Ugi's visit to his wife and child) is unfaithful, we are told Ugi's response: "Ugi had been badly hurt, and his first impulse was to leave David, to live only for his wife and children, to give up being a woman-man. But he loved David deeply, and when he surfaced after the initial shock he sensed that with time and patience the memory of that awful day would blur, and he would be able to forgive" (140). This is helpful, but perfunctory compared to the central narrative role of David's thoughts. After twelve years they go to Europe together, and David ponders Ugi's difference:

> David lay, thinking about Ugi's early days and the way he had changed. "I wish I knew what he thinks—how he thinks. To be taken out of a tribal society and thrust into this strange way of life is a challenge which has needed a superhuman adjustment, yet he seems to succeed without effort. I am so proud of him . . ." (150)

David allows Ugi to see that he is thinking along these lines. Ugi objects, forcibly: " 'I see David is still conscious that I am black. . . . I am no novelty. I am not different.' He stared hard at David. 'I have the same emotions, the same feelings, I have the same red blood.' " "David was hurt, and ashamed into silence" (151; my elisions). This is perhaps the only point at which a distance is allowed between David and the narration. Still, David feels able to pronounce that Ugi " 'now has a well-developed mind and a personality' " (165), as though he had previously lacked these attributes.

Similarly, in *Against the Tide*, it would be marvelous to know what Disley thinks about it all. We may infer, with Pete, that Disley is impressed with his lifestyle; he has thrown in his lot with education (while the rest of his township is rioting); Pete can take him forward. Pete's worry is that Disley will underestimate the gap between their social positions, and will imagine that by imitating Pete's amiable manner he can progress to a comparable state of affluence and self-determination. The predicament is manifest when Disley is returning to his township: there is no point in Pete giving him a hair drier because they have no electricity. However, Disley's self-possession, boosted by his success at school, enables him to inspire his people. If the narrator in *Time of Darkness* does not presume to take us into Disley's consciousness, the reader is encouraged to share a respect for the other dimensions in his life, in the township and in a rural area that they visit.

Perhaps it is not possible, still, for a white South African to presume to interpret the thoughts of a black person. J. M. Coetzee, in his prize-winning novel *Disgrace*, doesn't attempt this; we get only the viewpoint of the white, male protagonist. A black African has a large influence on the outcome of the action, but his thoughts and feelings remain mysterious and ominous. Perhaps such reticence is ultimately a sign of respect: what white people have done to black people in South Africa makes it impossible for one to speak for, or through, the other. Yet it must also undermine any humanistic or paternal argument, that all peoples are, or can become, one. Actually, as Patricia Duncker points out, Coetzee has another character of restricted representation, a white lesbian.[18] She also has no independent consciousness. She does have a lot of conversation with the protagonist, but, being traumatized, she is unable or unwilling to explain how she feels. This is not just a matter of fair shares, so to speak. If Coetzee were to assay the consciousness of these others, he would have to consider more carefully the claims these people might reasonably make upon each other and upon South Africa.

Homosexuality is shown as enhancing the opportunity for exploitation and humiliation in V. S. Naipaul's novella, *In a Free State*. Bobby, who is white, works as some kind of civil servant in an independent East African country, in which the president and the military are in the process of overthrowing the more traditional rule of the king. Bobby does this work not because it allows him to lord it over black African people, but because it enables him to abase himself before them in ways that are actually patronizing and condescending, and calculated to shore up his fragile emotional stability. He had a nervous breakdown; " 'Africa saved my life.' "[19] Bobby tells himself that he is recognizing the humanity of the African, but becomes crazily enraged when confronted with irrefutable indifference or hostility toward himself. He seeks to ingratiate himself with Africans by wearing what is called a native-style shirt; this annoys an army officer and he is severely beaten up.

Bobby acknowledges an effeminate side to his nature. For him Africa is empty spaces, long drives on open roads. " 'You want lift? You big boy, you no go school? No, no, you no frighten. Look, I give you shilling. You hold my hand. Look, my colour, your colour. I give you shilling buy schoolbooks.

Buy books, learn read, get big job. When I born again I want your colour' "
(109). The key moment is the color juxtaposition, the touching of the black
and white skin. Unfortunately for Bobby it doesn't always work. He chats
up a South African in a hotel bar: " 'If I come into the world again I want
to come with your colour.' His voice was low . . . his fingers moved until
they were over one of the Zulu's. . . . Then, without moving his hand or
changing his expression, the Zulu spat in Bobby's face" (107; my elisions).

Although Naipaul dwells upon the inadequacies of African regimes, he
appears to share the opinion of President Sam Nujoma of Namibia and
President Robert Mugabe of Zimbabwe, that homosexuality is a corrupt
European import. His main theme, in this offensive and tremendously written book, is that relations with Africans are impossible. When they are not
threatening or actually brutal, they are ridiculous: "The frightened boy
brought in the soup plate by plate, pressing his thumbs on the rims. He
walked with a stoop, raising his knees high; his big feet, loosely hinged at
the ankles, flapped up and down" (134). Above all, for Naipaul, these people are black; the narrative returns obsessively to their blackness. The only
man more objectionable than the black African is the white man who takes
him seriously, and no one but a pathetic, damaged queer is going to do that.
Naipaul's story shows, in effect, what happens when you allow the native
to get the whip hand.

Angus Wilson takes third world peoples more seriously, though his novel
As If by Magic is not free of suggestions that they may be amusing, irrational, mysterious, and dangerous. However, it does offer a significant challenge, from within a gay framework, to the complacency of empire. Hamo
Langmuir, a famous plant geneticist, tall and clumsy, has such exacting
fantasy requirements that he has driven away Leslie, his devoted partner,
because at twenty-five he is too old and has to shave. Hamo has found a
network of rent boys, but is unable to cope with any sexual relation that
might become personal. His sexual opportunities are transformed when he
is sent on a world tour to observe the success of "Magic," the new rice
which he has bred, and which is transforming the agro-economy of the
developing world. He passes in a haze through Japan, Indonesia, and South
Asia, becoming increasingly bold in pursuit of the Fairest Youth, and
grossly disrespectful toward his courteous and kind hosts, whose folly consists merely of embeddedness in a social milieu in which there are manners, decencies, and ongoing expectations. " 'Mr Langford, we are here a
small community. You have come among us without respect.' "[20]

Above all, it is difficult for the boys whom Hamo has accosted to carry
on as before in their communities; he imagines he can make it all right by

writing checks. His remark, that if a Singhalese serving boy, Muthu, gets into trouble he will take him to England, leads the boy to run away from a family where he has been well treated. " 'What can you do with the boy in England? He is a good boy. But he is ignorant. What will he do there?' " his mistress, Mrs. Dissawardene asks (282). This is a pertinent question—we know that Hamo's attraction to Muthu will last only while he is young. He catches fleeting glimpses of Muthu everywhere he goes (to him, one beautiful youth is much like another), and makes desperate attempts to find him. People die; the forces in play are entirely beyond Hamo's control.

These interferences in local mores are continuous with the intrusion effected by Magic rice, which is so productive that small farms on poor land are no longer viable. Muthu, for instance, might have returned to his village, but their land is marginal and Magic means that they wouldn't be able to feed him. A homophobic official accuses:

> I suggest that instead of insulting your host by buggering his servants, you look for your leavings in the slums of the cities of Asia. Luckily your very valuable scientific rationalisation of our local agriculture has made sure that the bazaars and public places are filled with the scum overflowing from the waters of hopeless paddy fields. If anyone has such low tastes, they are always ready to oblige for the price of a bowl of rice. (176)

Hamo submits a report calling for social conditions to be taken into account in agrarian innovation, but his employers ignore it. I admire *As If by Magic* for the sharp light it throws upon metropolitan gay mores, from within a gay perspective that may still endorse the quest for the Fairest Youth and his potential to respond. Also, it illuminates the continuity between psychosexual and sociopolitical hierarchies: Hamo's private quest is implicated in his professional practice.

On the opening page of Alan Hollinghurst's novel, *The Swimming-Pool Library*, Will Beckwith, the protagonist, admires a black maintenance worker on the Underground: "The black was looking at his loosely cupped hands: he was very aloof, composed, with an air of massive, scarcely conscious competence—I felt more than respect, a kind of tenderness for him."[21] There is a similar moment in the closing pages of the novel.

Will's new boyfriend, we learn at once, is black, seventeen, and from Stratford East (Will is twenty-five). Will is besotted: "Oh, the ever-open softness of black lips; and the strange dryness of the knots of his pigtails, which crackled as I rolled them between my fingers, and seemed both dead and half-erect" (3). Apparently the enthusiasm is reciprocated: "Then he would give up and fall recklessly on top of me on the sofa, panting in my face, kissing me, full of clumsy humour and longing" (13). Will is in charge. The relationship takes place entirely on his territory, and he expresses his passion with playful spankings.

Will admits to his friend James that his world and Arthur's are too far apart for a love relationship; "'It must be just an infatuation'" (20). Nonetheless, he does think of himself as "in love" with Arthur—the more so because of his (alleged) limitations:

> Even when he spoke, in his basic, unimaginative way, I felt almost sick with desire and compassion for him. Indeed, the fact that he had not mastered speech, that he laboured towards saying the simplest things, that his vocal expressions were prompted only by the strength of his feelings, unlike the camp, exploitative, ironical control of my own speech, made me want him more. . . . But in sex he lost his awkwardness. . . . It was a kind of gift for giving. (64; my elisions)

The dichotomy Will produces here is not ungenerous—his own mode of speech is not more attractive. Yet his is the language privileged in the book's narration. An antiracist will surely wonder whether Will might not have found more various qualities in Arthur if he had not been so ready to stereotype him.

In fact, Arthur is not quite as dumb as Will likes to believe. He finds Will's speech strange and funny: "Odd words seemed to amuse or offend him, and he gave urchin imitations of my speech. 'Arse-hale,' he would drawl. 'Get orf my arse-hale'" (presumably we should be hearing the entire narration in this upper-class accent). Will is quite disconcerted by such role reversals: "Sometimes I laughed graciously too, and did even posher imitations of his mimicry, knowing no one was listening. Sometimes I caught him and gave him what he was asking for" (14). Will is unnerved until he has reasserted his mastery.

When Arthur becomes trapped in the flat by some obscure, drug-related gangsterism in his family, their incompatibility becomes overwhelming for Will. They fall into a fluctuation between hostility, sexual violence, and sentimentality: "Now it became a murky business, a coupling in which we both exploited each other, my role as protector mined by the morbid emotion of protectiveness. I saw him becoming more and more my slave and my toy, in a barely conscious abasement which excited me even as it pulled me down" (31). It is unclear whether this is to be seen as an inevitable, natural corruption, or the consequence of Arthur's artificial confinement.

What, we may ponder, should Will and Arthur have been doing? They might have avoided each other, on the axiom that mixed-race couples are inevitably exploitative. They might each have retained their racial interest while looking out for someone of their own class and age, reasoning that taking on several hierarchies at once is too ambitious. They might have gone into therapy together, so that Will might learn to outgrow his domineering impulses and Arthur might receive assertiveness training. But would that have helped? Will positions Arthur as a simple and primitive counterpart because that is what turns him on. As James notes in his diary, " 'yet again he had picked on someone vastly poorer & dimmer than himself—younger too. I don't think he's ever made it with anyone with a degree' " (218). Is it wrong, or a mistake, to try to relate to someone of a different educational background? I like to think that they might have proceeded in something like the way they do in the novel, but with Will taking as much trouble to understand, engage, and please Arthur as Arthur is probably taking over him.

A partly comparable pattern is disclosed by Charles, who is eighty-three. His diaries of interwar life record an alternation between idealization of young black men and casual cottaging (sex in public toilets); the love of his life was a Sudanese boy, Taha, whom he brought back to London as his servant. Charles has regarded this as a noble commitment, but Will suggests that it is paternalistic, seeing adults as children (this is rich, coming from Will). Charles reasserts that there was in the colonial service " 'this absolute adoration of black people. . . . I've always had to be among them, you know, negroes' " (242; my elision). Whether Charles's mode is preferable, personally, politically, and ethically, is hard to say. Anyway, it appears to have degenerated in modern conditions: he now uses his hold over his retinue of beneficiaries to involve them in pornographic movies.

Racial hierarchy is not just Will's and Arthur's thing. It is the outcome of historic imperial relations. Will sees Abdul, the chef, "abstractly sharpening his knife on the steel and gazing at me as if I were a meal" (42). Eventually, Abdul is to have Will across a chopping table in the kitchen, tenderized with hard slaps and lubricated with corn oil. This is the only time Will is the insertee; Abdul is Taha's son; the empire fucks back. Again, Britain may retain the Falkland/Malvinas Islands, but imperial corruption is suggested by the exchange with Gabriel, a wealthy Argentinian, who is visiting London to buy pornography which he can't get in his own, less decadent country.

David Alderson rejects the idea that The Swimming-Pool Library is "an attempt to lay bare the roots of present-day sexual projections in historically grounded power relations."[22] I agree that the novel cannot be enlisted

for an anticolonial agenda; it does not sustain a coherent critique of imperial relations. Rather, as Alderson shows, it tends nostalgically to set an
imperialist and preliberation past against a degraded present, now (at the
time of narration) menaced additionally by AIDS. Nonetheless, the novel
does disclose structural relations between imperialism and racism, in the
formative mid-twentieth century and on into the present. Also, it exposes
Will's delusion that he can be free of history. His self-centered personal
life is of a piece with his general discovery that he has been arrogant in
supposing that he is free, autonomous, and without responsibility. Hollinghurst does not condemn imperialism, together with its interpersonal out-
growths; he explores the seductive and distasteful erotic opportunities for
people living in its wake, and locates the sexual energies which they may
still release.

What the protagonists find in *As If by Magic* and *The Swimming-Pool
Library* is that they are less in control of their destinies than they had
thought. This theme is to be expected when the decline of empire is at
stake: western Europeans do not rule the world any more. It is also continuous with the argument of this book, that our psychic life is organized along
the lines of the main hierarchies that determine our economic, social, and
political lives at large. Hamo and Will make their personal choices, but they
are structured by the imperial scenarios within which they operate. Hamo's
fantasies are those of the European intruder upon South Asia, from the
eighteenth century to the sexual tourism of today. Will's desires are continuous with those which Charles exercised in the Sudan.

SISTERS AND BROTHERS

For many lesbians and gay men of color, cross-racial relations such as I
have been describing spell bad news. The endemic complications and hesitations emerge in a candid and courageous late-night television discussion
among three lesbians of color and three gay men of color, *Doing It with You
Is Taboo* (SOI for Channel 4, 1993). Some of the contributors are in or ready
to contemplate relationships with whites, some not. Either way, two main
alternative propositions emerge: (1) black/white couples are to be avoided
because between such people race is bound to be important, and destructive; (2) a black/white couple is fine because, for the speaker and his or her
partner at least, race is insignificant. A third proposition, that black/white
difference might be both central and rewarding, is not entertained.

This pattern has occurred elsewhere in this book: difference is all right so long as it doesn't make any difference. It appears again in the British compilation, *Lesbians Talk: Making Black Waves* (1993). Relationships with white women are vastly problematic because, with the best will in the world, hegemonic white racism is so insidious. Some of the women canvassed eschew them altogether. Yet such relations may be "healthy," the editors say. One woman concurs: "I don't think making love to a White woman is any different from making love to a Black woman. All my life in this country I've had four beautiful relationships. Three were with White women and the fourth was with a Black woman." For another, conversely, "the issue of racism was always there. You cannot escape from racism."[23] The tendency of my argument, I realize, has been to endorse any kind of sexual agenda that promises to work. However, at certain points the psychological and political risks may be too great; these troubled accounts of cross-race liaisons reveal an intensity that bespeaks not only decades of personal discrimination but the histories of peoples.

Fictional and autobiographical treatments rehearse the problems. In Steven Corbin's novel *Fragments That Remain*, Skylar (black) and Evan (white) are probably breaking up, mainly because of continuous bickering about race. "I think Evan likes black people for all the wrong reasons," Skylar observes.[24] So what reasons are these? Judging from Evan, they appear to be taking the opportunity to be patronizing and self-congratulatory about one's liberalism, while maintaining a subdued but persistent level of racist sniping. Skylar declares, in anger, that Evan's attraction to blacks is like "the master leering at the slave" (173–74).

Progress between the two men occurs when Evan sees that Skylar has a point: " 'I do love black people, their passion, their exoticism, their colorfulness, but maybe I don't look beyond that' " (235). What would one see "beyond"? It might be the fullness of the individual, but Corbin encourages his reader to think rather of the lived realities of racial prejudice, at large and in the relationship. The main point, Corbin is perhaps saying, is not whether people's sexual fantasies follow racial divisions, but that each person should give adequate recognition to the situation of the other. This means the white man attempting to get some distance from an almost inevitable white viewpoint.

That is surely possible at a rational level. But what about the underlying fantasies? For if, after all, racial difference is the basis of the attraction, that difference is manifest, in our societies, as inequality. Unfortunately, Corbin gives little indication of what Skylar and Evan fantasize about or do in bed, so it is hard to envisage how far and in what ways their interaction depends on hierarchy.[25] Corbin protects Skylar from the sissy-stigma by having him tell his brother "a million times, all gay men don't get fucked. He's said it so much, I believe he's one of them" (260). In fact it is not easy to see what Skylar, who is unusually self-possessed about both gayness and race, gets from the relationship with Evan. While all the characters, including Skylar and Evan, make moral progress during the action of the novel, it remains unlikely, at the end, that Skylar and Evan can live together again.

In Larry Duplechan's novel *Eight Days a Week*, Johnnie Ray Rousseau is a singer, taking after his mother, in the shadow of his handsome brother. He experiences himself as unattractive and takes Barbra Streisand as his "hero" (note that Streisand's main film romances show Jews connecting with gentiles). Johnnie's desire-to-be produces a corresponding desire-for: he fantasizes that he might attract a blond hulk—"a lover. A husband. Some impossible combination of Tab Hunter, Rick Nelson and Steve Reeves."[26] At school Johnnie attaches himself to sporty white boys, abhorring his own "flat nose and (to me) overlarge lips" (25). A friend tells him that he has become " 'the all-too-willing victim of America's white-supremacist, master-race plantation mentality.' " Whatever the reason, Johnnie replies, he still likes blonds (28).

He seems to have found what he wants in Keith Keller. Johnnie's adulation of whites tends to place him in the "sissy" role, but he takes up body-building and is delighted when Keith likes to be fucked in turn. It transpires nonetheless that Keith really wants Johnnie in the role of housewife. He starts calling Johnnie "K. T.," because he looks like Tutankhamen ("King Tut," but also "Katie," I think; 186). Keith is unable to cope with Johnnie's musician's lifestyle, and his possessiveness breaks up the relationship. However, Keith is not altogether in the wrong. Johnnie admits that his response to the standard message in the contact ads—" 'No fats, fems or blacks, please' "—coming on top of his own initial lack of confidence, is to welcome, flirtatiously, every available instance of white sexual interest in him; he regards it as a triumph over the prevailing racist disconfirmation. "The prettier, the blonder, the more Aryan the man, the bigger (if not more permanent) the sense of victory at the sight of the man's fair head bobbing between my thighs. I suppose I truly am, as Snookie often tells me, a sick, sick woman" (197–98). Even at the moment of his proclaimed victory Johnnie types himself, self-deprecatingly, as female: race and gender line up in a classic conflation of subordinate roles. He cannot extract himself from disconfirmation and stigma while he stays within the hierarchical framework. Nonetheless, Johnnie moves on to a valuable relationship with another white man, so it appears that cross-racial affairs are not doomed.[27]

If feelings of racial inferiority and superiority may disturb cross-racial liaisons, they may also interfere with black-on-black relations. Audre Lorde's inspirational commitment to black women, as she presents it in *Zami*, does not occur spontaneously. Among school friends she "never mentioned how enticing and frightening I found their strange blonde- and red- and chestnut-colored secrets that peeked out from beneath their pulled-up half-slips."[28] Lorde's early affairs are with white women. Even in Mexico, where she feels suddenly at home, her main relationship is with a white woman. " 'How beautiful and brown you are,' " Eudora says (144). Back in New York in the 1950s, there appears to be little choice; the only organized scene is white. "It seemed that loving women was something that other Black women just didn't do" (155). The few that did found themselves "sleeping with the same white women. We recognized ourselves as exotic sister-outsiders who might gain little from banding together" (153). "[W]e seldom looked into each other's Black eyes lest we see our own aloneness and our own blunted power mirrored in the pursuit of darkness" (197–98). Lorde and her friends colluded in this scene, though they resented the racist admission policies of the bars, because it was the only one they could find. Muriel, her lover, admired by Lorde for her "paleness" (159), believed that lesbians were all equal in their outsiderhood: " 'We're all niggers,' she used to say, and I hated to hear her say it" (177).

Lorde makes progress as a lesbian and a black woman through a culminating affair with Afrekete (Kitty): "her chocolate skin and deep, sculptured mouth reminded me of a Benin bronze" (214). She evokes a Caribbean island in Harlem:

> And I remember Afrekete, who came out of a dream to me always being hard and real as the fire hairs along the underedge of my navel. She brought me live things from the bush, and from her farm set out in cocoyams and cassava—those magical fruit which Kitty bought in the West Indian markets along Lenox Avenue in the 140s or in the Puerto Rican *bodegas* within the bustling market over on Park Avenue. (218; Lorde's emphasis)

This is both impressive and limiting. Some black women may find such determined cultivation of the exotic a high price for a color-affirmative relationship. In the early 1970s, Lorde "began to live together permanently" with her daughter, her son, and her white lover, Frances.[29]

Lorde's achievement is to write positively of black-on-black lovers without suppressing the complications. She enlists her mother as an honorary dyke, on the ground that she was a "powerful woman" (6), but is this enough? She seems a monstrous abuser to me. Despite Lorde's famous skepticism about dismantling the house with the master's tools, the two projects she declares at the start of *Zami*—to be both male and female, and to replace the mother-father-child triad with grandmother-mother-daughter—aspire to co-opt the power system of the heterosexual family. Anna Wilson finds here "a crucial lack of alternative conceptualisations through which to imagine community."[30] In fact, Katie King notes, despite her lack of comment on butch/femme roles, Lorde characteristically assumes the dominant and protective role of a "top."[31] In her relationship with Muriel she adds fifteen years to her age in order to secure this role (*Zami*, 160, 165).

Lesbians of color continue to confront these questions. Ekua Omosupe ponders:

> when my white lover sees my Black face, does she read in it that I am the mythological, strong Black woman who is more stick than flesh? Am I the dark exotic? Am I the testimony to herself and others that she is not racist, but quite liberal? Does she see the face of her family's maid who was paid to love her and to take care of her because mother and father were too busy to be bothered?[32]

My argument is that we have to entertain the prospect that the answer to at least some of these questions is Yes; that such residues are inevitable; and that they may not always be unfortunate. Jackie Goldsby tells how she and her partner have carefully examined their motives to make sure that neither of them is "succumbing to internalized racism. We say this, even to ourselves, even though we know differently: where, in the context of lesbian political discourse on race, can we acknowledge that our knowingly crossing boundaries of race and class *is* part of our desire for each other?"[33]

For many African American gay men, the most significant pressures come from their own black communities. William G. Hawkeswood reports that gay black men in Harlem generally live there "because they prefer black men as friends and lovers and because they prefer to live closer to family and other relatives. Thus they avoid prolonged contact with whites," and rarely experience racism. They enjoy a generally supportive environment, despite occasional instances of verbal abuse, mostly from youths. "Generally they feel that gays are more tolerated and better accepted in Harlem than they are in mainstream America," partly because there are more pressing issues (poverty, unemployment, poor education, teenage pregnancies, drugs, AIDS).[34] This may be true. However, many of the contributors to major anthologies of African American gay experience—*In the Life*, edited by Joseph Beam, and *Brother to Brother*, edited by Essex Hemphill—record anguish, alienation, and damage in their childhood and youth, as they suffered catcalls of sissy and faggot from within the black community.[35] Indeed, they reveal a culture engrossed with the precariousness of male gendering. Reginald T. Jackson remarks that the taunt, "faggot," preceded any knowledge of homosexuality: had he known that this might involve "the love of a man. A black man," then he would gladly have endured the name-calling.[36] In the terms broached earlier in this book, gender identification precedes object-choice; the stigma attaches to effeminacy.

Marlon Riggs in his film *Tongues Untied* (1989), written around Riggs's poem of the same name, expounds a personal negotiation of sexuality and racial difference. Riggs experienced oppression in his own community as a sissy, more immediately than oppression as a black man. The solution was part of the problem:

> A whiteboy came to my rescue.
> Beckoned with gray/green eyes, a soft Tennessee drawl.
> Seduced me out of my adolescent silence.

Riggs found his way to San Francisco—the Castro, the gay district:

> I learned the touch and taste of snow.
> Cruising whiteboys, I played out
> adolescent dreams deferred.
> Patterns of black upon white upon black upon white
> mesmerized me. I focused hard, concentrated deep.[37]

Riggs was playing out racial relations as sexual relations. But it dawned upon him that this was not making him the person he sought to be: in the Castro he was "an invisible man"; the proffered black images were racist stereotypes. "I was a nigga, still." So he "went in search of something better," he says, listening to "Rhythms of blood, culture, / history, and race": black men must love one other (203–204). A concluding section of the film links civil rights marches with a black gay demonstration. The slogan on a banner is from an essay by Joseph Beam: "Black men loving Black men is the revolutionary act of the eighties."[38]

However, Riggs admits, the "absence of black images" occurred not only in the books, posters, and films dominated by white people, but in his "own fantasies" (*Tongues Untied*, 202–203). The film became controversial within black and gay communities when commentators noted that Riggs's personal life appeared to contradict his argument: his own partner was white.[39] B. Ruby Rich objects: "In a film full of the courage of coming out of the closet on the subject of queerness, it looked as though Riggs had stayed in the closet on the subject of race (as object of affection, not identity)."[40] In the credits Jack Vincent, the controversial partner, is thanked for his loving support; far less is at stake for the white man—he can afford to be sympathetic.

Questions have been raised also about the gendering of gay men in *Tongues Untied*. Goldsby remarks that drag queens are depicted as pathetic, lonely figures, to be displaced by more macho images.[41] Evidently, Riggs is under pressure from "Afrocentric" commentators who despise effeminacy:

> Because of my sexuality, I cannot be black. A strong, proud, "Afrocentric" black man is resolutely heterosexual, not *even* bisexual. Hence I remain a Negro. My sexual difference is considered of no value; indeed, it is a testament to weakness, passivity, the absence of real guts—balls. Hence I remain a sissy, punk, faggot. I cannot be a black gay man because by the tenets of black macho, black gay man is a triple negation. I am consigned, by these tenets, to remain a Negro faggot.[42]

The energy in this passage derives perhaps from an unstable combination of resistance to the way black manhood has been defined, and resentment at exclusion from that manhood. Is it that Riggs wants Afrocentrism to incorporate the sissy, or that he objects to being labeled a sissy? Gay-oriented commentators insist that emphasizing manliness is not the answer. Kobena Mercer calls it "another turn of the screw of oppression . . . when black men subjectively internalise and incorporate aspects of the dominant definitions of masculinity in order to contest the conditions of dependency and powerlessness which racism and racial oppression enforce."[43] Phillip Brian Harper, in comparable vein, rejects the "imagined solution": "a proper affirmation of black male authority."[44]

Finally I note that Riggs's appeal to sameness as the resolution of the dilemmas of racism converges upon a leading theme of this book. He has rediscovered and reaffirmed, in his case for black men loving black men, not a distinctive African American way of relating, but a purer, sharper version of the egalitarian ideology, which asserts that the most productive relations will be founded in sameness. The Castro, Riggs sees, proclaims the community of gayness and the unity of gay experience, while actually reinscribing the racist assumptions of American society generally; the task proposed in the film, then, is to make the egalitarian ideology succeed among black men. Yet Riggs's work is more important for the struggle it exposes, than for the watchword with which it ends.

SLAVES AND MASTERS

As I have said, S/M is best regarded, not as a speciality, but as continuous with the hierarchies that we all experience. Invocation of cross-racial masters and slaves does, however, raise the odds. In "Beneath the Veneer," in a recent collection of gay African American writing, Kheven L. LaGrone records his shock upon seeing at a party a white man leading a black man by a leash. Have black people forgotten the role of white supremacists in history? LaGrone demands.[45] No they haven't: that is what the leash is about.

Isaac Julien has made diverse approaches to these topics. His film *Looking for Langston* (1988) suggests that sexual relations between blacks and whites were regarded quite positively in Harlem in the 1920s and 1930s. This interpretation has been supported by Kevin J. Mumford, who finds that there was "a kind of affinity between homosexuals, black/white sex districts, and African-American culture more generally."[46] In a poem from around the same time as *Looking for Langston*, "Gary's Tale," Julien observes that race has infiltrated the psyche and infects every relationship:

> Because the last fight, the last battle, territory, will be with one's self,
> the most important terrain, the psyche.
> The mind will be the last neo-colonialised space to be decolonialised,
> this I know because I have been there, backwards and forwards.[47]

For Julien, this is not a reason to avoid cross-racial contact, or to give up hopes of positive change. In *Young Soul Rebels* (1991), the killer is a white boy who can't handle his attraction to black males. However, the film ends in utopian style, with a sexual liaison between Caz (black male) and Billibud (white male), another between Chris (black male) and Tracy (black female), a main-man comradeship between Caz and Chris, a special friendship between Tracy and Jill (white female), and everybody learning to funk.

Julien's short film *The Attendant* (1991) is set in an art gallery. The Attendant (Thomas Baptiste) is black; a visitor is white and wearing leather gear; they are drawn to each other. The gallery closes; the Attendant reimagines the paintings, replacing the original figures with men such as himself and the visitor, wearing contemporary leather gear. He focuses especially on an admired nineteenth-century painting by F. A. Biard, "Scene on the African Coast," showing episodes in the slave trade.[48] Two of the paintings become erotic cartoons by Tom of Finland. Other tableaux are composed of camp go-go boys. The Attendant whips the visitor. The Attendant sings in a theater—"Dido's Lament" from Purcell's *Dido and Aeneas* (Dido was abandoned on an African coast by an imperial visitor).

Julien has been criticized for depicting a black man with his psyche organized around imagery of historic humiliation. He has replied that images cannot be trapped in one meaning: the implements of slavery have been transformed into "sexualised, stylized fetish clothing for the queer body. The imperialist slave iconography is appropriated and repositioned." Gay subculture, including black gay subculture, makes its own use of the imagery. Furthermore, Julien adds, there are diverse ways of reading the film: it might be a parody, or transgressive; or it might be "moralistically read into the cheap sociology of a pathological, black/self-hating discourse."[49] The sickness resides in puritanical rejection, not in gay sex.

The problem with Julien's argument is that he wants to assert an open plurality of readings while disallowing some readings. He is on stronger ground when he asserts that morbidity resides with those who would deny "the psychic reality of black/white desire." These desires exist, and they may be more appealing than the restricted and restricting vision of puritans. "The out black snow queen draws attention to the fact of black desire for the white subject and contests pathological racial identities, the products of Afrocentric readings," Julien adds (125). He regrets what he regards as Riggs's retreat into Afrocentrism.

However, Riggs in fact bears witness on both sides of the argument. We may perhaps envisage a dynamic process; one in which Afrocentrism might be an appropriate stage on the route to self-affirmation, while investment in cross-racial imagery might be productive of political insights, but not destructive of the relations that promote them. The goal might be a point, not where one or the other is the right answer, but where they can inform each other. Of course, as we have seen in Corbin's *Fragments That Remain* and in Duplechan's *Eight Days a Week*, this depends as much on the white partner as the black. However, it is likely to be the latter who places himself most at risk.

These issues echo powerfully in the journals of Gary Fisher, published at the instigation of Eve Sedgwick after his death in 1994. Fisher tells of his fantasies and his encounters, and of the link between them and race relations in the United States. He writes a letter to a sexual partner, Master Park (*Slavery Defended* is a classic collection of "Views of the Old South"): "Here's that letter you wanted. I'm laying here sideways in the bed with *Slavery Defended* opened to about midway, sampling the arguments and thinking about how good it felt to serve. Not that it matters, but I enjoyed Thursday immensely, particularly the sleaze and humiliation of some of it" (extended pain he likes less). "The racial humiliation is a huge turn-on. I enjoy being your nigger, your property and worshipping not just you, but your whiteness."[50]

This is not a generalized masochism, nor just an individual thrill; it is about race, slavery, history, and skin color. In an earlier journal entry Fisher asks himself:

> Have I tried to oppress myself—as a black man and as a (passive) homosex-
> ual man—purely for the pleasure of it, or does that oppression go right to the
> point of my perceived weaknesses[?] . . . Can I divorce sexuality from power
> in the real world or do I want to[?] . . . I want to, in effect, give in to a sys-
> tem that wants to (has to) oppress me. (187; my question marks and elisions)

Is his submission to whiteness a personal pleasure, he asks, or does it bespeak a personal weakness? Is it not, rather, systemic?—the operations of real-world ideology in the psyche? Fisher is playing the part that is written for him in the racial script of the United States. Again: "Blackness is a state of frustration. There's no way out of this racial depression (I don't feel the frustration personally, but as part of a people I know that I'm being fucked, abused)" (199). Fisher experiences humiliating scenarios not just personally, but as the structural, racial exploitation which he knows to be their origin. In a manner of speaking, therefore, the fantasy is *not him*: "What is this fantasy that cuts across all of me, racial, intellectual, moral, spiritual, sexual . . . ?" (213; Fisher's hesitation).

As Sedgwick remarks in her Afterword to *Gary in Your Pocket*, it has seemed necessary in our time to handle S/M as a stigmatized minority practice, emphasizing the *dis*linkages between sexual fantasy and activity, on the one hand, and "the social realities of power and violence" on the other.[51] We are only playing, S/Mers are expected to say, our games are entirely separate from real-world violence. A theme of this book is that such a dislinkage is impossible to maintain and ultimately misleading. Yet, as elsewhere, we reach a point at which a violent disjunction becomes so inflammatory that we have to revert to the domains of ethical and political responsibility. Fisher is troubled: "Crandall calls me his nigger. He's much rougher with me than Ed and talks so genuinely I wonder if he doesn't believe what he's saying to me. It disturbs me to write what he says about carving 'White Power' into my flesh" (217–18). In fact it is a question, how far abuse is what Fisher wants: "I love snuggling up to him. We're on our sides. He has one arm beneath me and another round me. It's so warm. . . . I feel so safe next to him" (157; my elision). Again: "I want a loving master/daddy" (217). The desire for love and protection from a version of the abuser seems the key to this; the risk—the thrill—is in placing your trust in a person who might damage you. "So, particularly (especially or primarily) a white man, when he holds and protects me from others like him, brings me an excitement which strangely and uniquely parallels that which he causes me when he threatens or frightens me" (237).

This scenario seems to correlate with a persistent trope in black and white American gay writing: the violent and abusive father who gains excitement from punishing his son. Everyone he knows suffered some element of abuse in childhood, David Wojnarowicz says. He describes how his own father systematically beat all his family, and ordered David to play with his penis. He derives from this an abiding sexual preference: "I have always been attracted to dangerous men, men whose gestures intimated the possibilities of violence, and I have always seduced them into states of gentle grace with my hands and lips."[52] Rechy's narrator reports similarly in *City of Night*.[53] Tom in Monette's *Halfway Home* was tormented by his father and his brother, Brian, at the same time as being sexually drawn to the latter. This childhood experience has inhibited his love life, Tom believes: "I admit I have mixed them up, Brian and the man I never had." Now, as he makes a new relationship with Gray, a calm, caring, older man, he revises his model of manliness: *"This is what a brother is."*[54] The eponymous heroes in *Tim and Pete* both had hostile fathers; Joey's father was "a monster."[55] Gary Fisher reports a violent and abusive father. If his preferred mode of sexual expression mimics the relationship with his father, it also repudiates it. "The ultimate slap was to let it loose that I'd let some other man, not my dad, have me."[56] He does "finally meet a white man not twisted by the color thing," but their prospects are spoiled when Fisher declares his HIV status (*Gary in Your Pocket*, 245–46).

PHOBIA

I have tried elsewhere to distinguish phobic and structural racism. For only some individuals is racism phobic; for the rest of us, it gets structured into the language, into the prevailing stories through which the society seeks to understand itself. It becomes "common sense."[57] Structural racism is certainly not innocent; it affords a sympathetic milieu into which phobic racism may expand, and in some cases the two virtually merge. However, in other circumstances it is at least ameliorable: when pointed out it may be worked upon and changed.

Phobic racism, on the other hand, seeks to secure not just the economic, political, and general psychic well-being of the white man; the racial other is invoked as a way of handling profound personal inadequacy. The phobic racist cannot leave the topic—he or she looks for people of other races in order to exercise phobic feelings. Probably there is a more or less permanent phobic minority, the recruiting ground for fascist movements. At a certain point, enthrallment becomes obsessive, grotesque, violent, intolerable. I may seem in danger here of exonerating the system, by making it responsible for habitual structures, while phobic intensity is ascribed to individuals. However, it seems to me that phobia is usually dysfunctional, not actually sustaining the system. Its irrationalism is too unpredictable, too loose, too dangerous.

Homophobia, similarly, is a term that should not be used casually, for general anxiety and prejudice. It is best reserved for implacable, hostile fascination. Of course, racial and sexual phobias may occur together. The serial killer Jeffrey Dahmer was so drawn to his male victims, nearly all of whom were black or Asian, that he ate parts of their bodies.[58] This certainly attests to a consuming desire-for; we might regard it as a monstrous parody of desire-to-be (the ingested person).

The gay tradition includes powerful and equivocal evocations of phobia. In Tennessee Williams' story, "Desire and the Black Masseur," Anthony Burns, a nebulous and ineffective clerk (white) has been waiting, obscurely, for something to swallow him up. He finds it in the rough treatment of a black masseur (who isn't given a name).

> The knowledge grew quickly between them of what Burns wanted, that he was in search of atonement, and the black masseur was the natural instrument of it. He hated white-skinned bodies because they abused his pride. He loved to have their white skin prone beneath him, to bring his fist or the palm of his hand down on its passive surface. He had barely been able to hold this love in restraint, to control the wish that he felt to pound more fiercely and use the full of his power. But now at long last the suitable person had entered his orbit of passion. In the white-collar clerk he had located all that he longed for.[59]

This might be a mutually rewarding project—"The giant loved Burns, and Burns adored the giant" (221)—but the violence of the massage increases. While a preacher across the street invokes the atonement of Jesus, the masseur devours the body of Burns; he moves to another town and new customers.

All this, we are told, illustrates something about "the earth's whole population" as it "twisted and writhed beneath the manipulation of night's black fingers and the white ones of day" (223). The referent seems to be both color and humanity; guilt at historic racial exploitation is made to coincide with the Christian notion that everyone needs atonement. David Bergman emphasizes the racial implications: "Like Melville, Williams believes that an egalitarian relation between so-called civilized men and their primitive brothers can be achieved only through an act of cannibalism in which the civilized will be consumed."[60] Unfortunately, this is at the expense of reconfirming the black primitive. " 'What do you think this is? A jungle?' " the masseur's boss demands, not altogether unreasonably, when Burns's leg is fractured (221).

Getting eaten is the fate also of Sebastian in Williams' play *Suddenly Last Summer* (1958, filmed by Joseph L. Mankiewicz in 1959), where the agon of homosexuality again seems to coalesce with the supposed human condition. In a mythic Latin country, Sebastian is consumed by the native boys whom he has courted—"a flock of featherless little black sparrows," with gobbling birds on the Galapagos Islands, that prey upon the newly hatched turtles as they try to reach the sea, making "the sky almost as black as the beach."[61] How far Williams is in control of this scenario is in my view a question. It seems to me that he is making a melodramatic projection of queer guilt onto the universe, and positioning black males as angels of death.

James Robert Baker's novel *Testosterone* is, like *Tim and Pete*, a quest which takes the reader back and forth on the L.A. freeways. Whereas Tim and Pete mean well, Dean's mission is partly to get back together with Pablo Ortega so that they can share an ideal future—but mainly to kill him. This is because Pablo abruptly terminated their relationship. Dean doesn't consider whether he might have turned Pablo off in some way (Dean emerges as very strange), but interprets Pablo as an emotional serial killer. He tracks down Pablo's other lovers and finds ample confirmation of his malevolence. How much of this is true the reader cannot tell, since we have only Dean's word for it and he is evidently obsessive. He believes Pablo burned his house down, and took his dog for medical experiments or black magic. Anne, who says she had an affair with Pablo, claims he was a notorious doctor who tortured political prisoners in Chile in 1987, and Dean believes this, although Pablo would have been about twenty at the time. Anne retracts this story, but Dean goes on believing it. Then he credits another story, that Pablo was part of a notorious drug gang in Mexico, also in 1987. He becomes out of control and violent with people who frustrate him in any way. He attacks a man who looks rather like Pablo (he's not wearing his glasses). With increasing abandon, he imagines what Pablo might be saying or thinking.

What gradually becomes apparent is that Dean is preoccupied with Pablo's Latino race. Initially he reassures his friends that Pablo is not stereotypical: "He's Latino, but he doesn't have an accent (like your typical dumb beaner)."[62] Indeed, the stereotypes are reversed: Pablo is cool and dispassionate, Dean is spontaneous, expressive. This becomes an accusation: "I think his brown skin fooled me at first, so I didn't realize how much he was really like my father" (16). A sense of Dean as phobic develops when he laments the old days, when Southern California was a white boy's utopia, before "the killers of color shot you in the head and took your T-bird away." He has been noting contact ads in which Latinos offer to mistreat white boys, whereas the other way around would not be allowed because of "PC." "But I've made an effort through all this not to get racist. And I haven't. I really don't think I have" (51–52). This is a love/hate thing: Pablo's "skin was really amazing. So smooth and warm" (58); Dean imagines himself having a "faithful, young, smooth, brown-skinned fellow lifeguard/slave" (28).

The idea that Pablo has killed Dean's dog, either for scientific experiment or for Palo Mayombe black-magic rituals, depends on superstitious, racist notions of what Latino people are like: "Latino's do have this different feeling about cruelty to animals. I know that's a blanket statement. . . . Call me a racist if you want to, but it fucking happens. That's why it's taking a great effort on my part not to think all Latinos are sick" (94; my elision). Pablo becomes the dog: "He's like a mad cornered South American dog" (84). Dean believes a hairdresser who says that killing Pablo would not be enough to remove his curse; he takes the fact that the Sam Peckinpah horror movie *Bring Me the Head of Alfredo Garcia* is showing on TV as a sign that he must behead Pablo. He steals a machete and an ice chest to store the head. It is Dean, the white man from a Presbyterian background, who turns out to be the superstitious killer. The last sentence of the book shows Dean fixed in his obsession: "The smooth warmth of his brown skin" (200).

SHAME

Eve Sedgwick put the concept of *shame* into gay circulation in 1993, in an article heading up the new journal *GLQ* (*Gay and Lesbian Quarterly*). Her title, "Queer Performativity: Henry James's *The Art of the Novel*," announced a recognition of Judith Butler's work (performativity had been Butler's key contribution at that date), while moving, via James, toward a more inward, literary, intimate, and intense register. Sedgwick presents shaming as a condition of queer sexuality, and as constitutive of queer identity. Butler, in response, acknowledged an element of shame in performing queerness, while drawing the argument into collective and practical aspects of identity management and activism.[63]

I had not seen much potential for the development of shame; as Sedgwick remarks, it seems negative to dwell on the terms of our stigma. Then I noticed a line in Tennessee Williams' play, *Sweet Bird of Youth*, and its quotation in Neil Bartlett's novel, *Ready to Catch Him Should He Fall*. The Princess (an aging movie star) has been fencing verbally with Chance (a still-youthful hustler). In the last line of the scene she appeals to him: "Now get a little sweet music on the radio and come here to me and make me almost believe that we're a pair of young lovers *without any shame*."[64] Good lovemaking retrieves youth and confers emancipation from shame—*almost*. As I conclude this chapter on race—the most sensitive, threatening, and exciting hierarchy—it seems to me that, while shame is indeed loaded upon us by our societies, that does not altogether account for the cultural energy that attends it. In a parallel movement (for social structures, once more, are continuous with psychic structures) we generate shame among ourselves.

As I have said, people on the downside of the binary model are under the greater pressure. They put more at risk. Yet to exercise dominance also is to expose oneself; even the relatively powerful place themselves in jeopardy—of rejection, humiliation, and the sudden inundation of unwelcome self-knowledge. Shame, I suggest, derives from *awareness of exploitation*—both for the boy who turns over, and for the man who takes advantage of his willingness. It is a product of the hierarchies I have been discussing; it is integral with sexual passion, therefore; it is sexy. If this view is correct, the shame of exploiting and being exploited will be hard to exclude or evade. Maybe there are magical remedies—youth and beauty, according to Williams and Bartlett. And something for the older and less beautiful person to contribute—perhaps strength, accomplishment, style, generosity, validation, trust.

9

FICTION

I started out on this book with some ideas about desire and power. However, the great pleasure in the work has been encountering so many marvelous lesbian- and gay-themed novels and films. I have been delighted with the seriousness and humor, the inventiveness and responsibility, the imagination and abundance that have been revealed. As I say in chapter 1, my use of such resources is not designed to deduce facts from fiction, but to investigate the kinds of representations that have been circulating. My aim has been to explore how our experiences have fed into books, films, and cultural commentary, and how we, in turn, have read and pondered them, recognized and reframed ourselves through them. The pleasure in reading has derived partly from artistic achievement, but mainly it has been about registering the kinds of people that we have become, or aspired to become. If you read Leavitt or Monette differently from me, this will almost certainly be, not just a literary judgment, but a way of thinking about sexuality and power. We may have our most ambitious conversations and contests through fiction.

I am scarcely concerned, therefore, with whether a book is likely to become part of a literary canon. At the same time, if it transpires that the processes of subcultural exploration and self-recognition are effective, in part at least, and other readers and commentators frame their ideas through some of these texts, the outcome will *in practice* be something rather like a *lesbian and gay canon*. Now, insofar as canon means "law, rule, edict," that is not what I have in mind. However, "canonical" also means books that are accepted as "genuine and inspired," and those we have.[1]

In effect, this is what gay people have always done. There was little les-

bian fiction around when Alison Hennegan was young, but she cultivated her own investment in the classics. A passionate identification with
Achilles, distraught at the death of Patroclus, helped "by offering me a
world free from the assumption that human completeness exists solely in
the fusion of male and female." Hennegan went on to Petronius, Horace,
and Virgil, and subsequently to Siegfried Sassoon and Wilfred Owen, gay
poets of the Great War. "I did as most young gay and lesbian readers of the
time—older ones, too, for that matter—had to do. I created my own 'popular fiction,' developed my own much cherished canon."[2]

My ambition to make the discussion of texts subculturally effective has
been challenged by Stanley Fish, who takes me as exemplifying the
approach of "The Cultural Critic." This arises out of my book *Faultlines*,
where I agree with Fish that it is the academic profession that determines
which readings will pass as plausible, but accuse him of wanting to head
off such political potential as English literature may have.[3] Fish responds
by reiterating his assertion, that it must be futile for people working with
literature to aspire to political influence:

> Changing the mode of literary analysis or changing the object of literary
> analysis or changing the name of literary analysis will not change the mate-
> rial effectiveness of literary analysis and make it into an instrument of polit-
> ical action. That kind of change, if it is ever to occur, will require wholesale
> *structural* changes of which literary analysts might take advantage, but which
> they could never initiate.[4]

At one level this is plainly correct. Literary criticism is designed, precisely,
to head off any real-world engagement that literary intellectuals might
seek. The application of the categories "art" and "literature" amounts to a
way of distracting us from contemporary issues (which we might do something about), by asserting that the important writing will be "universal"
(and hence probably beyond remedy). The overthrow of such deep-set
ideas would indeed require a notable structural change. However, feminists, for instance, have succeeded in writing novels and criticism that both
create and respond to urgent political issues. I discern in Fish's pro-
nouncement a typical conservative strategy, whereby the terms for significant action are set at such a demanding level that they will never occur.
Revolution appears unlikely, so it is not worth trying to change anything. In
my view, writing of all kinds may change the boundaries of the plausible,
and hence of the effective scope for action, and it may be especially valuable in subcultural formations.

The most considered discussion from a radical perspective of minority reading has been made by John Guillory in *Cultural Capital*. He believes that the goal of minority groups must be to place a sample of their culture in mainstream venues—"opening out the canon." Such a process, Guillory says, falls within the American tradition of liberal pluralism: through *representation*, groups who have been excluded from full citizenship expect to make their presence felt. Insofar as this has the implicit aim of redressing the inadequacies of public political process, and of universities in particular, Guillory argues, it can be only an imaginary politics. Installing minority groups in canonical venues gestures toward a national oppression which it cannot affect.[5]

Partly for this reason, Guillory adds, the valorization of noncanonical texts tends to depend upon theoretically unsophisticated notions, such as the identity and authentic experience of the author, and reading is imagined, naively, as a transparent process. It is not inevitable, however, that the purposive invocation of texts by and about marginalized groups will succumb to these theoretical pitfalls. Compare the situation of racial minorities. Commentators such as Stuart Hall, bell hooks, and Paul Gilroy have pointed out that there can be no essential grounding for racial and ethnic identities. In an initial stage, Hall notes, black people sought to make their own images, challenging hegemonic versions of themselves; but today it is understood that representation is formative—active, constitutive—rather than mimetic. "Black," according to Hall, "is essentially a politically and culturally *constructed* category, which cannot be grounded in a set of fixed transcultural or transcendental racial categories and which therefore has no guarantees in Nature."[6] It is the same with lesbian, gay, and bisexual. There was a time for positive images—indeed, for visibility of any kind. Today a developed theory of ideology, the human subject, and cultural production affords opportunities for new engagements with textuality, and with the anxieties and hopes of a subcultural constituency.

Indeed, it is awareness of identity as constituted that affords opportunities for intervention. One inference from antiessentialist theory should be that we cannot simply throw off our current constructions. We are consequences of our histories—those that have been forced upon us and those that we have made ourselves. At the same time, it is because we believe that culture constructs the scope for our identities that we may believe those identities to be contingent and provisional, and therefore may strive to revise our own self-understanding and representation. If gay subculture is effective for its constituency, it is not because it evades poststructuralist insights, but because it responds to them.

The concept of "cultural capital" from which Guillory begins (in my view a very useful concept) leads him to present a static impression of how a group inhabits a culture. While it is true that mainstream cultures are under pressure to incorporate their treasures into authoritative state and national monoliths, subordinated groups have more urgent and particular concerns. For lesbians and gay men, though some ground may be gained by remarking how traditionally canonical authors have displayed a significant streak of homoeroticism, it is not important simply to possess this or that statusful icon.

The reply to Guillory is that the success of subcultural intervention may not reside primarily, or even at all, in infiltrating the mainstream. Indeed, insofar as that occurs, a consequence is usually distortion or appropriation; we are used to coping with hostile and patronizing images. The quality of our canon is not to be measured by the extent to which it impresses the mainstream, but in terms of its contribution to shared self-understanding. The point is to mark out a space in which to compare stories, for consolation, insight, and new imaginative awareness.

NOTES

1. INTRODUCTION

1. Reginald Shepherd, "On Not Being White," in Joseph Beam, ed., *In the Life* (Boston: Alyson, 1986), 53–54. Subsequent references are in the text. On white-on-black fixation, see Christopher Cutrone, "The Child with a Lion: The Utopia of Interracial Intimacy," *GLQ* (*Gay and Lesbian Quarterly*) 6 (2000): 249–85.

2. Jonathan Dollimore, *Sexual Dissidence* (Oxford: Clarendon, 1991), 65.

3. See R. D. Laing and D. G. Cooper, *Reason and Violence* (New York: Pantheon, 1971), 22–25.

4. See Alan Sinfield, *Cultural Politics—Queer Reading* (1994), 2d ed. (London: Routledge, 2005), chs. 1 and 2.

5. Louis Althusser, *Lenin and Philosophy*, trans. Ben Brewster (London: New Left, 1997), 160–65.

6. Althusser, *Lenin and Philosophy*, 190–91, 200.

7. Herbert Marcuse, *Eros and Civilization* (New York: Random House, 1955).

8. Michel Foucault, *The History of Sexuality*, vol. 1: *An Introduction*, trans. Robert Hurley (New York: Vintage, 1978), 11. I return to Foucault and power in chapter 4.

9. Joan Riviere, "Womanliness as a Masquerade" (1929), in Victor Burgin, James Donald, and Cora Kaplan, eds., *Formations of Fantasy* (London: Methuen, 1986), 37–38. See Vicky Lebeau, *Psychoanalysis and Cinema* (London: Wallflower, 2001), 101–15.

10. Michael Warner, "Homo-Narcissism; Or, Heterosexuality," in Joseph A. Boone and Michael Cadden, eds., *Engendering Men* (New York: Routledge, 1990), 200.

11. Lynne Segal, *Straight Sex* (London: Virago, 1994), 135.

12. For a defense and referencing of recent work, see Christopher Lane, "Psychoanalysis and Sexual Identity," in Andy Medhurst and Sally R. Munt, eds., *Lesbian and Gay Studies* (London: Cassell, 1997).

13. Alan Sinfield, *Out on Stage* (New Haven and London: Yale University Press, 1999).

14. Bertolt Brecht, "A Short Organum for the Theatre," in John Willett, ed. and trans., *Brecht on Theatre* (London: Eyre Methuen, 1978), 186.

15. Jim Grimsley, interview in *Gay Times* 288 (September 2002): 77.

16. Alan Sinfield, *Faultlines* (Berkeley: University of California Press, 1992; Oxford: Clarendon Press, 1992), ch. 2.

17. The terms *erotic dissidence, dissident sexuality,* and *sexual dissidence* are used for forbidden and/or stigmatized sex by Gayle S. Rubin in 1982. See Rubin, "Thinking Sex: Notes for a Radical Theory of the Politics of Sexuality," in Henry Abelove, Michèle Aina Barale, and David M. Halperin, eds., *The Lesbian and Gay Studies Reader* (New York: Routledge, 1993), 18, 22, 23. *Sexual Dissidence* is, of course, the title of Jonathan Dollimore's book.

18. Alan Sinfield, *Gay and After* (London: Serpent's Tail, 1998), ch. 3; Sinfield, "The Production of Gay and the Return of Power," in Richard Phillips, Diane Watt, and David Shuttleton, eds., *De-centring Sexualities* (London: Routledge, 2000); Sinfield, "Transgender and Les/bi/gay Identities," in David Alderson and Linda Anderson, eds., *Territories of Desire in Queer Culture* (Manchester: Manchester University Press, 2000).

19. Sinfield, *Gay and After*, 91, 103.

2. TAXONOMIES

1. David M. Halperin, *How to Do the History of Homosexuality* (Chicago: University of Chicago Press, 2002), 109–110.

2. Halperin, *How to Do the History*, 133–34.

3. David Halperin, "Pal o' Me Heart," *London Review of Books*, May 22, 2003, 32–33. See Jamie O'Neill, *At Swim, Two Boys* (London: Scribner, 2001).

4. Halperin, *How to Do the History*, 110, 134.

5. Bruce R. Smith, *Homosexual Desire in Shakespeare's England* (Chicago: University of Chicago Press, 1991); G. S. Rousseau, *Perilous Enlightenment* (Manchester: Manchester University Press, 1991), 9–13.

6. See David F. Greenberg, *The Construction of Homosexuality* (Chicago: University of Chicago Press, 1988); Stephen O. Murray, "The 'Underdevelopment' of Modern/Gay Homosexuality in MesoAmerica," in Kenneth Plummer, ed., *Modern Homosexualities* (London: Routledge, 1992); Gilbert Herdt, *Same Sex, Different Cultures* (Boulder, Colo.: Westfield, 1997).

7. Jeffrey Weeks, *Sexuality and Its Discontents* (London: Routledge, 1985), 90.

8. Eve Kosofsky Sedgwick, *Epistemology of the Closet* (Hemel Hempstead: Harvester Wheatsheaf, 1991), 23 (Sedgwick's emphasis).

9. Kenneth Lewes, *The Psychoanalytic Theory of Male Homosexuality* (London: Quartet, 1989), 35–42; C. A. Tripp, *The Homosexual Matrix* (1975) 2d ed. (New York: Meridian, 1987), 72–73; Kaja Silverman, *Male Subjectivity at the Margins* (New York: Routledge, 1992), ch. 8 (Silverman's third category has two subdivisions).

10. Sigmund Freud, *Three Essays on the Theory of Sexuality* (1905), in *The Penguin Freud Library*, vol. 7: *On Sexuality* (Harmondsworth: Penguin, 1977), 56.

11. Sigmund Freud, *Leonardo da Vinci* (1910), in *The Penguin Freud Library*, vol. 14: *Art and Literature* (Harmondsworth: Penguin, 1985). For a critique of this essay, see Earl Jackson Jr., *Strategies of Deviance* (Bloomington: Indiana University Press, 1995), 53–73.

12. E. M. Forster, *Maurice* (1971) (Harmondsworth: Penguin, 1972), 208.

13. Silverman, *Male Subjectivity at the Margins*, 344. However, Silverman also gestures toward the importance of class, age, and nationality, remarking: "Because their object-choice defies the libidinal logic of conventional masculinity, gay men are frequently viewed through the alternative screen of femininity" (353).

14. Sheila Jeffreys, "Butch and Femme: Now and Then," in Lesbian History Group, *Not a Passing Phase* (London: Women's Press, 1993).

15. Teresa de Lauretis, *The Practice of Love* (Bloomington: Indiana University Press, 1994), 240.

16. Elizabeth Grosz, *Space, Time, and Perversion* (New York: Routledge, 1995), ch. 10.

17. Rita Mae Brown, *Rubyfruit Jungle* (1973) (London: Corgi, 1978), 147. See Jonathan Dollimore, *Sexual Dissidence* (Oxford: Clarendon, 1991), 52–55.

18. Judith Butler, "Imitation and Gender Insubordination," in Diana Fuss, ed., *Inside/Out* (New York: Routledge, 1991), 20.

19. Freud's letter is quoted in Lewes, *The Psychoanalytic Theory of Male Homosexuality*, 32.

20. Michael Warner, "Homo-Narcissism; Or, Heterosexuality," in Joseph A. Boone and Michael Cadden, eds., *Engendering Men* (New York: Routledge, 1990), 192.

21. Carole-Anne Tyler, "Boys Will Be Girls: The Politics of Gay Drag," in Diana Fuss, ed., *Inside/Out*, 34.

22. Sigmund Freud, "Female Sexuality" (1931), in Freud, *The Penguin Freud Library*, vol. 7, *On Sexuality*, 376–77 (my elision).

23. Sigmund Freud, "On Narcissism: An Introduction" (1914), in *The Penguin Freud Library*, vol. 11: *On Metapsychology* (Harmondsworth: Penguin, 1984), 84. An editor's note directs readers to Freud's essay on Leonardo.

24. Freud, "On Narcissism," 81–82 (my elision). Tim Dean argues that narcissism need not exclude otherness: Dean, "Homosexuality and the Problem of Otherness," in Tim Dean and Christopher Lane, eds., *Homosexuality and Psychoanalysis* (Chicago: University of Chicago Press, 2001).

25. Lewes, *The Psychoanalytic Theory of Male Homosexuality*, 72.

26. Audre Lorde, *Zami: A New Spelling of My Name* (1982) (London: Pandora, 1996), 160, 165.

27. Freud, "Group Psychology and the Analysis of the Ego," in *The Penguin Freud Library*, vol. 12: *Civilization, Society, and Religion* (Harmondsworth: Penguin, 1985), 134.

28. Freud, "Group Psychology," 134.

29. Sedgwick, *Epistemology of the Closet*, 62.

30. Judith Butler, *Bodies That Matter* (New York: Routledge, 1993), 239.

31. Wayne Koestenbaum, *The Queen's Throat* (New York: Poseidon, 1993), 18.

32. John Fletcher, "Freud and His Uses: Psychoanalysis and Gay Theory," in Simon Shepherd and Mick Wallis, eds., *Coming On Strong* (London: Unwin Hyman, 1989), 99. See Warner, "Homo-Narcissism; Or, Heterosexuality," in Boone and Cadden, eds., *Engendering Men*, 197–98.

33. Sedgwick, *Epistemology of the Closet*, 86–90.

34. Ned Cresswell, *A Hollywood Conscience* (Brighton: Millivres, n.d.), 202.

35. James Robert Baker, *Tim and Pete* (1995) (London: Fourth Estate, 1996), 38 (my elision). Further on this novel, see below and ch. 4.

36. Quentin Crisp, *The Naked Civil Servant* (1968) (New York: Plume, 1977), 56.

37. Alan Sinfield, *Gay and After* (London: Serpent's Tail, 1998), ch. 3.

38. Jay Prosser explains that "transgender" was used initially to denote a stronger commitment to living as a woman than "transvestite" or "cross-dresser," and without the implications for sexuality in "transsexual." However, the tendency now is to use "transgender" in a coalitionary politics, to include all those subjects. In this essay I do the latter while retaining an emphasis from the former. See Jay Prosser, "Transgender," in Andy Medhurst and Sally R. Munt, eds., *Lesbian and Gay Studies* (London: Cassell, 1997); Prosser, *Second Skins* (New York: Columbia University Press, 1998), 176.

39. Leslie Feinberg, *Stone Butch Blues* (Ithaca: Firebrand, 1993), 143.

40. Judith Halberstam, "F2M: The Making of Female Masculinity," in Laura Doan, ed., *The Lesbian Postmodern* (New York: Columbia University Press, 1994), 212.

41. Don Kulick, "A Man in the House: The Boyfriends of Brazilian *Travesti* Prostitutes," *Social Text* 52–53 (1997): 133–60.

42. Prosser, *Second Skins*, ch. 5; Kate Bornstein, *Gender Outlaw* (New York: Routledge, 1994), 4. See Alan Sinfield, "Transgender and Les/bi/gay Identities," in David Alderson and Linda Anderson, eds., *Territories of Desire in Queer Culture* (Manchester: Manchester University Press, 2000).

43. Feinberg, *Stone Butch Blues*, 147.

44. See David Valentine and Riki Anne Wilchins, "One Percent on the Burn Chart: Gender, Genitals, and Hermaphrodites with Attitude," *Social Text* 52–53 (1997): 215–22; Anne Fausto-Sterling, "How to Build a Man," in Vernon A. Rosario, ed., *Science and Homosexualities* (New York: Routledge, 1997); Cheryl Chase, "Hermaphrodites with Attitude: Mapping the Emergence of Intersex Political Activism," *GLQ* (*Gay and Lesbian Quarterly*) 4 (1998): 189–211; Iain Morland, "Is Intersexuality Real?" *Textual Practice* 15 (2001): 527–47.

45. Clifford Geertz, *Local Knowledge* (New York: Basic Books, 1983).

46. See Sally R. Munt, ed., *Butch/Femme* (London: Cassell, 1998), 1, 41, 105, 143, 154, 159.

47. Judith Butler, *Gender Trouble* (New York and London: Routledge, 1990), 123.

48. Halberstam, "F2M: The Making of Female Masculinity," 220.

49. Stephen Maddison, *Fags, Hags, and Queer Sisters* (London: Macmillan, 2000), 191–92. This topic is much disputed; see Zachary I. Nataf, *Lesbians Talk Transgender* (London: Scarlet Press, 1996), 35–54.

50. Sigmund Freud, "A Case of Homosexuality in a Woman" (1920), in *The Penguin Freud Library*, vol. 9: *Case Histories II* (Harmondsworth: Penguin, 1979), 383–84.

51. Freud, "Group Psychology," 138.

52. Judith Halberstam, *Female Masculinity* (Durham: Duke University Press, 1998), 57.

53. Maddison, *Fags, Hags, and Queer Sisters*, 12.

54. Halberstam, *Female Masculinity*, 57–58.

55. See Alan Sinfield, *The Wilde Century* (New York: Columbia University Press, 1994), ch. 6; Sinfield, *Out on Stage* (New Haven and London: Yale University Press, 1999), 154–77.

56. Prosser, *Second Skins*, 165.

57. Baker, *Tim and Pete*, 35, 37.

58. Felice Picano, *Like People in History* (1995) (London: Abacus, 1996), 50.

59. Edmund White, *The Beautiful Room Is Empty* (London: Picador, 1988), 104.

60. Teresa de Lauretis, "The Essence of the Triangle; Or, Taking the Risk of Essentialism Seriously: Feminist Theory in Italy, the U.S., and Britain," in Naomi Schor and Elizabeth Weed, eds., *The Essential Difference* (Bloomington: Indiana University Press, 1994), 24.

61. Freud, *Three Essays*, 56.

62. See Arlene Stein, *Sex and Sensibility* (Berkeley: University of California Press, 1997); Lisa Power, "Forbidden Fruit," in Mark Simpson, ed., *Anti-Gay* (London: Cassell, 1996).

63. Aiden Shaw, *Wasted* (London: Gay Men's Press, 2001), 240.

64. Sarah Schulman, *Empathy* (1992) (London: Sheba Feminist Press, 1993), 4.

65. David T. Evans, *Sexual Citizenship* (London: Routledge, 1993), 45. See Donald Morton, "Queerity and Ludic Sado-Masochism: Compulsory Consumption and the Emerging Post-al Queer," in Mas'ud Zavarzadeh, Terese L. Ebert, and Donald Morton, eds., *Post-ality: Marxism and Postmodernism* (Washington, D.C.: Maisonneuve Press, 1995), 189–215; Sinfield, *Gay and After*, ch. 9.

66. Feinberg, *Stone Butch Blues*, 148.

3. FANTASY

1. Esther Newton and Shirley Walton, "The Misunderstanding: Toward a More Precise Sexual Vocabulary," in Carole S. Vance, ed., *Pleasure and Danger* (London: Routledge, 1984), 250.

2. Vicky Lebeau, *Psychoanalysis and Cinema* (London: Wallflower, 2001), 29.

3. Leo Bersani, *Homos* (Cambridge: Harvard University Press, 1995), 103–104.

4. See Leslie J. Moran, *The Homosexual(ity) of the Law* (London: Routledge, 1996), 180–91.

5. Laura Mulvey, "Visual Pleasure and Narrative Cinema," in Antony Easthope, ed., *Contemporary Film Theory* (London: Longman, 1993).

6. For Mulvey's later comments and a full debate, see Easthope, ed., *Contemporary Film Theory*. For an independent-minded assessment, see Brett Farmer, *Spectacular Passions* (Durham: Duke University Press, 2000). Teresa de Lauretis points out that there are important differences between film and fantasy: de Lauretis, *The Practice of Love* (Bloomington: Indiana University Press, 1994), 148.

7. Jean Laplanche and Jean-Bertrand Pontalis, "Fantasy and the Origins of Sexuality," in Victor Burgin, James Donald, and Cora Kaplan, eds., *Formations of Fantasy* (London: Methuen, 1986), 26, 22–23 (their emphases).

8. Sigmund Freud, " 'A Child Is Being Beaten' " (1919), in *The Penguin Freud Library*, vol. 10: *On Psychopathology* (Harmondsworth: Penguin, 1979).

9. James Robert Baker, *Boy Wonder* (1988) (London: Fourth Estate, 1996), 40 (Baker's emphases).

10. Chris Straayer, *Deviant Eyes, Deviant Bodies* (New York: Columbia University Press, 1996), 18–22.

11. Dorothy Allison, *Skin* (London: Pandora, 1995), 109–10.

12. Constance Penley, "Feminism, Psychoanalysis, and the Study of Popular Culture," in Lawrence Grossberg, Cary Nelson, and Paula A. Treichler, eds., *Cultural Studies* (New York: Routledge, 1992), 489. *Star Trek* is discussed also in Joanna Russ, *Magic Mommas, Trembling Sisters, Puritans, and Perverts* (Freedom, Calif.: Crossing Press: 1985), and in Allison, *Skin*, 95–97.

13. Richard Dyer, *Heavenly Bodies* (London: Macmillan, 1987), 168, 155–56.

14. Stephen Maddison, *Fags, Hags, and Queer Sisters* (London: Macmillan, 2000), 6.

15. David Wojnarowicz, *Close to the Knives* (1991) (London: Serpent's Tail, 1992), 26.

16. Lynne Segal, *Straight Sex* (London: Virago, 1994), 233; see 233–45.

17. Cora Kaplan, " 'A Cavern Opened in My Mind': The Poetics of Homosexuality and the Politics of Masculinity in James Baldwin," in Marcellus Blount and George P. Cunningham, eds., *Representing Black Men* (London: Routledge, 1996), 32.

18. Cheryl Clarke, "Living the Texts Out: Lesbians and the Uses of Black Women's Traditions," in Stanlie M. James and Abena P. A. Busia, eds., *Theorizing Black Feminisms* (New York: Routledge, 1993), 214.

19. Bia Lowe, "Mothers and Others, But Also Brothers," in Joan Nestle and John Preston, eds., *Sister and Brother* (London: Cassell, 1994), 127–28.

20. Sue-Ellen Case, "Tracking the Vampire," *Differences* 3.2 (Summer 1991): 1–20 (quote at 1).

21. Valerie Walkerdine, "Video Replay: Families, Films, and Fantasy," in Burgin, Donald, and Kaplan, eds., *Formations of Fantasy*, 169 (Walkerdine's emphasis; my elision).

22. Kaplan, " 'A Cavern Opened in My Mind,' " 30.

23. Segal, *Straight Sex*, 234.

24. Pai Hsien-yung, *Crystal Boys* (1990), trans. Howard Goldblatt (San Francisco: Gay Sunshine Press, 1995), 27, 100. See Alan Sinfield, *Gay and After* (London: Serpent's Tail, 1998), 59–68.

25. Alec Waugh, *Public School Life* (London: Collins, 1922), 137–38.

26. See Alan Sinfield, *Out on Stage* (New Haven and London: Yale University Press, 1999), 124–25.

27. Freud, *Three Essays on the Theory of Sexuality* (1905), in *The Penguin Freud Library*, vol. 7: *On Sexuality* (Harmondsworth: Penguin, 1977), 56.

28. Michel Foucault, *The Uses of Pleasure*, trans. Robert Hurley (Harmondsworth: Viking, 1986), 200.

29. See David M. Halperin, *How to Do the History of Homosexuality* (Chicago: Chicago University Press, 2002), 188–89.

30. Edmund White, *The Farewell Symphony* (London: Chatto, 1997), 402.

31. Jacqueline Rose, *The Haunting of Sylvia Plath* (London: Virago, 1991), 210.

32. Reginald Shepherd, "On Not Being White," in Joseph Beam, ed., *In the Life* (Boston: Alyson, 1986), 53–54.

33. Gary Fisher, *Gary in Your Pocket*, ed. Eve Kosofsky Sedgwick (Durham and London: Duke University Press, 1996), 203.

34. Earl Jackson Jr., *Strategies of Deviance* (Bloomington: Indiana University Press, 1995), 173, 132.

35. See Segal, *Straight Sex*, 282–97.

36. Robert Chesley, *Jerker, or the Helping Hand* (1986), in Chesley, *Hard Plays / Stiff Parts* (San Francisco: Alamo Square, 1990), 112 (Chesney's emphases [sic]).

37. Edmund White, *A Boy's Own Story* (1982) (London: Picador, 1983), 162.

38. Jonathan Dollimore, "Bisexuality, Heterosexuality, and Wishful Theory," *Textual Practice* 10 (1996): 523–39 (quote at 529; Dollimore's emphasis). For a slightly different version, see Dollimore, *Sex, Literature, and Censorship* (Cambridge, Eng.: Polity, 2001), 28-9.

39. Guy Willard, *Mirrors of Narcissus* (London: Millivres, 2000), 20–21, 25 (my elision).

40. Constance Penley, "Time Travel, Primal Scene, and the Critical Dystopia," in James Donald, ed., *Fantasy and the Cinema* (London: British Film Institute, 1989), 202.

41. De Lauretis, *The Practice of Love*, 140.

42. Judith Butler, *Gender Trouble* (New York and London: Routledge, 1990), 149.

43. Henning Bech, *When Men Meet*, trans. Teresa Mesquit and Tim Davies (Cambridge, Eng.: Polity, 1997), 217 (Bech's emphases; my elision).

44. John Clarke, "Style," in Stuart Hall and Tony Jefferson, eds., *Resistance Through Rituals* (London and Birmingham: Hutchinson/Centre for Contemporary Cultural Studies, 1976), 177.

45. R. D. Laing, *Self and Others* (Harmondsworth: Penguin, 1971), 136.

46. Dollimore, *Sex, Literature, and Censorship*, 56.

47. Andrew Holleran, *Dancer from the Dance* (1978) (London: Cape, 1979), 146.

48. Segal, *Straight Sex*, 161.

49. Jeanette Winterson, *The PowerBook* (2000) (London: Vintage, 2001), 4–5.

50. Mark Ravenhill, *Shopping and Fucking* (London: Methuen, 1996), 83.

51. Dennis Cooper, *Frisk* (1991) (London: Serpent's Tail, 1992), 44.

52. Oscar Wilde, *The Picture of Dorian Gray* (1891) (Oxford: Oxford University Press, 1981), 18.

53. Claudia Card, *Lesbian Choices* (New York: Columbia University Press, 1995), 231–35.

54. Dennis Cooper, *Try* (London: Serpent's Tail, 1994), 185 (Cooper's pause).

55. Dennis Cooper, *Guide* (1997) (London: Serpent's Tail, 1998), 155.

4. POWER

1. Jean Genet, *The Balcony* (1957), trans. Bernard Frechtman (London: Faber, 1966), 47 (my elision).

2. Paul Monette, *Becoming a Man* (1992) (London: Abacus, 1994), 66–68 (Monette's emphasis).

3. Paul Monette, *Borrowed Time* (New York: Avon, 1988), 13 (Monette's emphasis).

4. *Becoming a Man*, 175.

5. Theodore Redpath, ed., *The Songs and Sonets of John Donne* (London: Methuen, 1967), 2. Donne is usually thought of as a heterosexual poet, but see George Klawitter, "Verse Letters to T. W. from John Donne: 'By You My Love Is Sent,' " in Claude J. Summers, ed., *Homosexuality in Renaissance and Enlightenment England* (New York: Harrington Park, 1992).

6. Walt Whitman, *The Complete Poems*, ed. Francis Murphy (Harmondsworth: Penguin, 1996), 162.

7. Michel Foucault, *The History of Sexuality*, vol. 1: *An Introduction*, trans. Robert Hurley (New York: Vintage, 1978), 11; and 92–98.

8. Michel Foucault, *Discipline and Punish*, trans. Alan Sheridan (Harmondsworth: Penguin, 1979), 27. See Gail Mason, *The Spectacle of Violence* (New York: Routledge, 2002), ch. 6; Judith Butler, *Gender Trouble* (New York and London: Routledge, 1990), 91–106.

9. Teresa de Lauretis, *The Practice of Love* (Bloomington: Indiana University Press, 1994), 146 (my elision).

10. Geoffrey Gorer, *Sex and Marriage in England Today* (London: Nelson, 1971), 62, 65.

11. See Lillian Faderman, *Odd Girls and Twilight Lovers* (New York: Penguin, 1992); George E. Haggerty, *Men in Love* (New York: Columbia University Press, 1999).

12. David M. Halperin, *How to Do the History of Homosexuality* (Chicago: University of Chicago Press, 2002), 133–34.

13. Jeffrey Weeks, Brian Heaphy, and Catherine Donovan, *Same Sex Intimacies* (London: Routledge, 2001), 105.

14. Lynda Hart and Joshua Dale, "Sadomasochism," in Andy Medhurst and Sally R. Munt, eds., *Lesbian and Gay Studies* (London: Cassell, 1997), 345–46.

15. David Leavitt, *The Lost Language of Cranes* (1986) (Harmondsworth: Penguin, 1987), 169.

16. See Larry Gross, *Up from Invisibility* (New York: Columbia University Press, 2001), 146–47.

17. A. M. Homes, *Jack* (1989) (Harmondsworth: Penguin, 1991).

18. Anthony McDonald, *Adam* (London: Gay Men's Press, 2003).

19. Michael Cunningham, *Flesh and Blood* (New York: Farrar, Straus, and Giroux, 1995), 302, 303, 305 (my elision).

20. Edmund White, *The Farewell Symphony* (London: Chatto, 1997), 414–15, 298.

21. Samuel R. Delany, *The Motion of Light in Water* (1988) (London: Paladin, 1990), 267 (Delany's emphasis).

22. David Wojnarowicz, *Close to the Knives* (London: Serpent's Tail, 1992), 17 (my elision).

23. Ben Gove, *Cruising Culture* (Edinburgh: Edinburgh University Press, 2000), 156–59.

24. Dennis Altman, *The Homosexualization of America* (Boston: Beacon Press, 1982), 79–80; Leo Bersani, "Is the Rectum a Grave?" in Douglas Crimp, ed., *AIDS: Cultural Analysis, Cultural Activism* (Cambridge: MIT Press, 1988), 206.

25. Andrew Holleran, *Dancer from the Dance* (1978) (London: Cape, 1979), 40–43.

26. White, *The Farewell Symphony*, 298, 416.

27. Neil Bartlett, *Who Was That Man?* (London: Serpent's Tail, 1988), 220.

28. Larry Kramer, *Faggots* (1978) (London: Minerva, 1990), 382.

29. Oscar Moore, *A Matter of Life and Sex* (1991) (Harmondsworth: Penguin, 1992).

30. William M. Hoffman, *As Is* (1985), in Michael Feingold, ed., *The Way We Live Now* (New York: Theatre Communications Group, 1990), 25. The film was directed by Michael Lindsay-Hogg in 1986.

31. Thom Gunn, *The Man with Night Sweats* (London: Faber, 1992), 80.

32. Bersani, "Is the Rectum a Grave?" in Crimp, ed., *AIDS: Cultural Analysis*, 215.

33. Leo Bersani, *Homos* (Cambridge: Harvard University Press, 1995), 162, 170–71 (Bersani's emphases). Cf. Alan Sinfield, *Gay and After* (London: Serpent's Tail, 1998), ch. 7.

34. Leo Bersani, "Genital Chastity," in Tim Dean and Christopher Lane, eds., *Homosexuality and Psychoanalysis* (Chicago: University of Chicago Press, 2001), 365 (Bersani's emphasis).

35. Sigmund Freud, "From the History of an Infantile Neurosis" (1918 [1914]), in *The Penguin Freud Library*, vol. 9: *Case Histories II* (Harmondsworth: Penguin, 1979), 280.

36. Freud, *Three Essays on the Theory of Sexuality* (1905), in *The Penguin Freud Library*, vol. 7: *On Sexuality* (Harmondsworth: Penguin, 1977), 61–62 (Freud's emphases).

37. Freud, " 'A Child Is Being Beaten,' " (1919) in *The Penguin Freud Library*, vol. 10: *On Psychopathology* (Harmondsworth: Penguin, 1984), 180.

38. Ibid., 184–85 (Freud's emphasis).

39. Sigmund Freud, "The Economic Problem of Masochism" (1924), in *The Penguin Freud Library*, vol. 11: *On Metapsychology* (Harmondsworth: Penguin, 1984), 419; " 'A Child Is Being Beaten,' " 166.

40. Luce Irigaray, *Je, Tu, Nous* (New York: Routledge, 1993), 12 (Irigaray's emphasis).

41. Jean Laplanche, *New Foundations for Psychoanalysis*, trans. David Macey (Oxford: Blackwell, 1989); for Fletcher, see below. For some of the take-up of Laplanche's concept of implantation, see Elizabeth Cowie, "The Seductive Theories of Jean Laplanche: A New View of the Drive, Passivity, and Femininity," in John Fletcher and Martin Stanton, eds., *Jean Laplanche* (London: Institute of Contemporary Art, 1992); Catherine Belsey, *Desire: Love Stories in Western Culture* (Oxford: Blackwell, 1994), 51–52; Lynne Segal, *Why Feminism?* (Cambridge: Polity, 1999), 184–85.

42. Jean Laplanche, "Implantation, Intromission," in Laplanche, *Essays on Otherness*, ed. John Fletcher (London: Routledge, 1999), 135 (Laplanche's emphasis).

43. John Fletcher, "Gender, Sexuality, and the Theory of Seduction," *Women: A Cultural Review* 11 (2000): 102, 104 (Fletcher's emphasis).

44. "Interview: Jean Laplanche Talks to Martin Stanton," in John Fletcher and Martin Stanton, eds., *Jean Laplanche*, 10.

45. Fletcher, "Gender, Sexuality," 104.

46. Ibid., 106 (Fletcher's emphasis).

47. John Fletcher, "Recent Developments in the General Theory of Primal Seduction," *New Formations* 48 (2002–2003): 5–25 (quote at 9). See Dominique Scarfone, " 'It was *not* my mother': From Seduction to Negation," *New Formations* 48 (2002–2003): 69–76.

48. Laplanche, "Implantation, Intromission," 136.

49. Sheila Jeffreys, "Butch and Femme: Now and Then," in Lesbian History Group, *Not a Passing Phase* (London: Women's Press, 1993), 178.

50. Amber Hollibaugh and Cherríe Moraga, "What We're Rollin' Around in Bed With: Sexual Silences in Feminism," in Ann Snitow, Christine Stansell, and Sharon Thompson, eds., *Desire: The Politics of Sexuality* (London: Virago, 1984), 410–11.

51. Jeffreys, "Butch and Femme," 184 (my elision).

52. Hollibaugh and Moraga, "What We're Rollin' Around in Bed With," 406.

53. Cherrié Moraga, *Loving in the War Years* (Boston: South End Press, 1983), 125–26 (Moraga's emphasis).

54. Judith Halberstam, "Sex Debates," in Medhurst and Munt, eds., *Lesbian and Gay Studies*, 335.

55. Esther Newton and Shirley Walton, "The Misunderstanding: Toward a More Precise Sexual Vocabulary," in Carole S. Vance, ed., *Pleasure and Danger* (London: Routledge, 1984), 247.

56. Ursula Zilinsky, *Middle Ground* (1968) (London: Gay Men's Press, 1987), 146.

57. Sir Philip Sidney, *The Old Arcadia*, ed. Katherine Duncan-Jones (Oxford: Oxford University Press, 1985), 167.

58. Christopher Ricks, ed., *The Poems of Tennyson* (London: Longmans, 1969): *In Memoriam*, sec. 25 and 42.

59. W. H. Auden, *Collected Shorter Poems, 1927–1957* (London: Faber, 1969), 107–108.

60. Lynne Segal, *Straight Sex* (London: Virago, 1994), 248.

61. John Rechy, *The Sexual Outlaw* (1977) (London: W. H. Allen, 1978), 68 (my elision).

62. "Michel Foucault: Sex, Power, and the Politics of Identity," interview with Bob Gallagher and Alexander Wilson, *The Advocate* 400 (August 7, 1984): 30; quoted in Bersani, *Homos*, 88.

63. Bersani, *Homos*, 88.

64. Jeffrey Weeks, *Sexuality and Its Discontents* (London: Routledge, 1985), 44; Bersani, "Is the Rectum a Grave?" in Crimp, ed., *AIDS: Cultural Analysis*, 220–21.

65. Claudia Card, *Lesbian Choices* (New York: Columbia University Press, 1995), 221.

66. James Robert Baker, *Tim and Pete* (1995) (London: Fourth Estate, 1996), 150.

67. See Sadie Plant, *The Most Radical Gesture* (London: Routledge, 1992), 143–47.

68. See Graham White, "Direct Action, Dramatic Action: Theatre and Situationist Theory," *New Theatre Quarterly* 9.36 (November 1993): 329–40 (see 337).

69. See Peter Dickinson, " 'Go-go Dancing on the Brink of the Apocalypse': Representing AIDS," in Richard Dellamora, ed., *Postmodern Apocalypse* (Philadelphia: University of Pennsylvania Press, 1995).

70. Wojnarowicz, *Close to the Knives*, 81.

71. Sinfield, *Gay and After*, ch. 2 and 6. See Dennis Altman, *AIDS and the New Puritanism* (London: Pluto, 1986), ch. 8: "A Very American Epidemic?"

72. Andrew Sullivan, *Love Undetectable* (London: Chatto and Windus, 1998), 18.

73. Bersani, "Is the Rectum a Grave?" in Crimp, ed., *AIDS: Cultural Analysis*, 212.

74. Halberstam, "Sex Debates," in Medhurst and Munt, eds., *Lesbian and Gay Studies*, 333.

75. Bersani, *Homos*, 64.

5. GENDER

1. From Ned Ward, *The History of the London Clubs* (1709), printed in Ian McCormick, ed., *Secret Sexualities* (London: Routledge, 1977), 131.

2. Alan Bray, *Homosexuality in Renaissance England*, 2d ed. (London: Gay Men's Press, 1988), 86.

3. Ibid., 92.

4. Rictor Norton, *Mother Clap's Molly House* (London: Gay Men's Press, 1992).

5. Terry Castle, *The Apparitional Lesbian* (New York: Columbia University Press, 1993), ch. 5; Rictor Norton, *The Myth of the Modern Homosexual* (London: Cassell, 1997), 196–202.

6. Judith Halberstam, *Female Masculinity* (Durham: Duke University Press, 1998), 65–73.

7. Emma Donoghue, *Passions Between Women* (London: Scarlet Press, 1993), 61.

8. Terry Castle, ed., *The Literature of Lesbianism* (New York: Columbia University Press, 2003), 20.

9. George Chauncey Jr., "From Sexual Inversion to Homosexuality: Medicine and the Changing Conceptualization of Female Deviance," *Salmagundi* 58–59 (1982–83): 114–46 (quote at 123).

10. Gayle S. Rubin, "Thinking Sex: Notes for a Radical Theory of the Politics of Sexuality," in Henry Abelove, Michèle Aina Barale, and David M. Halperin, eds., *The Lesbian and Gay Studies Reader* (New York: Routledge, 1993), 33; Eve Kosofsky Sedgwick, *Epistemology of the Closet* (Hemel Hempstead: Harvester Wheatsheaf, 1991), 27–35.

11. John Fletcher, "Gender, Sexuality, and the Theory of Seduction," *Women: A Cultural Review* 11 (2000): 95–108, 95–96.

12. Tamsin Wilton, "Which One's the Man?" in Diane Richardson, ed., *Theorising Heterosexuality* (Buckingham: Open University Press, 1996), 137; William J. Spurlin, "Sissies and Sisters: Gender, Sexuality, and the Possibilities of Coalition," in Mandy Merck, Naomi Segal, and Elizabeth Wright, eds., *Coming Out of Feminism?* (Oxford: Blackwell, 1998).

13. David M. Halperin, *How to Do the History of Homosexuality* (Chicago: University of Chicago Press, 2002), ch. 4.

14. See Jennifer Terry, *An American Obsession* (Chicago: University of Chicago Press, 1999); Alan Sinfield, *The Wilde Century* (New York: Columbia University Press, 1994), 93–97.

15. Havelock Ellis and John Addington Symonds, *Sexual Inversion* (London: Wilson and Macmillan, 1897; New York: Ayer, 1994), 136–37; Sigmund Freud, *Three Essays on the Theory of Sexuality* (1905), in *The Penguin Freud Library*, vol. 7: *On Sexuality* (Harmondsworth: Penguin, 1977), 48–49. Only the suppressed first edition of *Sexual Inversion* bore Symonds' name, so in my text I follow the convention of referring to Ellis as the author.

16. Ellis and Symonds, *Sexual Inversion* (1897), 133.

17. Michel Foucault, *The History of Sexuality*, vol. 1: *An Introduction*, trans. Robert Hurley (New York: Vintage, 1978), 119.

18. Martin Scherzinger and Neville Hoad, "A/Symmetrical Reading of *Inversion* in Fin-de-Siècle Music, Musicology, and Sexology," in C. Lorey and J. Plews, eds., *Queering the Canon* (New York: Camden House, 1998).

19. Chauncey, "From Sexual Inversion to Homosexuality," 124. See Halberstam, *Female Masculinity*, 75–83.

20. David M. Halperin, *One Hundred Years of Homosexuality* (New York and London: Routledge, 1990), 16. A similar claim is made by Arnold Davidson, "How to Do the History of Psychoanalysis: A Reading of Freud's *Three Essays on the Theory of*

Sexuality," in François Meltzer, ed., *The Trial(s) of Psychoanalysis* (Chicago: University of Chicago Press, 1988), and by Jeffrey Weeks, *Sexuality and Its Discontents* (London: Routledge, 1985), 153–54.

21. Ellis and Symonds, *Sexual Inversion* (1897), 32.

22. Havelock Ellis, *Studies in the Psychology of Sex*, vol. 2: *Sexual Inversion* (Philadelphia: F. A. Davis, 1901); quoted from Aron Krich, ed., *The Sexual Revolution: Pioneer Writings on Sex: Krafft-Ebing, Ellis, Freud* (New York: Delta, 1964), 152, 156. These passages are revised and elaborated in Ellis's third edition of 1915: see Ellis, *Studies in the Psychology of Sex*, vol. 2, part 2 (New York: Random House, 1936), 2–4.

23. Ellis and Symonds, *Sexual Inversion* (1897), 119 (my elision; Ellis and Symonds' emphasis).

24. Ellis and Symonds, *Sexual Inversion* (1897), 120. Krafft-Ebing actually lists four stages or degrees: attraction to the same sex without effect on the manliness of a man; change of character, the man feeling himself to be a woman; sensation of physical transformation; delusion of sexual change. Richard von Krafft-Ebing, *Psychopathia Sexualis* (1886; 12th ed., 1903), trans. Franklin S. Klaf (New York: Scarborough, 1978), 190, 195, 200, 216.

25. Freud, *Three Essays*, 46. Freud's persistence in a gendered model of homosexuality is demonstrated by Christopher Craft, *Another Kind of Love* (Berkeley: University of California Press, 1994), 36–43. See also Sinfield, *The Wilde Century*, ch. 7.

26. C. A. Tripp, *The Homosexual Matrix* (1975), 2d ed. (New York: Meridian, 1987), 20, 71–74.

27. Sedgwick, *Epistemology of the Closet*, 45–47, 157–59.

28. Foucault, *The History of Sexuality* 1:43 (my emphases).

29. Gert Hekma, ' "A Female Soul in a Male Body': Sexual Inversion as Gender Inversion in Nineteenth-Century Sexology," in Gilbert Herdt, ed., *Third Sex, Third Gender* (New York: Zone, 1994), 236, 238.

30. Kaja Silverman, *Male Subjectivity at the Margins* (New York: Routledge, 1992), 342.

31. Neil Bartlett, *Who Was That Man? A Present for Mr. Oscar Wilde* (London: Serpent's Tail, 1988), xx (Bartlett's emphasis).

32. Gregg Blachford, "Male Dominance and the Gay World," in Kenneth Plummer, ed., *The Making of the Modern Homosexual* (London: Hutchinson, 1981); Jamie Gough, "Theories of Sexual Identity and the Masculinization of the Gay Man," in Simon Shepherd and Mick Wallis, eds., *Coming on Strong* (London: Unwin Hyman, 1989).

33. Dennis Altman, *The Homosexualization of America* (Boston: Beacon Press, 1982), 1.

34. Richard Dyer, *Only Entertainment* (London: Routledge, 1992), 165–66.

35. Simon Fraser, "Visions of Love," interview with Neil Bartlett, *Rouge* 8 (October-December 1991): 20–22 (quote at 21). See Alan Sinfield, " 'The Moment of Submission': Neil Bartlett in Conversation," *Modern Drama* 39 (1996): Special Issue on Lesbian/Gay/Queer Drama, ed. Hersh Zeifman, 211–21 (see 215).

36. Neil Bartlett, *Ready to Catch Him Should He Fall* (London: Serpent's Tail, 1990), 162.

37. See Harry Oosterhuis and Hubert Kennedy, eds., *Homosexuality and Male Bonding in Pre-Nazi Germany* (New York: Harrington Park Press, 1991).

38. George Chauncey, *Gay New York* (New York: Basic Books, 1994), 13.

39. Quoted in Donald Webster Cory, *The Homosexual in America* (1951), with a retrospective foreword (New York: Arno Press, 1975), 188.

40. David K. Johnson, "The Kids of Fairytown: Gay Male Culture on Chicago's Near North Side in the 1930s," and Allen Drexel, "Before Paris Burned: Race, Class, and Male Homosexuality on the Chicago South Side, 1935–1960," both in Brett Beemyn, ed., *Creating a Place for Ourselves* (New York: Routledge, 1997).

41. Edmund White, *The Beautiful Room is Empty* (London: Picador, 1988), 102-3, 33. The latter thought recurs: see 36 and 71.

42. John Marshall, "Pansies, Perverts, and Macho Men: Changing Conceptions of Homosexuality," in Plummer, ed., *The Making of the Modern Homosexual*, 135. See also Sinfield, *The Wilde Century*, ch. 6.

43. Quentin Crisp, *The Naked Civil Servant* (1968) (New York: Plume, 1977), 21.

44. Peter Wildeblood, *Against the Law* (London: Weidenfeld, 1955), 7.

45. Michael Bronski, *Culture Clash* (Boston: South End Press, 1984), 79–80.

46. Kenneth Marlowe, *The Male Homosexual* (Los Angeles: Medco, 1968), 12–13, 18.

47. Hall Carpenter Archives and Gay Men's Oral History Group, *Walking After Midnight* (London: Routledge, 1989), 87.

48. Mart Crowley, *The Boys in the Band* (New York: French, 1968), 45, 87 (Crowley's emphasis; my elision).

49. Leslie Feinberg, *Stone Butch Blues* (Ithaca: Firebrand, 1993), 11, 135–36.

50. Andrew Sullivan, *Virtually Normal*, 2d ed. (London: Picador, 1996), 4.

51. Andrew Sullivan, *Love Undetectable* (London: Chatto and Windus, 1998), 12–13.

52. Andrew Sullivan, "Mainlining Manhood," *Guardian Saturday Review*, April 8, 2000, 1–3.

53. Sullivan, *Love Undetectable*, 153.

54. Paul Monette, *Halfway Home* (New York: Crown, 1991), 246.

55. Joseph Hansen, *Steps Going Down* (1985) (London: Arlington, 1986), 24 (Hansen's emphasis).

56. Judith Butler, *Gender Trouble* (New York and London: Routledge, 1990), 25; Kate Bornstein, *Gender Outlaw* (New York: Routledge, 1994), 125, 138.

57. Sinfield, *The Wilde Century*, 75–78.

58. Tennessee Williams, *A Streetcar Named Desire* (1947), in Williams, "Sweet Bird of Youth," "A Streetcar Named Desire," "The Glass Menagerie," ed. E. Martin Browne (Harmondsworth: Penguin, 1962), 182–83.

59. John Rechy, *City of Night* (1963) (London: MacGibbon and Kee, 1964), 34.

60. John Rechy, *Bodies and Souls* (1983) (London: Star Books, 1985), 302–305 (Rechy's emphasis).

61. John Rechy, *The Sexual Outlaw* (1977) (London: W. H. Allen, 1978), 243 (Rechy's emphasis).

62. Ben Gove, *Cruising Culture* (Edinburgh: Edinburgh University Press, 2000), 43–46.

63. Edmund White, *The Farewell Symphony* (London: Chatto, 1997), 301.

64. Joseph Mills, "Dreaming, Drag," in Mills, *Obsessions* (Brighton: Millivres, 1998), 74.

65. Leo Bersani, "Is the Rectum a Grave?" in Douglas Crimp, ed., *AIDS: Cultural Analysis, Cultural Activism* (Cambridge: MIT Press, 1988), 208–209.

66. Leo Bersani, *Homos* (Cambridge.: Harvard University Press, (1995), 60–61.

67. See Patrick Paul Garlinger, " 'Homo-ness' and the Fear of Femininity," *Diacritics* 29 (1999): 57–71.

68. Tim Bergling, *Sissyphobia: Gay Men and Effeminate Behavior* (New York: Harrington Park, 2001), 9; Richard Green, *The "Sissy Boy Syndrome" and the Development of Homosexuality* (New Haven: Yale University Press, 1987), 141–43, 159–60, 169, 191.

69. Gove, *Cruising Culture*, 64–72 (at 50).

70. Jean Genet, *Our Lady of the Flowers* (1943), trans. Bernard Frechtman (London: Panther, 1966).

71. Ben Gove, "Framing Gay Youth," *Screen* 37 (1996): 174–92 (at 186–87).

72. John Hopkins, *Find Your Way Home* (1970) (Harmondsworth: Penguin, 1971).

73. See Stephen Maddison, *Fags, Hags and Queer Sisters* (London: Macmillan, 2000), 1–6.

74. Harvey Fierstein, *Torch Song Trilogy* (1979) (London: Methuen, 1984).

75. Richard Goldstein, *The Attack Queers* (London: Verso, 2002), 78.

76. Edmund White, *A Boy's Own Story* (1982) (London: Picador, 1983), 169.

77. White, *The Farewell Symphony*, 34.

78. James Kenneth Melson, *The Golden Boy* ((New York: Harrington Park, 1992), 191.

79. Richard Green, *The "Sissy Boy Syndrome" and the Development of Homosexuality* (New Haven: Yale University Press, 1987), 124; Todd's emphasis.

80. Bornstein, *Gender Outlaw*, 191.

81. See *Paradise Bent*, a documentary film produced and directed by Heather Croall (ReAngle Pictures, 1999).

82. Hugh McLean and Linda Ngcobo, "Abangibhamayo bathi ngimnandi (Those who fuck me say I'm tasty): Gay Sexuality in Reef Townships," in Mark Gevisser and Edwin Cameron, eds., *Defiant Desire* (London: Routledge, 1995), 164–65.

83. See Del LaGrace Volcano and Judith "Jack" Halberstam, *The Drag King Book* (London: Serpent's Tail, 1999).

84. Judith Halberstam, "What's That Smell? Queer Temporalities and Subcultural Lives," *International Journal of Cultural Studies* 6 (2003): 313–33.

85. Radclyffe Hall, *The Well of Loneliness* (London: Falcon Press, 1949), 29 (Hall's emphasis).

86. Jay Prosser, *Second Skins* (New York: Columbia University Press, 1998), 155–56.

87. For substantial evidence of the confused and formative reception of *The Well*, see Laura Doan, *Fashioning Sapphism* (New York: Columbia University Press, 2001), and Laura Doan and Jay Prosser, eds., *Palatable Poison* (New York: Columbia University Press, 2001).

88. Halberstam, *Female Masculinity*, 98.

89. Esther Newton, "The Mythic Mannish Lesbian: Radclyffe Hall and the New Woman," in Martin Duberman, Martha Vicinus, and George Chauncey Jr., eds., *Hidden from History* (New York: Meridian, 1990).

90. Prosser, *Second Skins*, ch. 4; Halberstam, *Female Masculinity*, 110.

91. Jean E. Mills, "Gertrude Stein Took the War Like a Man," *The Gay and Lesbian Review* 10.2 (March-April 2003): 16–17.

92. Feinberg, *Stone Butch Blues*, 13.

93. Sandy Stone, "The 'Empire' Strikes Back: A Posttranssexual Manifesto," in Julia Epstein and Kristina Straub, eds., *Bodyguards* (New York: Routledge, 1991), 298.

94. Butler, *Gender Trouble*, 137. Butler revises this argument in her book *Bodies That Matter* (New York: Routledge, 1993), 125. See further Moe Meyer, *The Politics and Poetics of Camp* (London: Routledge, 1994), and Fabio Cleto, *Camp: Queer Aesthetics and the Performing Subject* (Edinburgh: Edinburgh University Press, 1999).

95. Prosser, *Second Skins*, 204–205 (Prosser's emphasis).

96. Eve Kosofsky Sedgwick, *Tendencies* (London: Routledge, 1994), 221, 157–58.

97. Neil Duncan, *Sexual Bullying* (London: Routledge, 1999), 107–108. Girls in this school were more tolerant of male and female homosexuality, and tended to support each other in the face of accusations of lesbianism from boys (121–24).

98. Richard Smith, "Pretty Hate Machine," *Gay Times* 263 (August 2000): 19–20.

99. Wendy Wallace, "Is This Table Gay?" *Times Educational Supplement*, January 19, 2001, 9–10.

100. Moisés Kaufman, *The Laramie Project* (New York: Vintage, 2001), 90 (my elision).

6. AGE

1. Armistead Maupin, *The Night Listener* (London: Bantam, 2000), 42–43 (my elision).

2. *The Long Goodbye*, featuring Maupin and his partner Terry Anderson, BBC television, June 1, 1995. The series is about bereavement, in anticipation of Anderson's death.

3. Armistead Maupin, "Coming Home," in Edmund White, ed., *The Faber Book of Gay Short Fiction* (London: Faber, 1991), 355–56.

4. Eve Kosofsky Sedgwick, *Tendencies* (London: Routledge, 1994), 57–58 (my elision).

5. David M. Halperin, *How to Do the History of Homosexuality* (Chicago: University of Chicago Press, 2002), 115–16 (Halperin's emphases; my elision). Halperin, commenting on a draft from the present work, says that he means in this passage only "a largely lop-sided or non-reciprocal pattern of desire and pleasure" (ibid., 190). However, this strikes me as tautologous: when he writes of anomic relations, he only means anomic relations. This is the only place in his essay where Halperin addresses age difference.

6. Raymond Williams, *Problems in Materialism and Culture* (London: New Left Books, 1980), 38-42.

7. Simon LeVay and Elisabeth Nonas, *City of Friends* (Cambridge: MIT Press, 1995), 30–31. See Barry D. Adam, "Age Preferences Among Gay and Bisexual Men," *GLQ* (*Gay and Lesbian Quarterly*) 6 (2000): 423–33.

8. Edmund White, *The Married Man* (London: Chatto, 2000), 11.

9. Gregory Woods, *We Have the Melon* (Manchester: Carcanet, 1992), 60. See also Woods's Carcanet volumes, *May I Say Nothing* (1998) and *The District Commissioner's Dreams* (2002).

10. Paul Monette, *Halfway Home* (New York: Crown, 1991), 108 (Monette's emphasis).

11. Jack Dickson, *Oddfellows* (Brighton: Millivres, 1997), 50.

12. Simon Lovat, *Disorder and Chaos* (Brighton: Millivres, 1996), 159.

13. Paul Rabinow, ed., *The Foucault Reader* (Harmondsworth: Penguin, 1984), 344–45.

14. David Leeming, *James Baldwin* (Harmondsworth: Penguin, 1995), 286–87.

15. Alan Hollinghurst, *The Swimming-Pool Library* (New York: Random House, 1988), 284.

16. Lovat, *Disorder and Chaos*, 132.

17. Larry Kramer, *Faggots* (1978) (London: Minerva, 1990), 238–43.

18. Philip Osment, *This Island's Mine*, in Osment, ed., *Gay Sweatshop: Four Plays and a Company* (London: Methuen, 1989).

19. Paul Robinson, *Gay Lives* (Chicago: University of Chicago Press, 1999), 100.

20. Christopher Isherwood, *A Single Man* (1964) (London: Minerva, 1991) 130–31 (Isherwood's emphasis).

21. H. Montgomery Hyde, ed., *The Trials of Oscar Wilde* (London: Hodge, 1948), 236 (my elision).

22. See Jonathan Dollimore, *Death, Desire and Loss in Western Culture* (London: Routledge, 1998), ch. 19.

23. Mary Renault, *The Charioteer* (1953) (London: New English Library, 1990), 114. See Sinfield, *The Wilde Century* (New York: Columbia University Press, 1994), 143–45.

24. Allan Bloom, *The Closing of the American Mind* (New York: Simon and Schuster, 1987), 132–33.

25. Saul Bellow, *Ravelstein* (Harmondsworth: Penguin, 2000), 160.

26. Eve Kosofsky Sedgwick, *Epistemology of the Closet* (Hemel Hempstead: Harvester Wheatsheaf, 1991), 56–57 (my elision).

27. Patricia Duncker, *Hallucinating Foucault* (London: Serpent's Tail, 1996).

28. James Baldwin, *Another Country* (London: Michael Joseph, 1963), 181–82 (my elision, Baldwin's emphasis).

29. Kenneth Martin, *Aubade* (1957) (London: Gay Men's Press, 1989), 104.

30. Timothy Ireland, *Who Lies Inside* (London: Gay Men's Press, 1984), 17.

31. Guy Willard, *Mirrors of Narcissus* (London: Millivres, 2000), 121.

32. Jill Posener, *Any Woman Can* (1975), in Jill Davis, ed., *Lesbian Plays* (London: Methuen, 1987).

33. Jeanette Winterson, *Oranges Are Not the Only Fruit* (1985) (New York: Vintage, 1996), 153.

34. P-P Hartnett, *I Want to Fuck You* (London: Pulp Faction, 1998), 25.

35. Anonymous, *The Scarlet Pansy* (New York: Badboy, 1992), 42).

36. Edmund White, *A Boy's Own Story* (1982) (London: Picador, 1983), preface. See Ben Gove, "Framing Gay Youth," *Screen* 37 (1996): 174–92.

37. Iris Murdoch, *A Fairly Honourable Defeat* (1970) (Harmondsworth: Penguin, 1972).

38. Neil Bartlett, *Ready to Catch Him Should He Fall* (London: Serpent's Tail, 1990), 14.

39. Adam Mars-Jones, "Camp for Internal Exiles," *The Independent on Sunday*, October 14, 1990, Sunday Review 32. For this reference, and many rewarding exchanges about Bartlett, I am indebted to Linda Logie.

40. Alan Sinfield, " 'The Moment of Submission': Neil Bartlett in Conversation," *Modern Drama* 39 (1996): Special Issue on Lesbian/Gay/Queer Drama, ed. Hersh Zeifman, 211–21 (quote at 212–13).

7. CLASS

1. Eve Kosofsky Sedgwick, *Epistemology of the Closet* (Hemel Hempstead: Harvester Wheatsheaf, 1991), 31 (Sedgwick's emphases).

2. On Trotskyism, see Simon Edge, *With Friends Like These* (London: Cassell, 1995).

3. See Jeffrey Weeks, *Coming Out* (London: Quartet, 1977), 21; Ed Cohen, *Talk on the Wilde Side* (New York: Routledge, 1993), 145–48; Alan Sinfield, *The Wilde Century* (New York: Columbia University Press, 1994).

4. See Alan Sinfield, *Literature, Politics, and Culture in Postwar Britain*, 2d ed. (London: Athlone, 1997), ch. 5; Sinfield, *Gay and After* (London: Serpent's Tail, 1998), 95–99.

5. Michel Foucault, *The History of Sexuality*, vol. 1: *An Introduction*, trans. Robert Hurley (New York: Vintage, 1978), 120–21.

6. George Chauncey, *Gay New York* (New York: Basic Books, 1994), 118–21. See chapter 5, this volume.

7. Murray Healy, *Gay Skins* (London: Cassell, 1996), 16–36.

8. Sigmund Freud, "On the Universal Tendency to Debasement in the Sphere of Love" (1912), in *The Penguin Freud Library*, vol. 7: *On Sexuality* (Harmondsworth: Penguin, 1977), 248 (Freud's emphases).

9. H. Montgomery Hyde, ed., *The Trials of Oscar Wilde* (London: Hodge, 1948), 138.

10. C. H. Rolph, ed., *The Trial of Lady Chatterley* (Harmondsworth: Penguin, 1961), 17.

11. Peter Stallybrass and Allon White, *The Politics and Poetics of Transgression* (London: Methuen, 1986), 156, 153. See Leonore Davidoff, "Class and Gender in Victorian England: The Diaries of Arthur J. Munby and Hannah Cullwick," *Feminist Studies* 5 (1979): 87–141.

12. Liz Stanley, ed., *The Diaries of Hannah Cullwick, Victorian Maidservant* (London: Virago, 1984), 193.

13. Rodney Garland, *The Heart in Exile* (1953) (Brighton: Millivres, 1995), 179.

14. Jeffrey Weeks, "Inverts, Perverts, and Mary-Annes: Male Prostitution and the Regulation of Homosexuality in England in the Nineteenth and Early Twentieth Centuries," in Salvatore J. Licata and Robert P. Petersen, eds., *Historical Perspectives on Homosexuality* (New York: Haworth Press, 1985), 121.

15. Stephen Spender, *World within World* (London: Readers Union, 1953), 151.

16. Jonathan Harvey, *Beautiful Thing* (1993), in Michael Wilcox, ed., *Gay Plays 5* (London: Methuen, 1994); filmed by Hettie Macdonald (1995).

17. Jay Quinn, "The Kitchen Table," in Quinn, ed., *Rebel Yell* 2 (New York: Harrington Park, 2002), 189.

18. Tom Wakefield, *Mates* (London: Gay Men's Press, 1983), 18.

19. Edmund White, *The Married Man* (London: Chatto, 2000), 88.

20. Sally R. Munt, "Introduction," in Munt, ed., *Cultural Studies and the Working Class* (London: Cassell, 2000), 9. See Mary McIntosh, "Class," in Andy Medhurst and Sally R. Munt, eds., *Lesbian and Gay Studies* (London: Cassell, 1997).

21. Jean E. Howard and Scott Cutler Shershow, "Introduction: Marxism Now, Shakespeare Now," in Howard and Shershow, eds., *Marxist Shakespeares* (London: Routledge, 2001), 7–8. See also, in the same collection, Richard Halpern, "An Impure History of Ghosts: Derrida, Marx, Shakespeare," 43.

22. Leslie J. Moran, "Homophobic Violence: The Hidden Injuries of Class," in Munt, ed., *Cultural Studies and the Working Class*, 211–12, with reference to Ken Plummer, ed., *Modern Homosexualities* (London: Routledge, 1992), 22.

23. Carol M. Ward, *Rita Mae Brown* (New York: Twayne, 1993), 6. Ward's account is based on published interviews.

24. Dorothy Allison, *Bastard Out of Carolina* (London: Flamingo, 1993).

25. Dorothy Allison, *Skin* (London: Pandora, 1995), 23–24. Compare the arguments of Cherríe Moraga, discussed in chapter 4 above.

26. Andrew Holleran, *Dancer from the Dance* (1978) (London: Cape, 1979), 83.

27. David Bergman, *Gaiety Transfigured* (Madison: University of Wisconsin Press, 1991), 96–102. Other gay critics who have contributed to Whitman's importance, include Thomas Yingling, "Homosexuality and Utopian Discourse in American Poetry," in Betsy Erkkila and Jay Grossman, eds., *Breaking Bounds* (New York: Oxford University Press, 1996); Gregory Woods, *A History of Gay Literature* (New Haven: Yale University Press, 1998), 154–59, 176–80.

28. Jon Barrett, *Mark Bingham* (Los Angeles: Advocate, 2002), 71.

29. See Alan Sinfield, *Cultural Politics—Queer Reading* (1994), 2d ed. (London: Routledge, 2005), 35–36.

30. Ethan Mordden, *I've a Feeling We're Not in Kansas Anymore* (1983) (New York: St. Martin's, 1985), 105.

31. James Kenneth Melson, *The Golden Boy* (New York: Harrington Park, 1992), 58.

32. Steven Epstein, "Gay Politics, Ethnic Identity," in Edward Stein, ed., *Forms of Desire* (New York: Routledge, 1992), 282. See Sinfield, *Gay and After*, ch. 2.

33. James Robert Baker, *Tim and Pete* (1995) (London: Fourth Estate, 1996), 142.

34. Paul Monette, *Becoming a Man* (1992) (London: Abacus, 1994), 19.

35. Neal Drinnan, *Glove Puppet* (Camberwell, Victoria, Australia: Penguin, 1998), 158.

36. Paul Russell, *Boys of Life* (1991) (New York: Plume, 1992), 52.

37. Richard von Krafft-Ebing, *Psychopathia Sexualis* (1886; 12th ed., 1903), trans. Franklin S. Klaf (New York: Scarborough, 1978), 250 (my elision).

38. Richard House, *Bruiser* (London: Serpent's Tail, 1997), 77.

39. Joseph Hansen, *Steps Going Down* (1985) (London: Arlington, 1986), 74.

40. Phil Andros, *Below the Belt and Other Stories* (1982) (Boston, Mass.: Perinium Press, 1992). These stories were written by Samuel M. Steward.

41. Scott O'Hara, *Autopornography* (New York: Harrington Park, 1997), 151.

42. John Rechy, *City of Night* (1963) (London: MacGibbon and Kee, 1964), 32 (Rechy's elision).

43. Oscar Moore, *A Matter of Life and Sex* (1991) (Harmondsworth: Penguin, 1992), 162.

44. Donald J. West in association with Buz de Villiers, *Male Prostitution* (New York: Harrington Park, 1993), 162.

45. Michael Arditti, *Easter* (London: Arcadia, 2000), 335.

46. See Alan Sinfield, *Out on Stage* (New Haven and London: Yale University Press, 1999), 180–85.

47. Terrence McNally, *Love! Valour! Compassion!* (1994) (New York: Plume, 1995), 35.

48. Peter Cameron, *The Weekend* (1994) (London: Fourth Estate, 1996), 112.

49. Alan Hollinghurst, *The Spell* (London: Chatto, 1998), 47 (Hollinghurst's pause).

8. RACE

1. Ward Houser, "Black Gay Americans," in Wayne R. Dynes, ed., *The Encyclopaedia of Homosexuality* (Chicago and London: St. James Press, 1990), 149–50.

2. Edmund White, *The Farewell Symphony* (London: Chatto, 1997), 25, 90.

3. Andrew Holleran, *Dancer from the Dance* (1978) (London: Cape, 1979), 54.

4. David B. Feinberg, *Eighty-Sixed* (1989) (London: Gay Men's Press, 1991), 4.

5. Lyle Glazier, "Chester," in Michael J. Smith, ed., *Black Men—White Men* (San Francisco: Gay Sunshine Press, 1983), 101.

6. Rhonda Cobham, "Jekyll and Claude: The Erotics of Patronage in Claude McKay's *Banana Bottom*," in Cindy Patton and Benigno Sánchez-Eppler, eds., *Queer Diasporas* (Durham: Duke University Press, 2000).

7. Paul Thomas Cahill, "The Reunion," in Smith, ed., *Black Men—White Men*, 183 (Cahill's pause).

8. James Baldwin, *Another Country* (London: Michael Joseph, 1963), 337.

9. Eldridge Cleaver, *Soul on Ice* (London: Panther, 1970), 97, 100. See David Bergman, *Gaiety Transfigured* (Madison: University of Wisconsin Press, 1991), ch. 9; Lee Edelman, *Homographesis* (New York: Routledge, 1994), ch. 3.

10. Georges-Michel Sarotte, *Like a Brother, Like a Lover*, trans. Richard Miller (New York: Anchor/Doubleday, 1978), 97.

11. Marshall Moore, "Everybody Loves the Musée d'Orsay," in Jay Quinn, ed., *Rebel Yell 2* (New York: Harrington Park, 2002).

12. See bell hooks, *Outlaw Culture* (New York: Routledge, 1994); Lola Young, " 'Nothing Is As It Seems': Re-viewing *The Crying Game*," in Pat Kirkham and Janet Thumin, eds., *Me Jane: Masculinity, Movies, and Women* (London: Lawrence and Wishart, 1995).

13. Abdul JanMohamed, "The Economy of Manichean Allegory: The Function of Racial Difference in Colonialist Literature," *Critical Inquiry* 12 (1985): 59–87 (quote at 62).

14. John Sandys, *Against the Tide* (Penzance, Cornwall: United Writers Publications, 1984), 7.

15. Stephen Gray, *Time of Our Darkness* (London: Frederick Muller, 1988), 76.

16. Quoted in Shaun de Waal, "A Thousand Forms of Love: Representations of Homosexuality in South African Literature," in Mark Gevisser and Edwin Cameron, eds., *Defiant Desire* (London: Routledge, 1995), 240.

17. Tony Peake, "A Son's Story," in Peter Burton, ed., *The Mammoth Book of Gay Short Stories* (London: Robinson, 1997).

18. Patricia Duncker, *Writing on the Wall* (London: Pandora, 2002), 167–71. See J. M. Coetzee, *Disgrace* (London: Secker and Warburg, 1999).

19. V. S. Naipaul, *In a Free State* (1971) (Harmondsworth: Penguin, 1973), 106.

20. Angus Wilson, *As If by Magic* (London: Secker and Warburg, 1973), 283 (Wilson's emphasis).

21. Alan Hollinghurst, *The Swimming-Pool Library* (New York: Random House, 1988), 1. For a discussion of other aspects, see Alan Sinfield, "Culture, Consensus,

and Difference: Angus Wilson to Alan Hollinghurst," in Alistair Davies and Alan Sin-field, eds., *British Culture of the Postwar* (London: Routledge, 2000).

22. David Alderson, "Desire as Nostalgia: The Novels of Alan Hollinghurst," in Alderson and Linda Anderson, eds., *Territories of Desire in Queer Culture* (Manchester: Manchester University Press, 2000), 33.

23. Valerie Mason-John and Ann Khambatta, eds., *Lesbians Talk: Making Black Waves* (London: Scarlet Press, 1993), 30. See further B. Ruby Rich, "When Difference Is (More Than) Skin Deep," in Martha Gever, John Greyson, and Pratibha Parmar, eds., *Queer Looks* (New York: Routledge, 1993), 319–20; Biddy Martin, "Sexualities Without Gender and Other Queer Utopias," *Diacritics* 24.2–3 (1994): 104–21; see 114–15.

24. Steven Corbin, *Fragments That Remain* (1985) (London: Gay Men's Press, 1993), 69.

25. Chris Straayer regrets a similar lack of explicitness in Marlon Riggs's *Tongues Untied* (on which see below): Straayer, *Deviant Eyes, Deviant Bodies* (New York: Columbia University Press, 1996), 171.

26. Larry Duplechan, *Eight Days a Week* (Boston: Alyson, 1985), 17.

27. See further Wei-cheng Raymond Chu, "Some Ethnic Gays Are Coming Home; Or, the Trouble with Interraciality," *Textual Practice* 11 (1997): 219–36; Darieck Scott, "Jungle Fever? Black Gay Identity Politics, White Dick, and the Utopian Bedroom," *GLQ* (*Gay and Lesbian Quarterly*) 1 (1994): 299–321.

28. Audre Lorde, *Zami: A New Spelling of My Name* (1982) (London: Pandora, 1996), 100.

29. See Audre Lorde, *Sister Outsider* (Freedom, Calif.: Crossing Press, 1984), 74–77.

30. Anna Wilson, "Audre Lorde and the African-American Tradition: When the Family Is Not Enough," in Sally Munt, ed., *New Lesbian Criticism* (Hemel Hempstead: Harvester Wheatsheaf, 1992), 87.

31. Katie King, "Audre Lorde's Lacquered Layerings: The Lesbian Bar as a Site of Literary Production," in Munt, ed., *New Lesbian Criticism*, 71.

32. Ekua Omosupe, "Black/Lesbian/Bulldagger," *Differences* 3.2 (Summer 1991): 101–11 (quote at 104).

33. Jackie Goldsby, "What It Means to Be Colored Me," *Outlook: National Gay and Lesbian Quarterly* 9 (Summer 1990): 11; quoted in Rich, "When Difference Is (More Than) Skin Deep," in Gever, Greyson, and Parmar, eds., *Queer Looks*, 327 (Goldsby's emphasis)

34. William G. Hawkeswood, *One of the Children* (Berkeley: University of California Press, 1996), 155–57.

35. Joseph Beam, ed., *In the Life* (Boston: Alyson, 1986); Essex Hemphill, ed., *Brother to Brother* (Boston: Alyson, 1991).

36. Reginald T. Jackson, "The Absence of Fear," in Hemphill, ed., *Brother to Brother*, 207.

37. Quoted from Marlon Riggs's poem, "Tongues Untied," in Hemphill, ed., *Brother to Brother*, 202. The poem affords the backbone to the film.

38. Joseph Beam, "Brother to Brother: Words from the Heart," in Beam, ed., *In the Life*, 240.

39. See Ron Simmons, "*Tongues Untied*: An Interview with Marlon Riggs," in Hemphill, ed., *Brother to Brother*.

40. Rich, "When Difference Is (More Than) Skin Deep," in Gever, Greyson, and Parmar, eds., *Queer Looks*, 333.

41. Jackie Goldsby, "Queens of Language: *Paris Is Burning*," in Gever et al., eds, *Queer Looks*, 114.

42. Marlon Riggs, "Black Macho Revisited," in Hemphill, ed., *Brother to Brother*, 254 (Riggs's emphasis).

43. Kobena Mercer and Isaac Julien, "Race, Sexual Politics, and Black Masculinity: A Dossier," in Rowena Chapman and Jonathan Rutherford, eds., *Male Order* (London: Lawrence and Wishart, 1988), 112 (my elision). See Lynne Segal, *Slow Motion* (London: Virago, 1990), ch. 7.

44. Phillip Brian Harper, *Are We Not Men?* (New York and Oxford: Oxford University Press, 1996), x.

45. Kheven L. LaGrone, "Beneath the Veneer," in Charles Michael Smith, ed., *Fighting Words* (New York: Avon, 1999). On continuities in images of slavery, see David Marriott, *On Black Men* (Edinburgh: Edinburgh University Press, 2000). The issue is flagged in Lynda Hart and Joshua Dale, "Sadomasochism," in Andy Medhurst and Sally R. Munt, eds., *Lesbian and Gay Studies* (London: Cassell, 1997), 351.

46. Kevin J. Mumford, *Interzones: Black/White Sex Districts in Chicago and New York* (New York: Columbia University Press, 1997), 73.

47. Mercer and Julien, "Race, Sexual Politics, and Black Masculinity," in Chapman and Rutherford, eds., *Male Order*, 128. This Gary has no connection with Gary Fisher (on whom see below).

48. See Marcus Wood, *Blind Memory* (Manchester: Manchester University Press, 2000), 43–46.

49. Isaac Julien, "Confessions of a Snow Queen: Notes on the Making of *The Attendant*," *Critical Quarterly* 36.1 (Spring 1994): 120–26 (quotes at 123).

50. Gary Fisher, *Gary in Your Pocket*, ed. Eve Kosofsky Sedgwick (Durham and London: Duke University Press, 1996), 230–31. See Eric L. McKitrick, *Slavery Defended: The Views of the Old South* (Englewood Cliffs, N.J.: Prentice-Hall, 1963).

51. Fisher, *Gary in Your Pocket*, 282.

52. David Wojnarowicz, *Close to the Knives* (1991) (London: Serpent's Tail, 1992), 255, 266, 271.

53. John Rechy, *City of Night* (1963) (London: MacGibbon and Kee, 1964), 15–21.

54. Paul Monette, *Halfway Home* (New York: Crown, 1991), 32, 41 (Monette's emphasis).

55. James Robert Baker, *Tim and Pete* (1995) (London: Fourth Estate, 1996), 35–36, 166.

56. From a letter from Fisher to his sister, quoted in Eve Kosofsky Sedgwick, "Gary Fisher in Your Pocket," in Joshua Oppenheimer and Helena Reckitt, eds., *Acting on AIDS* (London: Serpent's Tail and ICA, 1997), 414.

57. See Alan Sinfield, *Literature, Politics, and Culture in Postwar Britain*, 2d ed. (London: Athlone, 1997), 121–24; Erroll Lawrence, "Just Plain Common Sense: The 'Roots' of Racism," in Centre for Contemporary Cultural Studies, *The Empire Strikes Back* (London: Hutchinson, 1982).

58. See Marriott, *On Black Men*, 34–41.

59. Tennessee Williams, "Desire and the Black Masseur," in Williams, *Collected Short Stories* (New York: Ballantine, 1985), 220.

60. Bergman, *Gaiety Transfigured*, 156–57. Bergman finds cannibalism linked with homosexuality also by Yukio Mishima, Herman Melville, Freud, and Tobias Schneebaum.

61. Tennessee Williams, *Suddenly Last Summer* (1958), in Williams, *"Orpheus Descending," "Something Unspoken," "Suddenly Last Summer"* (Harmondsworth: Penguin, 1961), 188, 142.

62. James Robert Baker, *Testosterone* (Los Angeles: Alyson Books, 2000), 7.

63. Eve Kosofsy Sedgwick, "Queer Performativity: Henry James's *The Art of the Novel*," *GLQ* (*Gay and Lesbian Quarterly*) 1 (1993): 1–16; Judith Butler, "Critically Queer," ibid., 17–32. See further Sally R. Munt, *Heroic Desire* (London: Cassell, 1998), ch. 4; Michael Warner, *The Trouble with Normal* (New York: Free Press, 1999), ch. 1; Douglas Crimp, "Mario Montez, For Shame," in Stephen M. Barber and David L. Clark, eds., *Regarding Sedgwick* (New York: Routledge, 2002).

64. Tennessee Williams, *Sweet Bird of Youth* (1959), in Williams, *"Sweet Bird of Youth," "A Streetcar Named Desire," "The Glass Menagerie"* (Harmondsworth: Penguin, 1962), 42 (my emphasis). See Neil Bartlett, *Ready to Catch Him Should He Fall* (London: Serpent's Tail, 1990), 13.

9. FICTION

1. *The Shorter Oxford English Dictionary*, 3d ed. (Oxford: Clarendon, 1964). The rules and books specified in the dictionary are those of the Christian churches. See Reed Woodhouse, *Unlimited Embrace: A Canon of Gay Fiction, 1945–1995* (Amherst: University of Massachusetts Press, 1998).

2. Alison Hennegan, "On Becoming a Lesbian Reader," in Susannah Radstone, ed., *Sweet Dreams* (London: Lawrence and Wishart, 1988), 169–71.

3. Stanley Fish, *Professional Correctness* (Oxford: Clarendon, 1995), 2; Alan Sinfield, *Faultlines* (Berkeley: University of California Press, 1992; Oxford: Clarendon Press, 1992), 288–90.

4. Fish, *Professional Correctness*, 44–45 (his emphasis).

5. John Guillory, *Cultural Capital* (Chicago: University of Chicago Press, 1993), 1–14.

6. Stuart Hall, "New Ethnicities," in James Donald and Ali Rattansi, eds., *"Race," Culture, and Difference* (London: Sage, 1992), 254 (Hall's emphasis). See Alan Sinfield, *Gay and After* (London: Serpent's Tail, 1998), chs. 1 and 2; Carrie Tirado Bramen, "Why the Academic Left Hates Identity Politics," *Textual Practice* 16 (2002): 1–11.

INDEX

BETWEEN MEN ~ BETWEEN WOMEN ■ LESBIAN, GAY, AND BISEXUAL STUDIES

Terry Castle and Larry Gross, Editors

Richard D. Mohr, *Gays/Justice: A Study of Ethics, Society, and Law*

Gary David Comstock, *Violence Against Lesbians and Gay Men*

Kath Weston, *Families We Choose: Lesbians, Gays, Kinship*

Lillian Faderman, *Odd Girls and Twilight Lovers: A History of Lesbian Life in Twentieth-Century America*

Judith Roof, *A Lure of Knowledge: Lesbian Sexuality and Theory*

John Clum, *Acting Gay: Male Homosexuality in Modern Drama*

Allen Ellenzweig, *The Homoerotic Photograph: Male Images from Durieu/Delacroix to Mapplethorpe*

Sally Munt, editor, *New Lesbian Criticism: Literary and Cultural Readings*

Timothy F. Murphy and Suzanne Poirier, editors, *Writing AIDS: Gay Literature, Language, and Analysis*

Linda D. Garnets and Douglas C. Kimmel, editors, *Psychological Perspectives on Lesbian and Gay Male Experiences* (2nd edition)

Laura Doan, editor, *The Lesbian Postmodern*

Noreen O'Connor and Joanna Ryan, *Wild Desires and Mistaken Identities: Lesbianism and Psychoanalysis*

Alan Sinfield, *The Wilde Century: Effeminacy, Oscar Wilde, and the Queer Moment*

Claudia Card, *Lesbian Choices*

Carter Wilson, *Hidden in the Blood: A Personal Investigation of AIDS in the Yucatán*

Alan Bray, *Homosexuality in Renaissance England*

Joseph Carrier, *De Los Otros: Intimacy and Homosexuality Among Mexican Men*

Joseph Bristow, *Effeminate England: Homoerotic Writing After 1885*

Corinne E. Blackmer and Patricia Juliana Smith, editors, *En Travesti: Women, Gender Subversion, Opera*

Don Paulson with Roger Simpson, *An Evening at The Garden of Allah: A Gay Cabaret in Seattle*

Claudia Schoppmann, *Days of Masquerade: Life Stories of Lesbians During the Third Reich*

Chris Straayer, *Deviant Eyes, Deviant Bodies: Sexual Re-Orientation in Film and Video*

Edward Alwood, *Straight News: Gays, Lesbians, and the News Media*

Thomas Waugh, *Hard to Imagine: Gay Male Eroticism in Photography and Film from Their Beginnings to Stonewall*

Judith Roof, *Come As You Are: Sexuality and Narrative*

Terry Castle, *Noel Coward and Radclyffe Hall: Kindred Spirits*

Kath Weston, *Render Me, Gender Me: Lesbians Talk Sex, Class, Color, Nation, Studmuffins . . .*

Ruth Vanita, *Sappho and the Virgin Mary: Same-Sex Love and the English Literary Imagination*

renée c. hoogland, *Lesbian Configurations*

Beverly Burch, *Other Women: Lesbian Experience and Psychoanalytic Theory of Women*